IRON PANTS

★ ★ ★

IRON PANTS

Oregon's Anti-New Deal Governor, Charles Henry Martin

Gary Murrell

WSU PRESS

Washington State University Press
Pullman, Washington

Washington State
SS University

Washington State University Press
PO Box 645910
Pullman, Washington 99164-5910
Phone: 800-354-7360
Fax: 509-335-8568
E-mail: wsupress@wsu.edu
Web site: www.wsu.edu/wsupress
Copyright 2000 by the Board of Regents of Washington State University
First printing 2000

Library of Congress Cataloging-in-Publication Data

Murrell, Gary, 1947–
    Iron pants : Oregon's anti-New Deal governor, Charles Henry Martin / Gary Murrell
    p. cm.
    Includes bibliographical references (p.) and index.
    ISBN 0-87422-196-X (pbk.)
    1. Martin, Charles H. (Charles Henry) 1863–1946. 2. Governors—Oregon—
Biography. 3. Oregon—Politics and government—1859–1950. 4. United States—
History, Military—19th century. 5. United States—History, Military—20th century.
6. United States. Army—Biography. 7. New Deal, 1933–1939—Oregon. 8. United
States—Politics and government—1933–1945. I. Title.

F881.M36 M87 2000
979.5'04'092—dc21   00-033405
[B]

TABLE OF CONTENTS

For my loving friend and teacher Bill Gaboury. His passion for history, his belief that through study and application, humans would eventually achieve their fulfillment and liberation, inspired a generation of students.

ACKNOWLEDGMENTS

T HE DEBT OF GRATITUDE I owe to Michael Gyde, my friend and companion in all that matters, I can hardly express except that to acknowledge it here may again impress upon him all that he means to me.

Fellow historians, colleagues, and friends alike have encouraged my work and/or read sections of this manuscript, offering their invaluable suggestions, criticisms, and encouragement. Bill Gaboury passed away before he could see his mentoring at Southern Oregon State College come to fruition. He was a good friend and an exacting, critical historian. He helped mold my passionate interest in history as an older, returning undergraduate student to the needs and necessities of the professional historian. Through his guidance, above all other historians save Herbert Aptheker, I came to know with certainty that to understand the history of the United States, a historian of the American experience must first and foremost know the history of African-Americans and working people.

Senator Mark Hatfield proved to be a delightful interviewee and insightful critic of the manuscript. I offer thanks to Daniel Pope, Ed Bingham, and Howard Brick at the University of Oregon who together suffered through the military portions of the biography when it was my Ph.D. dissertation. For directing my interests in historical biography to productive use, I am much indebted to Ed Bingham. Quintard Taylor always encouraged, trusted, and directed my interests in African-American history. I hope my work validates that trust. To Richard Maxwell Brown and Jeff Ostler I owe a deep gratitude for reading and offering criticisms and suggestions on the final draft of the manuscript.

Karen Gernant at Southern Oregon State College and Jacek Lerych at Grays Harbor College provided invaluable assistance by making sense of Chinese place names for the chapter dealing with the Boxer Uprising. My former professor Bill Meulemans offered valuable suggestions on areas related to Oregon politics. Over the years Ellen Givins helped tame a sometimes out of control polemical style by editing drafts of many chapters and always made my writing better.

I cannot thank my Grays Harbor College friend and colleague Lynne Lerych enough for taking time from her family and recreational summer reading to expend hours editing the manuscript. Also at Grays Harbor College, Russ Jones, Genie Fox, and Myles Robinson read drafts of the manuscript and offered valuable criticisms and observations, and my economics colleague, Mark Zerr, used some of his precious sabbatical time to translate 1920s and 1930s dollars into modern-day equivalents for which I am grateful. I thank other faculty colleagues at Grays Harbor for the stipend from the Faculty Excellence Award and the Board of Trustees for approving the award which aided my research during the summer of 1996.

Twice while doing research, I could not have continued the work without the invaluable assistance of dedicated librarians who acquired materials through inter-library loan. At Grays Harbor College, Don Cates and Elsie Evans worked diligently on my behalf, as did the inter-library loan staff at Southern Oregon State College. Although I have never met him, a situation which I hope soon will be rectified, I thank E. Kimbark MacColl for sharing notes and recollections with me. His books on the history of Portland proved to be of enormous assistance in understanding Oregon politics and personalities.

Considering the subject areas that I had to cover that reside outside of my historical specialty, I have inevitably blundered. I hope specialists in the various fields and eras will excuse unintentional faux pas, for which I claim unequivocal responsibility.

In regard to archival materials, I had the valuable assistance of professionals. At the National Archives in Washington, D.C., the archivists helped a neophyte understand the system and went out of their way to provide guidance. At the City of Portland Archives, my friend and graduate school colleague Marcus Robbins helped locate materials on the Red Squad, and archivists at the State of Oregon, the University of Oregon Library, and the Lane County Historical Society also provided valuable assistance. I can say the same for those at the U.S. Army Military History Institute in Carlisle, Pennsylvania, and the Grayville Historical Society in White County, Illinois, from whom I received research assistance and documents through the mails. I also gained capable and extremely professional work and assistance from Todd Welch, Kris White, M.C. Cuthill, and the photographic archivists at the Oregon Historical Society in Portland, Oregon.

Throughout the long process of readying the manuscript for publication, the entire team at the WSU Press has been enormously helpful and supportive. Keith Petersen, the editor with whom I was associated longest prior to his leaving for a new position, made invaluable suggestions after reading early drafts and the peer reviews, which improved the book. The able editors who took over the project, Glen W. Lindeman and Jennifer Greifenkamp Hay, worked diligently on finishing the book, kept an anxious author pacified, and made significant contributions to the text's content and structure. Sue Emory's work in promoting the book is much appreciated and she has been very patient in shepherding a neophyte through the marketing process. I also wish to thank typesetter Nancy Grunewald and cover designer David C. Hoyt. Overall, the support of Associate Director Mary B. Read and Director Thomas H. Sanders proved decisive in seeing the project through to completion.

Finally, I would have had hefty hotel bills if my friends Helen Libonati and Fran and Robb Voss had not, over the years, put me up while I puttered around in archival collections.

It is not the consciousness of men that determines their existence, but, on the contrary, their social existence determines their consciousness.

—Karl Marx

Chapter One

FROM GRAYVILLE TO VANCOUVER BARRACKS

Most of my life has been spent in support of superior authority and in exercising authority in my own sphere.
—Charles Henry Martin

Strange as it may seem, while the Americans are a very non-military people, they are yet a very war-like people.
—Charles Henry Martin

STANDING ON A BLUFF called Oxford Hill, at the junction of Edwards and White counties in southeastern Illinois, one can gaze at lowland farms with winding streams and chart the course of the Wabash River. To the east, one sees Posey and Gibson counties across the Indiana border. Just below the bluff, on the banks of the Wabash, sits the picturesque town of Grayville. In this bucolic setting, on the six-hundred-forty acre Orange Farm, Charles Henry Martin was born, October 1, 1863, the third of ten children, eight sons and two daughters.[1]

Little information exists about Charles Henry's mother Mary Jane (Hughes) Martin. She was an obviously sturdy, plucky, and determined farm woman, characteristics she held in common with many nineteenth-century women. Mary Jane bore ten children, seven of whom survived to adulthood. Unwilling to give up the familiar surroundings of White County, Illinois, shortly after her marriage, she abruptly canceled the move to Oregon Territory planned by her husband. She insisted instead that they buy the Orange Farm, acreage originally developed as a British settlement.[2]

Samuel Holly Martin, Charles Henry's father, began life in the bluegrass country of Kentucky's Shelby County, April 18, 1821. By the 1860s, he typified the majority of the Illinois population who either migrated from the southern states or were descended from southern people. At the age of two, Samuel's parents sent him to live with a childless uncle. Raised to the life of the farm, at seventeen Samuel struck out on his own, following the river as a laborer until 1843 when he began a political career. As the elected constable for Grayville, he took an active part in the 1844 presidential election as an advocate of James K. Polk, resulting in his patronage appointment as postmaster in 1845. Later that year, Samuel won election as justice of the peace for his precinct. With the outbreak of the war with Mexico in 1846, President Polk appointed Samuel a second lieutenant in the regular army. Assigned to the Fourteenth Infantry, the twenty-six-year-old Samuel served with General Winfield Scott's army at Veracruz. After Scott captured Mexico City, Samuel spent most of his remaining service in a hospital bed stricken by an unnamed disease. Nursed back to health by Mexican nuns, he left the army and settled in Grayville where he opened a small grocery store.

Samuel, a determined, obstinate, and stubborn man, often exhibited the characteristics of a "stern old Spartan," according to his daughter-in-law. He became a leading Democratic politician in southern Illinois, "one of the most eminent men of White County for his public services and historical knowledge," and something of a novelty as an ardent, outspoken Democrat. He served as a county judge and as a member of both the House and Senate in the Illinois legislature, being first elected to the House in 1850. He was "a great friend of Stephen A. Douglas . . . [and] voted for him for United States senator against Abraham Lincoln in '58." People evidently knew what Judge Martin, as Samuel liked to be called, stood for. He displayed his determination; he could be counted on as "steady in his principles and prompt to his word."[3]

Because he was a "stand-pat democrat, friend of Douglas, an opponent of Lincoln, it is safe to assume that Samuel Martin probably mirrored the Douglas position on slavery—opposition to slavery on political and economic, rather than philosophical grounds. Douglas certainly seems never to have had any moral antipathy to slavery; through inheritance, his first wife and children owned slaves, though Douglas himself did not. Douglas attacked disunion, not slavery, advocating maintenance of the integrity of the union at all costs including, if need be, the continuation of that odious practice. At first, Illinois Douglas Democrats supported the war. That support began to wane, however, as the war dragged on, and from 1862 to 1865, many Illinois Democrats opposed continuing the war.

The Illinois legislature, controlled by the Democrats in 1862, adopted resolutions against further conflict and counseled an armistice and peace negotiations. Following the lead of other mid-Western states, at the constitutional convention called that same year, Douglas Democrat delegates put forward clauses for a revised state constitution, later passed by the voters, that "prevented Negroes and mulattoes from immigrating into the state and from voting and holding office." In July 1863, the Democratic Party sponsored a mass meeting in Springfield that adopted resolutions that, among other things, endorsed the doctrine of state sovereignty—a disguised endorsement of the right of states to choose whether to allow slavery—and called on President Lincoln to withdraw the Emancipation Proclamation. As a leading Democrat and doctrinaire Douglas supporter, Judge Martin would have been uncharacteristically out of step if he had not supported these measures.[4]

Mary Jane gave birth to Charles Henry Martin three months after that mass meeting. Throughout his life, Charles Henry had a plethora of nicknames: Harry, a name commonly used by only his intimates; Charlie Harry; Charles Harry; C. Harry; and Tommy for a short period in the 1890s when he performed in amateur theatrical presentations at Fort Vancouver, Washington. Charles Henry took to life on the farm and expected to follow in his father's footsteps as farmer and state politician. Family tragedy, however, intervened to alter the course of Charles Henry's life. On the same day, one trying to save the other, Charles Henry's two older brothers, Thomas Jefferson and Samuel Holly drowned in the Wabash River. Ten years later, that same rapacious river also claimed one of his younger brothers, Franklin Pierce. Judge Martin's plans for a career of public service to the United States for his eldest son collapsed with the deaths of Thomas and Samuel. "According to the ideals of those days, one son must be dedicated to the service of his country," Charles Henry's wife Louise recalled. With the deaths of the two older boys, the responsibility for service to country devolved to Charles Henry. The judge charted a course to ensure that his surviving eldest son would execute the father's ideals.[5]

However, teenager Charles Henry had his own ideas about a career that did not include his father's plans. "He wanted to be a farmer-writer and succeed his father in politics." Seriously interested in a writing career, Charles Henry put off the day of reckoning with his father by convincing him both men's ideals could be satisfied if Charles Henry started out by getting an education. Adroitly sidestepping his father, Charles Henry pursued his dream by enrolling at Ewing College, a Baptist institution in southern Illinois, to study law and the classics.[6]

Charles Henry's maneuver placated his father for only a short time. Judge Martin demanded that his son put aside the law. He informed Charles Henry that the duties of a good son and patriot would be fulfilled only through a life of soldiering. Charles Henry "hated the thought of military service" and resisted, vociferously, clashing repeatedly with his father. The "stern old Spartan" pressed ahead regardless. Judge Martin succeeded in using his influence, through his political crony U.S. Representative Richard W. Townsend, to secure an appointment for Charles Henry at the U.S. Military Academy at West Point. Finally, sensing the inevitable, Charles Henry relented to parental authority. On July 1, 1882 "poor shy little country lad" Charles Henry entered West Point with the class of 1886.[7]

Charles Henry arrived at Highland Falls, New York, lacking the preparation of many of his classmates and determined to hate West Point. "He had a hard time there, where he came for the first time up against boys from first-class preparatory schools," Louise wrote. "How often has he told me of those cruel days of homesickness—loathing of military drill—hazing by the upper-classmen. It was a test of character."[8]

The plebe, or first year, proved a grueling, "terrible experience" for cadet Martin, fresh from Illinois. He found seclusion and comfort only in his room, in the company of his roommate. Out of their room, Charles Henry lived a life of hour-by-hour regimentation, hours filled with humiliation and crushing discipline, ordered even so far as having a prescribed way to walk—come down first on toes then on heels. For performing the walk and other rituals properly, plebes earned a reward: the appellation "beasts."[9]

Cadet Martin's first trial at the academy came with the entrance exams. He competed successfully with other cadets who had taken several month's preparatory work at the nearby Braden and Huse academies. Comprehensive written and oral exams in reading, writing, orthography, arithmetic, grammar, descriptive geography, and U.S. History measured a cadet's preparedness for entrance to West Point. Despite his wife's later laments, Charles's Illinois schooling proved more than adequate to pass the exams.[10]

Having gained entrance to the academy, cadets spent the first few weeks of their new life learning military drills and sleeping in tents on the academy's parade ground. Plebes swept the camp's dirt streets twice daily and when upperclassmen came to inspect the "beasts'" work, they often harangued the new recruits for being filthy and dusty. Spurred on by the constant harangue, the "beasts" spent a great deal of time attempting to keep person, clothing, and tents clean for inspection.

Charles Henry resisted the regulations, regimentation, and routine at every turn. His letters home contained outpourings of misery. That summer he begged his father to allow him to "toss up the army career that he had not chosen for himself. But his father remained adamant." Charles Henry stayed at West Point.[11]

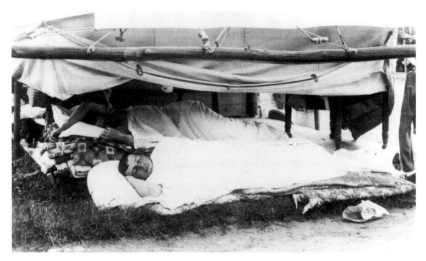

Cadet Martin asleep on the West Point parade grounds in the "Beast Barracks." *Oregon Historical Society, 96790*

With summer over, the plebes moved into the "beast barracks" where the rigorous academic training commenced in earnest. "Studious qualities counted for almost everything now, and all energies centered on learning." The U.S. Army expected cadets to master a broad range of subject matter. Charles Henry found himself grappling with plane and analytical geometry, spherical trigonometry, English grammar and rhetoric, and French grammar and literature. Cadets rounded out the scholarly routine with lectures in ethics and history. If they made it to the fourth year, infantry and artillery tactics and small-arms practice joined the already hectic schedule.[12]

Military discipline, as strict as the scholarly discipline at West Point, proved sheer torture for Charles Henry. He resented the cruel hazing of plebes orchestrated by upperclassmen. In fact, hazing caused such a continuing problem at West Point that to finally put an end to it, the War Department appointed Brigadier General Oliver Otis Howard, of Civil War and Indian-fighting fame, to serve as commander. General Howard's sanctions did not succeed in ending hazing. Upperclassmen "forced plebes to do exhausting physical exercises that sometimes resulted in permanent physical damage, to eat or drink unpalatable foods, and in various ways to humiliate themselves." As vicious as hazing could sometimes become, it served, in the minds of most cadets, as a bonding ritual, a symbol of camaraderie.[13]

One exception to hazing did, however, develop. Black cadets became the only cadets never subjected to hazing. In the fifty years after the Civil

War, thirteen African-American cadets graduated from West Point. One graduated with Martin in 1887. They lived an isolated, silent existence during their four years, being ostracized by all the white cadets. The very few black cadets who eventually graduated served in segregated regiments under the command of white officers. Prior to becoming West Point commander, General Howard had an exalted reputation among African-Americans, having been head of the Freedmen's Bureau, the founder of all-black Howard University, and the organizer of an integrated Congregational church in Washington, D.C. As commander, General Howard wanted more African-Americans admitted into West Point, but he met stiff resistance from General in Chief of the Army, William T. Sherman. From the beginning of the selection process for commandant, Sherman opposed Howard's nomination, and when, after a year and a half, discipline broke down in Howard's West Point command, Sherman replaced him with Colonel Wesley Merritt.[14]

Despite his diffidence, Charles Henry survived through the first year. But first-year cadets did not merit the summer respite accorded upperclassmen. Military officials wanted to ensure that "beasts" shed their civilian personas, that they became thoroughly indoctrinated in military discipline and culture. To reach that goal, "the cadets [were] kept at West Point without a leave to return home, for the two first years." Charles Henry managed to complete his second summer camp and begin his second full school year. His letters home continued to plead for relief. Just as consistently, he met the stern, unbending will of his father.[15]

Carrying his rancor at his father's immovable position into the second full year, Charles Henry maintained his determination to leave West Point. His work lacked enthusiasm. The 1884 election provided Charles Henry with the diversion he craved. An ardent Democrat, following in his father's footsteps, Charles Henry threw himself into politics—the presidential campaign of Grover Cleveland. Instead of studying, Charles Henry spent hours pouring over the *New York World* plotting presidential campaign strategy with his roommate.[16] Cleveland won the presidency, but Charles Henry lost his West Point appointment. At the end of the second year, the question of Judge Martin forcing Charles Henry to continue in the career he hated became moot. Charles Henry received his dismissal from West Point for failing to master the French language.

Though continual antagonism to paternal authority had not altered Charles Henry's situation, he could not then, nor ever, accept failure. He abruptly changed his mind concerning a military career. Booted out of West Point? "He decided that they couldn't do that to him." After two years of rebellion and begging to be permitted to quit, Charles Henry went home in the summer of 1885 and told his disillusioned father that he "wanted to get back into the academy."[17]

Judge Martin went immediately to work. Mustering what must have been considerable political influence, Judge Martin accomplished a remarkable feat. He convinced U.S. Senator John A. Logan and U.S. Representative Samuel S. Marshall to intercede on his son's behalf. Logan and Marshall years earlier had steered Wesley Merritt's appointment to the academy through Congress. With Merritt now in command at West Point, Judge Martin, Senator Logan, and Representative Marshall found a sympathetic ear. In an unprecedented move, the only such instance to come to light in the history of the academy, Colonel Merritt persuaded the West Point academic board to readmit Charles Henry with the class of 1887.[18]

Employing the same diligence and determination with which he attempted to thwart his father's will, Charles Henry now focused all his attention on mastering his academic studies and two years later, in June 1887, graduated nineteenth in a class of sixty-four. Cadets chose their career appointments by order of class ranking, so while more glory attached to service with the cavalry, Charles Henry, ranked number nineteen, now more than ever the dutiful son, chose the Fourteenth "Fightin' Irish" U.S. Infantry, his father's Mexican War regiment. Second Lieutenant Martin's orders directed him to join the great westward migration, to report to Vancouver Barracks in Washington, across the Columbia River from Portland, Oregon.

The West Point Class of 1887. *Oregon Historical Society, 020188*

★ ★ ★

The Hudson's Bay Company built Fort Vancouver in 1824–25 as a trading post in its fur empire. By the late 1880s Vancouver Barracks housed the headquarters for the U.S. Army's Department of the Columbia, the hub for a series of small garrisons scattered throughout the Pacific Northwest, virtually forgotten outposts at the far reaches of the American continental empire. After the Civil War, and once Indian resistance to American expansion had subsided, Congress and most citizens virtually ignored the army, especially the units so far removed from the centers of power. "Prior to the Spanish-American War the army was a tiny band of scattered remnants," Martin later recalled, "administered through a bureaucratic department which, in the knowledge of every trained officer was obsolete and inadequate." Soldiers whiled away their time in service at their duty stations desperately searching for diversions to fill their days. Officers knew few opportunities existed for advancement in rank—promotion came with demonstrations of military abilities and without a war to prove their capabilities, officers stagnated. Consequently, except in widely scattered instances of Indian uprisings which became fewer and fewer, military officers could do no more than concern themselves with routine administrative details. Not even Vancouver Barracks' glorious past stirred much interest among the bored officers. Prior to its abandonment in 1947, Vancouver Barracks provided a training ground for some of the army's brightest stars: Ulysses S. Grant made desperate attempts to curb his drinking and used his spare time to augment his meager income by raising potatoes; Phil Sheridan left Vancouver to start his meteoric rise to fame during the Civil War; and others stationed there included George B. McClellan, Oliver O. Howard, Arthur MacArthur, and George C. Marshall.[19]

By the time Martin arrived at Fort Vancouver, the only mission assigned to the U.S. Army was surveillance and demonstration marches parading the flag around the Pacific Northwest every summer. Earlier in the nineteenth century, Vancouver Barracks served as an active, strategic bulwark supporting continental imperialism. But by 1887, except for the army massacre at Wounded Knee, South Dakota, during the winter of 1890–91, the Indian wars and uprisings had ceased. The Department of the Columbia, covering all of the Pacific Northwest and Alaska, maintained surveillance over the Indian reservations within its jurisdiction. The widely scattered subordinate forts, including Fort Canby, Fort Sherman, Fort Spokane, and Boise Barracks, located near the reservations, enhanced the department's surveillance capabilities.

Then just twenty-five years old, Lieutenant Martin spent six days on the Northern Pacific Railroad travelling across the country. Visions of gallant, brave soldiers, distinguishing themselves in wars against bloodthirsty savages, filled his thoughts as his train passed sites where he supposed the cavalry valiantly extended the frontier of civilization. Years later he likened this journey to the invasion of China where he led chivalrous Christian soldiers engaged in teaching other heathen savages to respect the might and power of the United States.[20]

Arriving in Portland cocky and full of enthusiasm, Charles Henry ran straight into military formality and rebuff. Though he and his luggage both arrived safely at their destinations, they arrived at separate locations. Undaunted, he hired a horse and buggy, drove the old military road seven miles north out of Portland, crossed the long trestle over the flats near the Columbia, and took the ferry across the river to Vancouver Barracks. The uncompromising and perfectionist commander, General Thomas N. Anderson, informed the young Lieutenant that without a uniform he could not report for duty. Without hesitation, Martin climbed back into his buggy, retraced the arduous trip to Portland where he borrowed a uniform, from whom remains unclear, and the next day reported for duty.

Lieutenant Martin settled contentedly into eleven successful, although militarily uneventful, years of service at Vancouver Barracks. He lived with other unmarried officers in quarters where they were cared for by Chinese cooks and servants. Each officer paid for the cooks and for food, and each had a private Asian servant to whom he paid five dollars per month. During this time Martin became enamored with Portland, where he would eventually own considerable real estate holdings and wield considerable political power and influence. He "had visions of Portland and Oregon's future greatness," his wife Louise wrote, "and put his savings into real estate in three different counties."[21]

Aside from dealing with chronic problems associated with drunkenness among officers and enlisted men, Lieutenant Martin alternated the routine of garrison duty at Vancouver Barracks with an active social calendar and the annual display of the flag at the various Indian reservations situated in the Department of the Columbia military district. His first march came during the summer of 1888, and for the 1889 summer march he commanded fifty men and twenty-two decrepit six-horse wagons, relics of the Civil War.

Early that summer, after crossing the Columbia River, Lieutenant Martin led his command toward Pendleton along the Barlow Trail, a formidable pioneer path over the Cascade Range. The trail remained as narrow, crooked, rutted, and rocky as when Sam Barlow first assaulted the forest in 1845. At times it proved so difficult to traverse, especially near Mount Hood, that the wagons managed only two or three miles per day. The aged wagons continually broke down, adding further delays. In that summer of 1889, Lieutenant Martin eventually brought his command to the Umatilla Indian Reservation near Pendleton, Oregon, joining up with the rest of the regiment which had travelled more leisurely by ferry up the Columbia.

Martin maneuvered his command among the Indians west and south of Pendleton, then under settlement by white migrants as a cattle and wheat region. His simple orders directed him "to let the tribes know that they [the army] were on the job," even though "there had been no recent trouble with the redskins."[22]

Having duly impressed the assorted tribes with a show of strength, Lieutenant Martin's command retraced its path back to Vancouver Barracks over the Barlow Trail.

For many at Vancouver Barracks, especially enlisted men, the unvarying routine passed in monotony until 1894. That spring the army's show of force turned from impressing defeated Indians to putting down an unemployed workers' uprising when the Fourteenth Infantry became embroiled in confrontations with followers of Jacob Coxey, the Populist political agitator behind a plan to march an "army" of unemployed workers to Washington, D.C.

On March 25, 1894, from points across the United States, Coxey's followers began their march to Washington to demand relief for the unemployed and starving. A severe financial collapse in 1893, which precipitated runs on banks, business failures, and massive unemployment, settled into economic depression by 1894. Coxey galvanized the unemployed throughout the country with his call for a march on Washington to petition the federal government for relief. Workers in the west eagerly signed on to Coxey's army, joining the pilgrimage to the nation's capital by commandeering trains to carry them east. Simultaneously, the American Railway Union strike, which started at the Pullman Railroad Works near Chicago, expanded to threaten the entire U.S. railroad system. The government, alarmed by the open resistance to authority, called out the army in the most massive movement of troops since the Civil War.[23]

A contingent of Coxey's army, composed of unemployed workers from the forests of the Pacific slope, railroad laborers, and other desperate unemployed men, formed in Portland. Martin later described these desperate men as "the distressed, the freaks and the rats in this part of the northwest."[24]

Leaders of the Portland Coxey contingent obeyed a municipal judge's orders to leave Portland. One thousand strong, they marched a few miles east from Portland to Troutdale where they took possession of some freight cars parked on a siding. Outnumbered, the frantic U.S. marshal sent Oregon's Populist governor Sylvester Pennoyer an urgent request for reinforcements, asking the governor to muster troops to dislodge the Coxeyites from the train. Governor Pennoyer refused.[25]

Government superiors ordered Brigadier General Elwell S. Otis, in command of the Department of the Columbia, to enforce a United States court injunction issued on April 27 ordering the Coxeyites to relinquish the train. The next day, a special train carrying railroad company dignitaries arrived in Troutdale. The encamped Coxeyites "surrounded it, manned the engine, ran the cars upon a siding, coupled the engine to the box cars which they had occupied the night before, and started east," exemplifying what Carlos Schwantes has called "the distinguishing badge of the western Coxeyite . . . the stolen train." Newly promoted First Lieutenant Charles Martin went with other army units pursuing the labor outlaws. Racing to intercept the insurgents, the army captured the Portland Coxeyites and their stolen trains at Arlington, Idaho. Later that night U.S. marshals herded the Coxeyites aboard a special train that returned the men to Portland. Judge Charles B. Bellinger released the men on the afternoon of April 30. Within a week, the Coxeyites again headed for Washington, D.C. quietly slipping "out of town in small bands." Rounded up once again and put on trial, in late May federal judge James H. Beatty, saying that the defendants "bore the indelible stamp of the criminal," and calling "the movement a conspiracy," confined the convicted Coxeyites "in a special prison . . . located in the sagebrush wilderness where the Union Pacific crossed the Snake River from Oregon into Idaho, not far from Farewell Bend, where the old Oregon Trail left the river." Throughout the summer, the Portland contingent languished at "Camp Despair" a "depressing wasteland of sand and sage . . . devoid of all signs of human habitation," guarded by two hundred and fifty soldiers. Ill-prepared to care for large numbers of prisoners, the army did nothing to alleviate the primitive conditions in which their captives suffered. No proper facilities existed to house the prisoners, and lacking funds, the army could not buy food and clothing. Finally, as the oppressive summer heat gave way to the first indications of fall, the army broke the Coxeyites up into small detachments to prevent their reassembling and sent the detachments back to Oregon accompanied by their army guards. While part of the forces from the Department of the Columbia guarded the Coxeyites in Idaho, others

(Martin served with both groups) transported the U.S. mail, which had been halted by the railroad strike.[26]

Though their leader Eugene V. Debs languished behind bars, the American Railway Union (ARU) continued the strike begun at the Pullman works. After receiving orders from Washington, General Otis ordered Lieutenant Martin's unit to run the trains idled by the ARU strike. Throughout the summer the Fourteenth ran the Northern Pacific from Portland to Missoula, Montana. Soldiers, neophytes at railroad operations, became brakemen and engineers. Lieutenant Martin and others of the Fourteenth kept watch on telephone lines and bridges as the trains made their daylight-only runs. "It was dangerous to run at night," Martin later recalled, "with the threat ever present of barriers thrown across the rails . . .[and] strikers were out to cut the hose between cars, to burn the trains."[27]

Finally, the U.S. government broke the ARU strike. The emerging labor movement, aroused to action by the 1893–94 depression, capitulated to irresistible force. With Debs's strike broken and Coxey's army routed, the Vancouver soldiers resumed their mundane life at the post. Officers at least escaped the enlisted men's gloomy existence with some notable diversions, making frequent trips to Portland where they played an important part in the city's social life.

Vancouver's officers sought invitations to Portland events just as eligible young women from Portland's elite vied for invitations to activities at the fort. At dinner parties, dances, or amateur theatrical presentations where his boyish good looks often landed him the role of the shy, bashful lover, Martin's natural gregariousness and self-assurance often made him the center of attention. He welcomed the diversions and used the opportunities provided by these social occasions to find a suitable partner with whom to share his life.[28]

At one of the many social affairs in Portland, Charles Henry met the very eligible Louise Jane Hughes, the daughter of Ellis G. Hughes, one of Portland's leading lawyers "and the man whose fighting ability resulted in creation of the Port of Portland." After a short courtship, Lieutenant Martin married Louise Hughes on April 15, 1897.[29]

The Martins settled into domestic tranquility in the married-officer quarters at Vancouver Barracks. The quietude through long years of peace after the Civil War would soon be broken as the United States joined the European imperialist order by declaring war on Spain in Cuba and the Philippines. War demanded an army, an expeditionary force to leave the confines of the continental United States, and Charles Henry Martin would be among the first to answer the call of duty.

NOTES

1. Throughout the Notes, the following abbreviations will be used: CHM for Charles Henry Martin, LM for his wife, Louise Martin; CHMC for the Charles Henry Martin Collection, OHS for the Oregon Historical Society, Portland, Oregon. Spelling has been corrected in the quotes throughout the book.
2. Duane Hennessy, *Oregonian,* December 4, 1938.
3. LM to Harry E. Dutton, September 19, 1934, CHMC, OHS; *History of White County Illinois* (Chicago: Inter-State Publishing Company, 1883), 354–56; Hennessy.
4. *Encyclopedia Britannica,* 1960 ed., s.v. "Illinois."
5. LM to Harry E. Dutton, September 19, 1934, CHMC, OHS.
6. Ibid.
7. Ibid.; Hennessy.
8. LM to Harry E. Dutton, September 19, 1934, CHMC, OHS.
9. Ibid., and Hennessy.
10. Frank E. Vandiver, *Black Jack: The Life and Times of John J. Pershing,* Vol. 1 (College Station: Texas A&M University Press, 1977), 27–28.
11. Hennessy.
12. Vandiver, 30.
13. Ibid.; Hennessy; Stephen E. Ambrose, *Duty, Honor, Country: A History of West Point* (Baltimore: The Johns Hopkins Press, 1966), 222.
14. Ibid, 231, 232, 236; Hennessy.
15. LM to Harry E. Dutton, September 19, 1934, CHMC, OHS.
16. Hennessy; typescript obituary of Charles Henry Martin, 1946.
17. Hennessy.
18. Ibid.
19. Congressional Record, V 78, 73D Congress, 2D Session, March 1–14, 1934, 3927–29. Timothy K. Nenninger, *The Leavenworth Schools and the Old Army* (Westport, Connecticut: Greenwood Press, 1978), 16; Victoria L. Ransom, "Officers' Row at Vancouver Barracks," *Clark County History,* Vol. 3, 1962, 38–43.
20. Hennessy.
21. LM to Harry E. Dutton, September 19, 1934, CHMC, OHS.
22. CHM as quoted in Duane Hennessy, *Oregonian,* December 11, 1938.
23. Donald L. McMurry, *Coxey's Army* (Seattle: University of Washington Press, 1968), 4.
24. Duane Hennessy, *Oregonian,* December 11, 1938.
25. McMurry, 217–18.
26. Ibid., 215, 218; Carlos A. Schwantes, *Coxey's Army: An American Odyssey* (Moscow: University of Idaho Press, 1994),195–207; Hennessy, December 11, 1938; CHM was promoted on April 16, 1894. Information on the pursuit of the laboring men is contained in an incomplete military biography with no author noted, CHMC, OHS.
27. Hennessy, December 11, 1938.
28. Hennessy, December 4, 1938.
29. Ibid.

The bachelor's mess at Vancouver Barracks. Martin is at left. His friend and eventual business partner, Henry Cabell, is in the back at center left. *Oregon Historical Society, 020198*

Fourteenth Infantry officers pose while on duty in the Philippines. Martin is seated at the left in the front row. *Oregon Historical Society, 004886*

Chapter Two

THE SPANISH-AMERICAN-PHILIPPINE WAR

We are told that history repeats itself. Is Aguinaldo to become a George Washington & General Otis a Sir Henry [Thomas] Gage?
—Charles Henry Martin

And if you go down in the shock of battle go down with your face to the enemy.
—Samuel H. Martin

TRAVELLING ACROSS THE CONTINENT to his assignment in Vancouver, the new West Point graduate, uninitiated in battle, conjured visions of heroic deeds for God and country. When confronted with an actual combat situation, more mundane issues, even doubts, crept into Martin's consciousness. During January 1899, after serving several months in the Philippine Islands, Lieutenant Martin began to feel uneasy about his role and that of the United States in the occupation of the Philippines subsequent to the Spanish military defeat. "We are now," he wrote his wife Louise on January 13, 1899, "face to face with the Filipinos who as we now know hate us and will fight us if we remain here." Curiously, for Martin considered the Filipinos an uncivilized people, "they have acted very shrewdly." "What [would] happen," Martin wondered, when the U.S. Army attempted to take away the weapons they had given the Filipinos to fight the Spanish? He believed the Filipinos would fight.[1]

When the Martins married on April 15, 1897, the Philippine Islands would hardly have been any concern. The couple busied themselves with a full social life centered among Portland's elite. Louise's father, Ellis G. Hughes, railroad entrepreneur, attorney, and real-estate speculator, belonged to the small circle of men who composed the ruling class in Portland. Hughes introduced Martin into that circle, where he made political and economic contacts from which he would benefit all his life. At the social headquarters for Portland's ruling elite, the Arlington Club, where he would later become a lifetime member, Martin rubbed shoulders with Henry Failing, president of the First National Bank, George B. Markle, president of the Oregon National Bank, William S. Ladd, real estate speculator, William M. Killingsworth, wealthy realtor, and others. Hughes's enthusiasm convinced young Martin that Portland would someday be the most important city on the West Coast. With a secure position among the most wealthy men in Portland, Martin began dabbling in real estate himself, guided by and always deferential to his father-in-law's desires.[2]

As February passed into March 1898, the Martins anxiously anticipated the birth of their first child, expected in early June. But an explosion in Havana Harbor on February 15 set in motion events that altered the course of their lives and propelled Lieutenant Martin into his first test as a soldier.

During the closing decade of the nineteenth century, proponents of U.S. expansionism flexed their collective muscles when, in January 1893, a group of sugar planters, bankers, and clergymen deposed the queen of the Hawaiian Islands. Held as a "protectorate" for five years while imperialists and anti-imperialists argued the merits of annexation, Hawaii eventually capitulated to annexation in 1898. During that five-year interval while efforts to annex Hawaii stalled, imperialists discovered a fresh cause in Cuba, where Spain fought a desperate battle against Cuban revolutionary nationalists to maintain the last vestiges of its fading colonial empire.

The Cleveland and McKinley administrations attempted to negotiate with the Spanish, but by January 1898 the deteriorating situation threatened significant U.S. economic interests on the island. As severe riots erupted in the Cuban capital, President McKinley dispatched the battleship *Maine* to Havana Harbor "as a 'gesture of friendship.'" Three weeks later, on February 15, 1898, an explosion ripped through the *Maine* killing two hundred and fifty-four sailors of the U.S. Navy. Seven weeks later, after tremendous public outcry for reprisals against Spain, fueled most notably by Hearst's "yellow" press, the U.S. Congress, without a direct request from the president, declared war on Spain.[3]

The declaration of war provided an important symbol for national unity. Now, at last, the sectional breach caused by the Civil War could be healed. The United States could be made whole again through war. "For the first time in a third of a century the tocsin of war has been sounded . . . There is no North or South; no East or West. Seventy million Americans are now marching side by side, under the same flag, to the martial airs of a United People." Young men stampeded to enlist. With jingoistic speeches ringing from lectern and pulpit, conscription became unnecessary; in fact, military planners never even considered using it. Patriotic speakers urged Northwest-erners to join the cause. In Eugene, Oregon, one hundred miles from Vancouver Barracks, future Oregon Supreme Court Justice Lawrence T. Harris echoed the calls heard around the country. "For the people of the United States," Harris thundered, "a race that is bound to dominate more and more of the earth's surface, there is in store a great and incomparable destiny," a "Manifest Destiny," as newspaperman John L. O'Sullivan prophesied ear-lier in the century. "This nation is expanding, growing, and extending its influence and power to every mart and hamlet of the known world," Har-ris said, which should cause "no man [to] tremble at the mention of terri-torial expansion. Territorial expansion under such circumstances is simply the natural and destined growth of a mighty nation."[4]

Once the *Maine* exploded, the officer corps at Vancouver Barracks re-garded war with Spain as an inevitability even before the actual declaration of war on April 25, 1898. As rumors swirled around the post, Lieutenant Martin made preparations. At thirty-five, Martin knew that the only path to promotion led directly to participation in the war. Fearing that he would somehow miss out on the battle for Cuba, Martin tried to use his father-in-law's political influence among friends in the state of Washington to se-cure an appointment as colonel of Washington volunteers. When the news reached Vancouver Barracks on May 2 announcing Admiral Dewey's destruc-tion of the Spanish fleet at Manila Bay, Martin quickly revised his plans. He recognized instinctively that his best chance at action on the battlefield would be in the Philippines, not in Cuba. He reasoned, correctly, that Dewey's fleet could capture the islands but that the navy needed an army to main-tain their hold on the captured territory.[5]

On April 22, prior to the declaration of war, President McKinley cabled Dewey with orders to attack the Spanish military. Nine days later Dewey smashed the Spanish fleet in Manila Bay. On May 2, while Philippine revo-lutionary leader Emilio Aguinaldo's forces surrounded Manila, President McKinley, before knowing of Dewey's victory, ordered Major General Wesley Merritt to lead a U.S. Army expeditionary ground force to the Philippines, calculating, just as Lieutenant Martin had predicted, that Dewey would need combat troops to complete his conquest of the islands. The president did not formulate nor put forward for discussion any political policy concern-ing the Philippines. He ordered the expeditionary forces under General Merritt to battle with no clear objective except to provide the United States with a claim to some portion of the Philippines in future peace negotiations with Spain.

Within ten days of Dewey's victory, Lieutenant Martin and the Fourteenth Infantry arrived in San Francisco where General Merritt, Martin's commander at West Point, consolidated his forces for an invasion of the Philippines. When Martin's former commanding officer at Vancouver, General Thomas N. Anderson, led the first of the invasion forces out of San Francisco, Martin seethed with resentment at not being with them. When he arrived in San Francisco, the lieutenant assumed duties as regimental quartermaster. As chief supply officer, Martin remained behind to procure and transport military necessities for the expeditionary army. Instead of pursuing glory in battle or earning promotion citations, Lieutenant Martin scoured San Francisco for underwear and wiped out "practically all the shoe stores" in the city. He amassed clothing, camp and garrison equipment, ships, gunpowder, and rifles to supply what he described as departing troops who "were a pretty hard looking outfit," on their way to the United States' first declared overseas war.[6]

Never losing sight of his goal, Martin remained as determined as ever to participate in the battle for the Philippines and vigorously pursued, through his political connections, an appointment as colonel of Washington Volunteers. Ellis Hughes laid the groundwork with Washington's lieutenant governor, Thurston Daniels, and Henry J. Snively, commissioner of Public Institutions. They pressured Washington's governor, John R. Rogers, on Martin's behalf. Louise wrote to her husband in San Francisco fearing that her father's influence might not prove sufficient. Knowing her husband's talents with the certainty only a wife can possess, her frustration at the political maneuvering broke through in her letters. "Actual worth, experience and capability go for nothing," she wrote. Hughes's intervention almost paid off. "You . . . understand that you will receive the appointment of Colonel, of the 2nd Regiment . . . the governor has promised me," Henry Snively wrote to Lieutenant Martin on May 28. But with Martin already in San Francisco, communications evidently broke down. Under the mistaken impression that Martin sailed for Manila with the Fourteenth Regiment, Governor Rogers claimed, "I did my best to secure the services of Lieut. Martin but as he has gone with his regiment . . . that must, of course, be given up."[7]

When the army eventually ordered Martin to duty in the Philippines, his deliverance from quartermaster duty in San Francisco came as a bittersweet victory. Louise gave birth to their first son, Ellis Hughes "tiddlie-winks" Martin, less than a month before Martin's ship set sail. Louise had great difficulty with the birth and spent several months recovering, unable to nurse the child. They both worried about the baby's health, and Martin, torn between family and military obligations, wanted to be with his wife and son. Louise tried to reassure her husband. She promised not to let him down but lamented her "failure" in performing a mother's duties.[8]

With the prospect of her husband actually participating in the fight, Louise found that her worries about her own health and that of the baby could not dislodge dark thoughts of war and concern for Martin's safety. The war invaded her life as surely as the U.S. military invaded the Philippines. She avidly followed events in the newspapers, making predictions and relaying her hopes to Martin as his ship headed for the Hawaiian Islands. "I really do not see how the Spaniards can fight much longer," she said in one letter. "I hope," she continued, "I shall have a long letter from Honolulu. The chances are that war will be over before you reach there and in that event you may get no further."[9]

When Martin boarded the *City of Pueblo* on July 28, 1898, he did so as a newly promoted captain, reaping the fruits of war early. Amidst the exhilaration and anticipation of the trip, he had ample time during the twenty-five-day voyage to digest a letter he received from his father just prior to sailing. "I may never meet you again on this Earth," the elder Martin wrote, "but I hope you may by the providence of [our] lord be spared many years and enjoy the pleasure of a happy and pleasant life with your wife and dear little son." Be "brave and patriotic," the father cautioned, "be cool and determined in the face of the enemy." If death should come, "face it bravely," the father warned. Make it an honorable death, one with purpose and meaning. "If you go down in the shock of battle," he said, "go down with your face to [the] enemy."[10]

The *City of Pueblo* made stops in Honolulu and Hong Kong on the 9,000-mile journey to the Philippines. In Hawaii Martin managed to try his hand at surfing. His description of that experience prompted Louise to suggest that because the sea was his "native element" he might consider a career in the navy "instead of the U.S.A." "What fun it must be," she wrote lightheartedly, "to ride the breakers like that!" In a series of letters, written as the *City of Pueblo* made its way across the Pacific, Louise continued to keep her "C. Harry" informed about events taking place in Cuba and the Philippines. The letters reveal anxiety about the war and exhibit some insecurity about her place in Martin's life. She elucidated both the confusion that United States imperialism met at home and her personal insecurity. "The papers now are filled with peace negotiations," she informed her husband, "and the great question at stake is whether to relinquish our claim to the Philippines—simply controlling a coaling station—or to keep them with Porto-Rico and demand no further indemnity." She explained the "great

diversity of opinion," over the United States actually holding colonial pos-
sessions but maintained that "the majority are strongly in favor of holding
what we have horribly won." She predicted trouble ahead if the United States
attempted to subdue Emilio Aguinaldo's revolutionary forces, "for the insurgents . . . are not to be so easily subdued and I am quite sure that gentleman will not submit to being governed or being taught the new methods
of our Christian and humane government without a desperate struggle."
Aguinaldo's visage evidently assured Louise of his stubbornness: "His pic-
tures show him to be a doggerd self-opinionated [unreadable]." Turning to
their relationship, she wondered if war would drive thoughts of her from
Martin's consciousness. "Do you really miss me very much?" she asked. "I
would give worlds for a glimpse into your thoughts and heart. You are living in the midst of such stirring scenes and surrounded by so many old time
friends I am afraid you have very little time to think of poor little Louise.
But I love you devotedly nonetheless."[11]

On August 13, one week before Martin's arrival in the Philippines, the
U.S. expeditionary army defeated the Spanish in a sham-battle for Manila.
Three days later, completely forgetting her predictions about Aguinaldo,
Louise gushed over the victory of the United States. "From the various accounts received here," she wrote, "I think you will find Manila delightful,
and oh, but I am glad sir, that the fighting is all over. Manila is in our hands
and peace an accomplished fact. Of course I know how disgusted you will
be at getting there the day after the fair, . . . you blood thirsty villain." In
her assessment that peace was an "accomplished fact" and that Martin arrived too late for the fighting, Louise could not have been more wrong.[12]

As the first ground forces commander in the Philippines, General
Thomas Anderson led the fight against the Spanish at Manila. Revolutionary leader Emilio Aguinaldo, whose forces began the struggle with the Spanish
four years prior to U.S. involvement, complicated Anderson's task. When
Aguinaldo sought out tentative contacts with Rounceville Wildman, the U.S.
consul-general in Hong Kong, Commander Edward P. Wood, responding
to instructions from Wildman and Dewey, "assured [Aguinaldo] of American support in the event that the United States went to war with Spain."
Having spent some time in Hong Kong as the result of temporary peace
agreements with the Spanish, Aguinaldo eagerly awaited his return to the
Philippines as an ally of the United States. Dewey sent one of his ships to
Hong Kong three weeks after the battle at Manila Bay to fetch Aguinaldo
back to the Philippines. Aguinaldo pressed for written commitments of
support from the U.S. government. When Wildman demurred, Aguinaldo,
nonetheless, maintained his belief that the United States would not just move

in to replace the Spanish as the Philippine's colonial master. He viewed U.S. foreign policy as traditionally anti-colonial and besides, he considered the act of transporting him to the Philippines aboard a U.S. warship to be a de facto alliance. All of his assumptions proved wrong.[13]

Following orders, General Anderson, who actually assigned diplomatic significance to Dewey's assistance to Aguinaldo, treated the Filipino as a junior partner, in a patronizing and paternalistic way. While he and Dewey maintained direct communication with Aguinaldo, in meetings with him, they attempted to maintain the impression that they acted unofficially, that the talks did not constitute recognition of Aguinaldo's nascent government. They "went to almost childish lengths to impart an air of informality," contriving "to forget their swords, to show up without tunics, or to leave them carefully unbuttoned."[14]

Consolidating his command of the revolutionaries on all the islands once he returned, Aguinaldo surrounded Manila and bottled up the Spanish forces at a time when the United States had only a handful of marines on land. He created a revolutionary government and promulgated a declaration of independence modeled on and quoting that of Thomas Jefferson. Throughout the summer Aguinaldo made numerous appearances before his troops to praise U.S. democracy and to thank the United States for its help in defeating the Spanish. "The Filipino forces were allied to 'the great North American nation, the cradle of liberty, and therefore the friend to our people,' he told his troops." But as the summer progressed, and more and more U.S. troops streamed ashore, Aguinaldo's suspicions deepened. He pressed ahead with his campaign to acquire as much territory as possible before the arrival of the complete U.S. expeditionary army. "Thus, he calculated, he could improve his bargaining stance with the Americans. For the same reason, he decided to declare the independence of the Philippines."[15]

General Wesley Merritt replaced General Anderson on July 25, 1898. General Merritt, who as superintendent of West Point had reinstated Cadet Martin after his expulsion from the academy, sought, at age sixty-one, his last chance at glory. As one of the Civil War's "boy generals," cited six times for gallantry, he accompanied General U.S. Grant to Appomattox. Through his service during the Indian wars, having fought with George Armstrong Custer, he felt he knew how to deal with "savages." Imperious and devoid of any diplomatic inclinations, "he envisioned nothing less than the complete conquest of the Philippines," and predicted to President McKinley that in all probability the United States would also have to fight the "so-called insurgents." Merritt's first directive upon assuming command forbade any further communication with Aguinaldo's headquarters.[16]

General Merritt wanted to defeat the Spanish troops who still held the city of Manila and to do it without aid from Aguinaldo. To accomplish this, he embarked on a duplicitous campaign, directing Dewey to persuade Aguinaldo to let U.S. forces occupy the front lines, which the insurgents had already established around the city. At the same time, without informing Aguinaldo, Merritt and Dewey negotiated with the Spanish commander, who, already reconciled to defeat, preferred surrendering to the United States rather than dealing with Aguinaldo's revolutionaries. Together with the Spanish commander, Merritt and Dewey concocted a charade battle—details of which never intruded on the celebration of the "great victory" in the United States because they remained secret—that would save the Spanish commander's reputation back in Madrid while affording the United States the victory. The Spanish commander and General Merritt informed very few of their own officers about the plan, which resulted in unnecessary deaths on both sides of the phony battle when communications broke down. However, having duly resisted, the Spanish finally surrendered Manila to the forces of the United States on August 13. Ironically, the war had been over before the battle, but neither the Spanish nor the U.S. governments could communicate to their military forces the contents of the peace protocol they had signed because the cable to Hong Kong had been cut.

During the protracted peace negotiations, the Spanish had regrets about their participation in this fraud. Aguinaldo, totally unaware of the deception, could not understand why the United States denied his troops participation in the battle and pressed for joint occupation of Manila. The Filipino soldiers, frustrated in their attempts to broaden their hold on Manila, eventually exchanged a few warning shots with U.S. forces, but General Merritt adamantly refused a joint occupation—a decision that President McKinley eventually supported.

Eight days after the defeat of the Spanish, General Merritt boarded the Spanish governor general's personal launch, "the most valuable article of his capture," to head the welcoming committee at the arrival of the *City of Pueblo* in Manila Bay. From the ship, with obvious pride in the moment, Martin related the events of the splendid welcome to his wife. Merritt's officers "rushed on board" the *Pueblo,* Martin said, "grinning like school boys," with news of the great victory over the Spanish. General Merritt, "the finest of our generals," told the reinforcements that the revolutionaries then surrounding Manila "are susceptible to [my] gentle influences." They would soon be going home, he informed the new arrivals, so "have a good time & impress everybody with the idea that we are the best fellows on the face of the earth." Martin eagerly anticipated some action. "We go ashore at dawn," he said, "to join the rest of the 14th at the walls of the city in keeping the insurgents out. As I predicted," he reassured Louise, "you'll see me home soon."[17]

General Merritt left the islands several days later bound for Paris to attend the peace commission meeting and negotiate a treaty between Spain and the United States. The majority of President McKinley's peace delegation eagerly accepted Merritt's rationale for occupation of the entire Philippine archipelago when he argued that any single island would be militarily indefensible. When Merritt "totally distorted for the commission the political conditions in the Philippines, and depicted Emilio Aguinaldo . . . as 'a Chinese halfbreed adventurer,'" he assured a longer stay for U.S. forces than Captain Martin anticipated.[18]

Martin occupied sumptuous quarters in Manila. "After many vexatious delays," he wrote home, "we have finally gotten settled in the Spanish barracks at Malare [Malata?] a fashionable—if such a word may be used with reference to anything in this place—suburb of the city. . . . Our quarters are palatial," he continued, "so elegant that we expect the occupants to return . . . any day to reclaim them." General Elwell S. Otis, the new commander in the Philippines, under whom Martin had also served at Vancouver Barracks, named the Captain to the Provost Marshal General's office as chief of the Department of Streets, Parks, Fire and Sanitation. Martin faced staggering sanitation problems in a city crowded with refugees. "Garbage . . . [that] had accumulated during the siege littered the streets, . . . [and one] American team even devoted weeks to the repulsive task of removing the human excrement piled up under houses, whose toilets consisted of a hole in the floor." The ardent Martin applied what Louise called his "unusual executive ability" to the task. His superiors agreed. "He has shown himself to be zealous, efficient and capable," his commanding officer, Colonel E.B. Williston, wrote some months later. "The stupendous work accomplished by Captain Martin in cleaning the city and disposing of the accumulations of filth, can never be fully appreciated . . . in fact, it is much cleaner than many cities in America." Martin, however, loathed the assignment. Up to his proverbial neck in scatological duties, he lamented his fate to Louise, wondering, "when will this cruel separation end . . . my miserable existence?"[19]

As the U.S. occupation of Manila continued, the volatile situation within the city grew more tense with the potential for violence between the armed camps simmering just below the surface. General Otis kept Aguinaldo's troops in place, but they still formed a circle around Manila and its suburbs. Gradually, Otis allowed Aguinaldo's troops into the city "a few at a time." As the forces from the two sides mixed, confrontations occurred nearly daily. Almost uniformly, with the notable exception of some sympathetic African-Americans then serving in segregated army units, the U.S. soldiers shared with U.S. government officials a racist ethnocentrism toward Filipinos. While U.S. soldiers verbally assaulted Filipinos with colloquial racist vulgarities, "nigger" or "goo-goos," their counterparts in the United States Senate couched their prejudices in loftier language. "They are a barbarous race," Senator Albert J. Beveridge told his fellow senators, "they are, as a people, dull and stupid." Captain Martin proved no exception. "The natives have not a single virtue to redeem them," he wrote of Filipinos. "They are infinitely lower and viler than our own Indians . . . All the Filipinos are a lazy shiftless set who would rather steal than work."[20]

Ugly incidents multiplied around the city, especially at entry points where U.S. sentries harassed and degraded Filipinos attempting to enter Manila. Filipinos seethed at being treated so unfairly in their own country. "We are almost at hostilities with the insurgents," Martin warned, "who hate us almost as much as they did the Spanish troops." General Otis, who claimed to have stared down Sitting Bull in a confrontation at the Yellowstone River in 1876, saw no reason to alter the actions of his troops. While the army continued to insult Aguinaldo's forces, Otis persisted in making provocative moves against the revolutionaries and presented outlandish ultimatums to Aguinaldo.[21]

As the debate between imperialists and anti-imperialists in the United States over the question of Philippine annexation occupied the citizenry, Martin sided with the anti-imperialists and wanted the United States out of the Philippines. "There is nothing in this country for us," he told Louise. "Let us hope that . . . we shall not hold the Philippines." In fact, a month later, senatorial candidate Albert J. Beveridge enunciated the rationalization for imperialism that prevailed in the councils of government.[22]

On September 16, Beveridge, who would win election to the United States Senate four months later, delivered his "The March of the Flag" speech in Indianapolis, Indiana. He masterfully articulated the ideas of geographical predestination, God-given title, divine mission, duty, paramount interest, political affinity, and self-defense intrinsic to "Manifest Destiny":

> It is a noble land that God has given us . . . a people imperial by virtue of their power, by right of their institutions, by authority of their Heaven-directed purposes. . . . Shall the American people continue their march toward the commercial supremacy of the world? Will you remember that we do but what our fathers did—we but pitch the tents of liberty farther westward, farther southward—we only continue the march of the flag? Distance and oceans are no arguments. The fact that all territory our fathers bought and seized is contiguous, is no argument. The

riches of the Philippines have hardly been touched by the finger-tips of modern methods. Within five decades the bulk of Oriental commerce will be ours.[23]

Anti-imperialists attempted to counter Beveridge's arguments with contentions of their own, ranging from lofty idealism to the blatantly racist. Former Secretary of the Interior Carl Schurz warned against acquisition of the Philippines because the "various savages and half-savages . . . [are] animated with instincts, impulses and passions bred by the tropical sun . . . What will become of American labor and the standards of American citizenship," he asked, "[when] they would take in the mixtures of Indian and negro blood, . . . and other unspeakable Asiatics . . . ." Martin, who would later echo many of Schurz's racist sentiments, confined his comments for the moment to the concerns of an officer watching his troops die of tropical diseases. To Louise, in an October 1898 letter, he berated "some of our enthusiastic annexationists . . . [who should] pause and consider whether the sacrifice of so many lives were worth the dollars a few adventurers would make out of the islands."[24]

President McKinley finally ended his silence on the question of annexation on October 25 when he declared officially that he favored keeping all of the Philippine Islands. As he later told a group of Methodist missionaries, he had had, while on his knees in prayer, a revelation from God defining the duty of the United States to uplift and Christianize the Philippine people. Martin believed McKinley made a poor choice. "Poor old Spain. We have all been very much depressed the last few days on the news that the United States had demanded of Spain all the Philippines. [W]e had been led to believe that all [McKinley's] demand over here would be the cession of a coaling station," Martin wrote, obviously disappointed. Not to worry, he assured Louise, "the feeling here is that should Spain grant our exorbitant demands the Senate will refuse to ratify the treaty."[25]

Some officers' wives joined their husbands in the Philippines, but Martin advised Louise not to come. "What a joy it would be to have you here with me but of course while [the baby] is so young and tender it is completely out of the question," he wrote tenderly. Moreover, "our friend Mrs. Gale now makes no secret of her dislike for the place. She says that had she known what a place it was she would never have come, that it is no place for a white woman." So Louise remained in the Northwest. The void created by his absence from Louise added to Martin's already considerable isolation. Having missed out on the action in Cuba and the battle for Manila, Martin resented all the more keenly the boredom of garrison duty so reminiscent of his days at Vancouver Barracks. Sleep seems to have occupied much of his time. "You used to laugh at me sleeping so much at Vancouver," he wrote Louise, "should you see me now I am quite sure that you would be shocked."[26]

Martin spent hours traveling around the city in a covered cart provided for his official duties. As he roamed Manila searching out unsanitary conditions, he maintained, at the insistence of Louise, the tourist's eye for souvenirs. "I will keep my eyes open for curios as you suggest. But I am doubtful of the result. I am too proud to loot," he claimed, but with U.S. troops madly looting everything in sight, "when you are now found with anything valuable in your possession the means of possession are at once questioned."

By December, however, his noble intentions succumbed to practicality. His efforts to provide Louise with "curios" compelled him to become a looter. His initial reluctance "came at the expense of growing richer by looting," he told Louise. "I [have] become a robber like many of these other gentlemen," he admitted. He assured Louise that honorable motives precipitated his theft. "I . . . have taken a hat from the very head of one of Aguinaldo's minions," he told her. "As soon as I saw his hat—a curiosity I assure you—I determined that it should be yours. I stopped my driver, got out and deliberately seized it." The power gave him a thrill. "So proud am I of my late success I shall repeat it when . . . [it] pleases me." While to Martin the hat itself was virtually worthless, except as a curiosity, for a desperately poor people who had virtually nothing to begin with, the indignity of the theft, and the accompanying impotence with which to respond, typified the Filipino experience with Americans. The incongruity of the disparity between himself and Filipino peasants generally escaped Martin's consciousness. With no sense of the irony, he concluded the same letter to his wife with the admonition to "tell the young man [baby Ellis] in one of your evening talks that the kids here have absolutely nothing."[27]

Spain and the United States finally reached agreement on treaty terms, December 10, 1898. The agreement called for U.S. forces to occupy the Philippine Islands as a U.S. possession. President McKinley cabled General Otis on December 26 with a proclamation, to be made public, in which he said in part that "America's 'earnest and paramount aim' . . . was to 'win the confidence, respect and affection' of the Filipinos by 'proving to them that the mission of the United States is one of benevolent assimilation.'" General Otis, confident that he knew more about the situation in the Philippines than the president, rewrote the proclamation, inserting what he believed to be less belligerent and inflammatory rhetoric, attempting to assuage Aguinaldo. The general's good intentions were for naught, however, because Aguinaldo obtained a copy of the original and, believing that the United States meant to seize the Philippines, prepared for war. "General Otis' proclamation was published yesterday, a copy being sent to Aguinaldo at Malolos. We are now waiting for the effect," Martin wrote on January 6, 1899.[28]

While they waited, the 20,000 U.S. soldiers grew increasingly more hostile toward the Filipinos. Many "were 'just itching to get at the niggers' ... [wondering] just what it would take to get these 'insolent natives to fight.'" When Aguinaldo posted his "open, defiant rejoinder," to McKinley's proclamation "on all the walls of the city," officers prepared their restless soldiers for battle.[29]

Martin, who up to that point believed that no fighting would occur, abruptly changed his mind because "things now look very serious." He believed the only way that open hostilities could be avoided would "be by accident." If the United States annexed the islands, "the Filipinos are going to fight and I don't see how we can retreat from the stand which we have taken." When Aguinaldo followed his first proclamation with one even more belligerent the next day, Martin admitted that "Aguinaldo has matched Otis so far both in Generalship and diplomacy. . . . Otis' proclamation is a masterpiece, so is Aguinaldo's answer." General Otis led his officers to believe that "the Filipinos were fighting among themselves," but Martin now realized that "all the time Aguinaldo was gathering around him the strong men of his people, strengthening his outposts around Manila, arming his troops . . . filling his treasury . . . bringing back the faltering, encouraging the faithful. . . . [He] is supreme over all the islands." Martin believed the situation had gone terribly awry. The U.S. Army fought a war of liberation against the Spanish. What was wrong with the Philippine people? Liberators should be met "with [a] surging mass of Filipinos on the way to make peace." What do we get for an answer to our efforts? Martin asked. "Give us our independence or we [will] fight you to the death." What if the fight replicated the American Revolution? "We are told that history repeats itself," he said. "Is Aguinaldo to become a George Washington & General Otis a Sir Henry [Thomas] Gage?"

General Otis, despite his orders to maintain the peace, followed a course of provocative maneuvers and demands "designed to incite the Filipinos to warfare." Now no less "itching" for a fight than his soldiers, Otis dispatched troops to the port of Iloilo, three hundred miles from Manila on the Island of Panay, to dislodge the Spanish garrison that remained there despite the treaty. When the Spanish forces finally departed on Christmas Day and the U.S. fleet sat offshore awaiting orders to storm the city, Aguinaldo's forces moved in ahead of the Americans. General Otis hesitated. McKinley's orders, which Otis found incomprehensible, demanded that he "capture the town without risking a fight." While the American troops sat in the tropical sun aboard their ships, Aguinaldo's forces taunted them from shore. "Our troops . . . are jeered at, called cowards," Martin fumed.[30]

While the standoff continued, General Otis clung tenaciously to the belief that Aguinaldo had no legitimate claim to power. Captain Martin nurtured his private doubts. "We are now face to face with the Filipinos who as we now know hate us and will fight us if we remain here." The liberating mission that began the war changed so that "our actions of May are not our actions of December." Would the rest of the world view the United States as just another imperialist power? Martin feared so. "I am not so sure that Aguinaldo's able papers will not convince the people of the world that we have been guilty of bad faith," he fretted. The precarious position of U.S. forces worried him. "Here in the walled city we are surrounded by 13,000 disarmed Spaniards & 35,000 of their sympathizers. In our front are 30,000 Filipinos." Tempers reached the breaking point. One night, when someone killed a dog in one section of Manila, U.S. troops three miles away, hearing the shot, opened fire on Aguinaldo's forces. Martin feared that "a few hot headed fools" would precipitate a bloodbath.[31]

Three weeks later, he ignored his apprehensiveness and predicted a swift resolution to the "insurgent troubles." His confidence led him to reverse his earlier decision about bringing Louise to the islands. "I am so glad that you are willing to come out . . . [I] want you to come as soon as possible 'if not sooner,'" he wrote her on February 4, 1899. Later that night, while Martin sat in the officers' club, Private William Grayson killed an unarmed Filipino peasant in downtown Manila, igniting the Philippine-American war."[32]

"The expected has happened," Martin wrote four days later. "We have commenced our conquest of the Philippines in a battle which has proved that the insurgents were braver men than we have given them credit of being." He predicted earlier that the Filipinos would never stand and fight the Americans, "there will never be more than one pitched battle." Though that part of his prediction proved false, the remainder proved quite accurate. After the first battle, Martin wrote, "the Filipino will have to be hunted in the mountains and swamps. But with their intense hatred of us I believe they will fight in ambush to the bitter end." When the fighting actually broke out Martin grabbed a "sword and pistol—my own had been left at my office" and joined his regiment "in the trenches." The swiftness with which the battle ignited threw General Otis off balance. Communications broke down. Fighting raged through the night. In the morning, Captain Martin, acting as regimental adjutant, led an assault on an earthen-works Filipino bunker. After a prearranged four shot naval bombardment, Martin's forces advanced on the Filipino block house only to have to run for cover as the navy lobbed three more shells on their own troop's position. The shells landed behind the advancing soldiers but created panic and terror nonetheless. Martin "rushed to Brigade Hdqrs. over a path lined with sharpshooters" to report the mistake and stop the friendly fire, "and I was frightened to death all the way," he told Louise. "The navy," he said, "has been of no material assistance . . . [and should] clear out for Hong Kong."[33]

Martin, echoing his father's advice, acknowledged the bravery of Aguinaldo's soldiers. "Although the insurgents have uniformly and with frightful losses been driven back," he wrote Louise, "[t]hey have died in the field of honor as becomes the brave—with their faces and not their backs to us." Acknowledging the military prowess of the Filipinos caused him grief, though, because "our little national cemetery is filling—too rapidly filling with our bravest and best men."[34]

The lofty rhetoric with which the United States embarked on its war with Spain notwithstanding, the United States now instigated a war of territorial conquest, directed against a native, anti-colonial government established by a revolutionary independence movement with wide popular support. That government pronounced its revolutionary right to self-determination in Jeffersonian language every citizen of the United States should have recognized.

Much to his chagrin, Martin experienced no more of the battle in the Philippines beyond that first night. After the fiasco at the block house, General Otis recalled him from the fighting to continue his duties with the Department of Sanitation in Manila. Louise and Ellis, whose presence he anxiously anticipated, did not arrive for another year. The reunion lasted an aggravatingly short time; within five months of Louise's arrival, Captain Martin was on his way to China to protect the "Open Door Policy" by helping to crush the Boxer Uprising.

NOTES

1. CHM to LM, January 13, 1899, CHMC, OHS.
2. E. Kimbark MacColl, *Merchants, Money, and Power: The Portland Establishment 1843–1913* (Portland: The Georgian Press, 1988), 134, 292.
3. Stanley Karnow, *In Our Image: America's Empire in the Philippines* (New York: Random House, 1989), 88; Stuart Creighton Miller, *Benevolent Assimilation* (New Haven: Yale University Press, 1982), 21, 94, 95. Though nearly everyone blamed the explosion on the Spanish, we now know that the explosion occurred inside one of the holds on the ship, perhaps as the result of coal dust build-up.
4. Lawrence T. Harris, typescript of a speech, July 4, 1898, Lawrence T. Harris collection, Lane County Historical Society, Eugene, Oregon.

5. Duane Hennessy, "The Life of Martin," *Oregonian,* December 11, 1938. This date is taken from Hennessy's article and presumably came from Martin during an interview. Martin's memory of when word reached Vancouver is probably in error. Dewey had cut the cable between Manila and Hong Kong to deny its use to the Spanish. According to Karnow, the first word to reach the United States regarding Dewey's victory was on the morning of May 7, 1898.

6. Hennessy; Karl Irving Faust, *Campaigning in the Philippines* (San Francisco: The Hicks-Judd Company Publishers, 1899), 302.

7. LM to CHM, May 28, 1898, Henry J. Snively to CHM, May 28, 1898, Governor Rogers to Henry Snively, May 28, 1898, CHMC, OHS.

8. LM to CHM, July 17, 1898, CHMC, OHS.

9. Ibid.

10. Samuel H. Martin to CHM, May 10, 1898, CHMC, OHS.

11. LM to CHM, August 1 and 18, 1898, CHMC, OHS.

12. LM to CHM, August 18, 1898, CHMC, OHS.

13. Miller, 35.

14. Ibid.

15. Ibid., 37; Karnow, 116.

16. Miller, 42, Karnow, 107.

17. CHM to LM, August 21, 1898, CHMC, OHS.

18. Miller, 20.

19. CHM to LM, September 3, 1898; CHM to LM, August 28, 1898, CHMC, OHS; Karnow, 130, 131; LM to Harry E. Dutton, September 19, 1934; Colonel E.B. Williston to Adjutant General, U.S. Army, Washington, D.C., May 23, 1900, CHMC, OHS.

20. CHM to LM, August 28, 1898, CHMC, OHS; The Staff, Social Sciences 1, the College of the University of Chicago, *The People Shall Judge,* Vol. 2 (Chicago: The University of Chicago Press, 1949), 295, 298.

21. CHM to LM, August 28 and 30, 1898, CHMC, OHS.

22. Ibid., August 28, 1898.

23. Albert J. Beveridge, in Daniel J. Boorstin, ed., *An American Primer* (Chicago: The University of Chicago Press, 1966), 622–29.

24. Carl Schurz, quoted in Manfred Jones, ed., *American Foreign Relations in the Twentieth Century* (New York: Thomas Y. Crowell Company, 1967), 21–25; CHM to LM, October 17, 1898, CHMC, OHS.

25. Karnow, 128, 129; Miller, 23; CHM to LM November 4, 1898, CHMC, OHS.

26. CHM to LM, October 17 and November 21, 1898, CHMC, OHS.

27. Ibid., October 26 and December 2, 1898, CHMC, OHS.

28. Karnow, 134; Miller, 24; CHM to LM, January 6, 1899, CHMC, OHS.

29. Stuart Creighton Miller, "The American Soldier and the Conquest of the Philippines," in Peter W. Stanley, ed., *Reappraising an Empire: New Perspectives on Philippine-American History* (Cambridge: Harvard University Press, 1984), 15.

30. Miller, "The American Soldier," 15; Karnow, 134; CHM to LM, January 12, 1899, CHMC, OHS.

31. Ibid., January 13, 1899.

32. Ibid., February 4 and 8, 1899; Karnow, 139.

33. CHM to LM, February 8 and 12, 1899, CHMC, OHS.

34. Ibid.

Chapter Three

THE BOXER UPRISING

It is very slow work, for the Chinese are supposititious and egotistical and are afraid of us and think their own Confucianism is as good as our religion.
—Eva Jane Price, missionary

The foreign troops in the Legations still hold their position and wait for outside relief. Kill them all, so that the mouths of the foreigners will be silenced.
—A memorial submitted to the Throne

Perhaps after all we may arouse the sleeper only to cause him to overrun the world.
—Charles Henry Martin

AFTER TWELVE YEARS in the army and a taste of battle in the Philippines, Martin's ambition exceeded the two silver bars of his captaincy. His early rebellion had vanished, replaced, through the years of military training and duty, by the soldier's stoic masculine virtues—discipline, obedience, bravery, fatalism. His life exemplified the counsel of Marcus Aurelius whom he studied at the Academy: "When a man has once taken up his stand, either because it seems best to him or in obedience to orders, there I believe he is bound to remain and face the dangers, taking no account of death or anything else before dishonor." At thirty-seven, as a member of the multinational expeditionary army making its way to relieve the diplomats under siege at their legations in China, Martin had taken his stand. He obeyed orders, he willingly faced danger; he now lived the soldier's creed with fervor: duty, honor, country.[1]

The Fourteenth Infantry departed Manila for duty in China with the allied invasion force on July 15, 1900. After a "pleasant voyage of six days," Martin's ship put into Nagasaki, Japan, where he wrote a reflective letter to his father-in-law, Ellis Hughes, for whom the Martins had named their first son. Having housed his "little family" safely and comfortably, he assured Louise's father, he regretted nonetheless having to leave them. But, at the same time, getting out from under the strain at the sanitation department brought great relief.[2]

Martin's thoughts did not stray far from China as he wrote this letter, with customary formality to "Mr. Hughes." He said that most of the men in his unit feared for the safety of the Americans "suffering" in China. He felt confident, though, "that the mobilization of the allied forces will make short work of Brother John." Despite the "frightful conditions over there," Martin envisioned a great adventure. "To see and be with the allied armies and navies of the world will certainly be the event of a life."[3]

While still bogged down in the quagmire of its first land war in Asia attempting to overcome the nationalist revolution in the Philippines, the United States dispatched its China force, opening its second war in Asia. The 2,700 U.S. troops joined the allied forces—20,000 Japanese, 10,000 Russians, 4,000 English, and much smaller contingents from Australia, Germany, and Italy. Together, the allies intended to destroy the "Boxer Rebellion" and free the missionaries and diplomats held hostage in the foreign legations at Beijing and Tianjin.

Martin's impressions of Asians, like those of most citizens on the West Coast, came principally through the stereotypes that developed during the latter half of the nineteenth century as the railroads brought Chinese laborers to the United States to build the lines that spanned the continent. Depending on the audience, antagonists reviled the Chinese for their "heathenish ways," rebuked them as being a source of "cheap labor," condemned their "fatuous ignorance" and "treacherous mendacity," and described them, without irony, as "opium-sodden." In periodical literature, many writers describing the Chinese and their culture "drew a picture of a people with strange and devious ways whose presence pointed out the contrasts between the civilized Christian West and the barbaric pagan East."

In the 1890s, Portland's Chinatown embraced a population as high as 10,000 when hostility and federal exclusion acts convinced many Chinese that the United States really did not want them. The Chinese in Portland fared no better than Chinese did most everywhere else on the West Coast. Duress and discrimination invaded their daily existence. Portland laborers, fearing competition from Chinese labor, used vigilante tactics to intimidate Chinese workers and eventually organized an "Anti-Coolie" Association.[4]

While Chinese immigrants in the U.S. labored under these conditions, China suffered national humiliation throughout the nineteenth century. Through a series of wars, from the Opium War against the British early in the century to the wars against Japan and Russia at the end of the century, China proved unable to overcome foreign domination. The victors forced China, by treaty, to grant increasingly extensive commercial and political concessions. They carved out pieces of China over which they carried out exclusive domination. Foreign companies, protected by foreign governments, made monopolistic arrangements over banking, trade, construction, and mineral rights.[5]

In 1897–98, Germany, Italy, England, France, Russia, and Japan all made new demands on China. Eying the supposed vast potential for trade, the United States joined the other powers for the first time in 1899. With U.S. missionaries leading the call for a more activist U.S. foreign policy in China, the U.S. government stepped into the imperialist fray to stop the formal colonialist dismemberment of China, and incidentally, to secure its own trading rights. "We want our own markets for our manufactures and agricultural products," President McKinley explained, "we want a foreign market for our surplus products." Former U.S. Minister to China Colonel Charles Denby pressed throughout the last decade of the nineteenth century for investment from the United States to build a railroad system in China that "would provide cheap access to China's interior and to the teeming millions who lived there."[6]

Secretary of State John Hay issued the Open Door Notes during late 1899 and early 1900, conceptualizing a framework for the proposition that the U.S. sphere of influence included all of China. The Open Door Notes "distilled the conglomeration of motives, pressures, and theories into a classic strategy of non-colonial imperial expansion,"—informal empire—the imperialism of free trade.[7]

The resentment "at last touched off hidden mines in the Chinese soul," Herbert Hoover recalled, when "there swept over North China one of those blind emotional movements not unusual among Asiatic masses."[8]

Many Chinese developed an intense hatred for colonialists from the United States, Europe, Russia, and Japan. As the nineteenth century drew to a close, the "Boxers," an extraordinarily powerful and popular movement, arose in central China's Shan Dong Province: "a ruthless, anti-foreign, anti-Christian movement that swept China with hurricane force."[9]

The Boxers' antipathy toward Christians had deep historical roots, going back to the sixteenth century when Western traders and missionaries arrived in China to establish trading relations and convert the "heathen Chinee." This marriage between business and religion formed "the inextricably linked engines of Western empire-building." After each military defeat, the treaties included not only cessions of land, they contained clauses protecting the rights of Christians to proselytize.[10]

With a haughty demeanor and supreme self-assurance, alien customs, and "indisputable religious truth," some missionaries remained oblivious to the hostility and contempt they engendered among the Chinese people. Christian missionaries, in many instances, did not learn the Chinese language and showed even less interest in Chinese history or civilization. Many "were contemptuous of Asian civilization and communicated their arrogance and condescension in their dealings with the Chinese." However much the Chinese resented their domination by Western imperialism in its capitalistic guise, imperialism in its religious guise aroused the most implacable hatred in China.[11]

The Boxers commanded an international audience after capturing the attention of the world in the summer of 1900; "above all they stood as a dramatic example of ordinary Chinese peasants rising up to rid China of the hated foreign presence."[12]

The Boxer movement swept out of Shan Dong Province in early 1900. Called "Boxers" by foreigners, the best translation of their Chinese name would be "Boxers (or Fists) United in Righteousness or Boxers of United Righteousness." Their boxing "was really a set of invulnerability rituals— to protect them from the powerful new weapons of the West," rituals remarkably similar to those practiced in the 1880s and early 1890s by Indian adherents of Wovoka's "Ghost Dance" religion in the United States.[13]

By May 1900, when foreign ministers could no longer ignore increasing Boxer ferociousness, a contingent of foreign troops—"75 Russian, 75 British, 75 French, 50 Americans, 40 Italians, and 25 Japanese"—arrived in Beijing to provide protection for foreign diplomats at their legations. U.S. Minister to China Edwin Conger cabled repeatedly for instructions from Secretary Hay, but Hay, suspicious of European motives and apparently having serious misgivings about the capabilities of Conger, avoided taking a firm stand. "We have no policy in China," he cabled Conger as late as June 10, "except to protect with energy American interests, and especially American citizens and the legation. There must be nothing done which would commit us to future action inconsistent with your standing instructions. There must be no alliances."[14]

On June 8, the Boxers moved to take control of the area between Beijing and Tianjin, cutting off the railroad that provided access for the legations to the port at Dagu where the allied naval flotilla waited offshore. The Boxers killed Christians living west of Beijing and destroyed enough sections of the railroad to cut off any means of escape for the Beijing legations. That day, Chinese troops joined the Boxers for the first time as the Boxers began moving in on Tianjin.

Boxers appeared on Beijing's Legation Street on June 12. Members of the legations, feeling real fear for their lives, hastily constructed temporary barricades of furniture and other household materials. On June 21, Chinese troops and Boxers opened fire on the Legation Quarter, beginning the siege of the foreign legations in Beijing. The next day China declared war on the allied forces.

Six weeks later, Captain Martin settled into his quarters in the compound of the Methodist Episcopal Church Mission in Tianjin. "So far," he wrote to Ellis Hughes, "I have enjoyed the campaign very much except the march through Tianjin from the depot to our camp." Two weeks after allied forces routed the Boxer siege of Tianjin, bodies "in a fearful state of decomposition . . . partly eaten up by dogs, still lay in the streets. Here the stench two weeks after the capture was so bad that it was almost unbearable."[15]

To understand the siege at Tianjin and learn how the allied forces recaptured the city, we must go back almost two months. On June 10, Boxers began shelling the American compound. Unlike their counterparts in Beijing, the foreigners at Tianjin did not hesitate to act once the Boxers moved. The 1,100 sailors and marines stationed at the compound organized themselves into a cohesive force under the command of a Russian colonel and with the civilians, began constructing defenses.[16]

Once the actual siege began on June 17, the combined Boxer and Chinese military forces subjected Tianjin to almost continual rifle and artillery attack. Future President of the United States Herbert Hoover, then living in Tianjin, estimated that from beginning to end, the Chinese fired approximately 60,000 shells into the settlement. As the battle raged in Tianjin, allied naval commanders overran and captured the Chinese forts at Dagu some thirty miles downriver from Tianjin. The U.S. naval force, still lacking explicit directions from their government in Washington, did not participate.[17]

With the Dagu forts neutralized, a force of 8,000 allied marines battled their way up the river to relieve the siege at Tianjin, arriving there on June 23. They found "a sight of heartbreaking desolation . . . What a sight!" The troops passed through "miles of windowless, one-storied houses [that] looked like rows of skulls in some vast mausoleum." The city's Chinese inhabitants had vanished. Except for the sound of their horses' hooves and the clumping of their own boots, the empty streets echoed with a "profound death-like stillness." Amid the destruction and desolation, one British observer travelling with the relief army deplored the lack of colonial amenities: What could a "proper gentleman" do, he wondered? "There was no Chinese coolie to help" with his luggage.[18]

The allied forces defeated the Boxer siege at Tianjin on July 14. The next day, Captain Martin and the 1,135 men of the Fourteenth Infantry, under the command of Colonel A.S. Daggett, left the Philippines bound for China. Attempting to "present a creditable appearance" to the other allied military forces, U.S. Philippine commander General Arthur MacArthur loaded his troops down with "new clothing, arms, and equipment." In addition to military supplies and coffins, soldiers packed footlockers (some packed two or three), boxes of red cross supplies, cots, books, and magazines. When the regiment arrived in Tianjin, it quickly became "the laughing stock of the other forces in loading ourselves down with such trash." Eventually, after separating out essential military supplies, Colonel Daggett put the torch to the rest.[19]

At the invitation of Presbyterian minister Dr. Lowry, Colonel Daggett moved the men of the Fourteenth into two compounds, one belonging to the American Missionary Board and another just across the street. The French forces wanted to use the two compounds for a hospital, but Colonel Daggett and Reverend Lowry told them to look for quarters elsewhere. Because Lowry detested the French, thwarting their desires gave him enormous pleasure.[20]

While Martin set up camp in these temporary quarters, "like a gentleman in the field," the allied military commanders laid plans for the eighty-mile march to relieve the legations at Beijing. He shared quarters with Lieutenant H.S. Wagner, who was, Martin reported, "quite a swell. He has come on this campaign as though he were going to a season's fight at Newport." Martin too did not lack for comforts. Officers' excess baggage did not meet the same fate as enlisted men's, so the captain unpacked his trunks, setting his books and trinkets around his room.[21]

As Martin watched the actions of the other allied armies, he cast his critical eye on them. He accounted the U.S., British, and German forces as the most civilized. "[We] are the only people who give a Chinaman the benefit of a Court Martial. All the others kill them at sight. The Russians and Japs even torture before killing." He believed the French cowards, complimented the Japanese on being "neat and clean in their personal appearance," and thoroughly detested the Russians. He admitted their prowess as soldiers, but felt repelled by them personally, calling them a "bunch of dirty drunken beasts," almost as bad as the French.[22]

When commanders postponed plans for the attack on Beijing while the allied forces waited for reinforcements, Martin began to doubt whether the Chinese would be defeated as easily as he had previously thought. He now predicted "a bloody campaign is ahead of us." The Chinese, "strange to say, know how to use modern artillery." In fact, during the battle for Tianjin, the Chinese use of artillery "proved more effective than that of the allies." He pondered the fate of Western civilization should the Chinese prove too successful at modern warfare. "Perhaps after all," he wrote with trepidation, "we may arouse the sleeper only to cause him to overrun the world." Martin did not hold this view in isolation. He echoed much sentiment passing through the corridors of power in the United States where fear that the awakening of the quiescent Chinese dragon held more peril than promise.[23]

The same day that Martin penned those lines to Ellis Hughes, many hundreds of miles to the north, at Fenzhou, U.S. missionary Eva Price came to similar conclusions about the bloody nature of the conflict. With a sense of foreboding, she contemplated the deaths of thirty-three fellow missionaries beheaded nearby on July 8. "If only foreign soldiers could soon come into the province we would probably be saved," she wrote, in her last letter before meeting her own death at the hands of the Boxers.[24]

But no foreign soldiers or politicians ever envisioned moving into the countryside to evacuate missionaries. President McKinley, who at one time contemplated ordering U.S. citizens to leave the Chinese interior, yielded to Hay's urging that to do so would in effect "be a sign that the United States lacked faith in the pledges [of southern-Chinese Viceroys to protect foreigners in their districts] and might well increase tension in their still peaceful provinces. Hay also looked disagreeably on the immense responsibility such withdrawal would later place on the government for the missionaries' subsistence and repatriation."[25]

Major General Adna R. Chaffee, Civil War hero and Indian fighter, arrived in Tianjin to take command of United States forces on July 30. Still, the order to advance on Beijing did not come. Martin blamed the delay on the failure of Russian General Linivitch "to enter into counsel and there are not enough troops here to move forward without his command." Since no agreement provided for an officer of one army to give orders to officers of any other army, General Linivitch finally agreed to a consensus arrangement: "it was decided that a conference of commanders should be held every evening . . . to determine movements."[26]

On the afternoon of August 4 "raising clouds of dust on the road and rattling the heavy gun carriages over the rickety wooden bridges outside Tianjin," allied forces, numbering 18,600 including 2,500 from the United States, moved out from Tianjin to relieve the siege in Beijing. Diarist Henry Savage-Landor, who accompanied the "holy" expedition, chafed at the delays as the forces began the march. The allied armies idled, he said, "and let men, women, and children of our blood be slaughtered by these barbarians."[27]

When at last the Fourteenth Regiment joined the line of march, Captain Martin fumed. General Chaffee ordered officers to travel light. Martin had to leave his "stuff" behind. What could Chaffee be thinking, Martin wondered. "We are ordered to go forward simply with a poncho or shelter tent half, one change of underclothing, shoes and kakhie, toilet articles limited to towel, cake of soap and toothbrush and comb." Enlisted men could not even carry a change of shoes or uniform. The captain's attitude mellowed somewhat when General Chaffee allowed U.S. forces to "capture . . . twenty coolies . . . to carry food and extra ammunition." In fact, the allied armies indiscriminately enslaved hundreds of Chinese, pressing them into service as "coolies." Once captured, the men took their place "amongst a row of coolies, of whom there was always an inadequate supply." When someone protested, "the prick of a bayonet made him quickly realize that his protestations would be of no avail." Hundreds of the captured civilians pulled "Chinese-junks" loaded with provisions up the very crooked, meandering Bei He River that sometimes wandered many miles from the army's campsites.[28]

The armies marched approximately four miles that first day, camping in the rain about seven that night. The soldiers leading the column began setting up camp before those at the end passed over the wooden bridges at Tianjin where the march began. That night, the allied forces made their first contact with the Chinese Imperial Army. The Japanese led the attack, but by the time Martin's unit reached the firing line the Chinese had already retreated. The next afternoon, after chasing the Chinese forces about the countryside, Martin's unit got "out of touch." He passed the time sitting in the road writing to Louise while a newspaper correspondent waited to take the letter to Tianjin. "This is expected to be the last big stand of the Chinos unless they stand at Pekin," he wrote, sitting in the dusty road.[29]

Martin's reference to "getting out of touch" portrayed the situation charitably. The U.S. forces charged after the Chinese with such abandon that they became hopelessly lost in the vast Chinese farmland. Henry Savage-Landor, a British civilian who accompanied the armies on their march, claimed that "for some unaccountable reason," the Americans "lost their way, and therefore were not in the position assigned to them, nor did they take any part in the engagement." Nevertheless, the Japanese engaged the Chinese army for about two hours that day before the Chinese made a hasty retreat. The allied forces spent the remainder of the day chasing the Chinese army north toward Beijing.[30]

The next day, August 6, the U.S. forces moved out on the left bank of the Bei He as flanking cover for the Japanese. The march through corn and

sweet-potato fields that hindered their movement irritated officers and enlisted men alike. The weather brought sheer exhaustion. "The sun was scorch-
ing," Colonel Daggett wrote. "It seemed to have more power to prostrate
men than I had witnessed in our Southern States or Cuba or the Philippines."
Martin coped as best he could with the heat, surprising even himself. Three
other officers in his unit succumbed to the summer sun, two enlisted men
died from sunstroke, and many others suffered crippling disabilities brought
on by heat prostration.[31]

With the Fourteenth Infantry in the lead, the U.S. and British forces
marched approximately ten miles before engaging Chinese Imperial forces
supplemented by Boxers at Yang Cun. As the allied commanders deployed
their troops, Colonel Daggett ordered Martin to take his company into the
lead position. As Martin led his men around a bend in the road, "the 14th
. . . came under the fire of the gun which the Chinese had placed on the
embankment near the water-tower, and also from the rifles of the Chinese
infantrymen in houses and behind trees." Captain Martin made a daring
400-yard dash with Company M directly at the Chinese gun, capturing it
with the help of his friend and junior officer from Vancouver Barracks, Lieutenant C.N. Murphy.[32]

After four hours of bloody fighting, the Chinese forces retreated once
again and the battle ended. Martin's company suffered "the heaviest of any
organization engaged." Of the 102 men he led down the road, "I had fifteen men hit . . . 2 died in the field, 4 were mortally wounded, all [the] rest
except one very seriously." Colonel Daggett wrote glowingly about Martin's
heroic actions. "Patriotism, sustained by Anglo-Saxon pluck, won," he said,
"and the flag was honored at Yang Cun in the presence of foreign nations."[33]

U.S. commanders buried the dead with military pageantry. The regimental band, the only band among the allies on the march to Beijing, preceded the dead to a large common grave. The military chaplain read a
"touching service . . . and then the bodies were laid to rest side by side until
they could be conveyed at the expense of the State, back to America."[34]

All accounts of the battle, including Captain Martin's to the Adjutant,
Third Battalion, agreed on at least one point: the sweltering August heat in
China exacted a fierce toll on the troops. "So exhausted were the men,"
Martin wrote that day in his report, "that few were able to fire on the
retreating enemy. . . . Three of our seven enlisted men who made it fainted
from exhaustion afterwards." Colonel Daggett recalled that many of his
troops had "fallen out from heat-exhaustion."[35]

The allied forces spent August 7 camped near Yang Cun waiting for
their supplies coming up the river to reach the troops. Many U.S. soldiers

attempted to swim in the river or wash the dust and heat from their bodies but the number of human corpses and dead horses made the water unfit and hindered the progress of the "junks."[36]

Martin spent his day reflecting on the battle in letters to Louise and his father-in-law. He bemoaned Colonel Daggett's leadership, complaining, erroneously, that the colonel took no interest in his heroic actions. The captain believed that his actions deserved a battlefield promotion, but he doubted Daggett would recommend him for the honor.[37]

Others among the U.S. troops occupied their time in a less reflective way. Perhaps the perceived image depicting the "Heathen Chinee" that permeated American society and infected U.S. soldiers or the racist dogma that placed the Chinese a species below the human level led to the actions that day. Most soldiers after all "are able to kill and be killed more easily in warfare if they possess an image of the enemy sufficiently evil to inspire hatred and repugnance." Or was it the belief that the Chinese despised the Christian God that motivated their vengeance? Maybe the heat clouded men's minds and hardened their hearts. Whatever the reason—and it is unlikely we will ever know—there occurred that day "a disgusting bit of cruelty . . . a few yards from the American camp."[38]

A group of U.S. soldiers dragged a bound Chinese prisoner before an officer and asked what they should do with him. "Take him away, . . . and do with him what you d— please," the officer responded. Given the license, and evidently inured to cruelty, the soldiers dragged the Chinese man off under a railway bridge where they administered a group-beating. During the process some French and Japanese soldiers joined their U.S. colleagues. A French soldier pulled a revolver and shot the Chinese man in the face. "With his skull smashed, the man fell, and lay still breathing and moaning, with a crowd of soldiers around him, gloating over his sufferings." The French soldier then shot the man again and a Japanese stamped on the prostrate, mortally-wounded man's head.[39]

"For nearly an hour the fellow lay in this dreadful condition, with hundreds of soldiers leaning over him to get a glimpse of his agony, and going into roars of laughter as he made ghastly contortions in his delirium." Colonel Daggett later claimed that U.S. soldiers always avoided "any wanton injury to the defenseless." He may have been wrong about U.S. troops participating, but Daggett called those savage actions of other nations, "[a] disgrace of humanity, especially to soldiers of Christian nations." As one chronicler of the expedition wrote, "[a] horrible lust of cruelty developed amongst the private soldiery of all nationalities, and pervaded them like some subtle miasma emanating from this evil-smelling land."[40]

As the march to Beijing proceeded, U.S. forces suffered more staggering daily losses from sun stroke. General Chaffee insisted on marching his troops during the middle of the day, subjecting them to the most intense heat. The Japanese and Russian forces occupied the lead position in the marching order, so they led the way beginning at 4 a.m. in a relatively cool part of the day. Martin's regiment rarely left their camp before eight or nine in the morning and spent the entire day choking on the dust from the 12,000 troops ahead of them. The day after leaving Yang Cun, Martin's regiment lost 171 men to the sun. The next day seventy-six men fell, and on the day following that, ninety-six. The U.S. forces became a running joke among the other allied armies. If one wanted to find the way from Tianjin to Beijing, not the shortest way, just a way, the story went, "all you had to do was to follow the trail of blankets, water-bottles, haversacks, and other articles that the American boys had thrown away on the march, as they had not sufficient strength to carry them."[41]

Day after day, as Martin's troops passed through deserted Chinese villages, they saw the corpses of entire Chinese families executed by the Japanese and Russian forces. Some bodies they found "suspended from the rafters of their houses, where they had committed suicide." Sometimes they stuck to the road; other times they careened off through the treeless plain covered with full-grown corn rising ten or fifteen feet from the dry ground, obstructing any movement of air that might fan the burning soldiers' faces or blow away the dust. As thousands of soldiers marched through the corn fields, they raised "the dust of ages" with each step.[42]

General Chaffee exacerbated these miserable conditions. From the time they left Tianjin until they arrived in Beijing, Chaffee invariably directed U.S. troops to make camp for the night in the middle of the corn fields. Even when better grounds existed not more than a few yards away, Chaffee consistently chose the hollow, where "myriads of mosquitoes and midges" plagued his soldiers. Other commanders just as consistently picked open places "with the breeze and fresh air." Allied observers wondered why Chaffee made his men "suffer unnecessarily."[43]

Captain Martin seethed with resentment for Chaffee and even drew up a bill of particulars outlining the general's incompetence. Martin claimed that the general possessed the "physical courage and swagger of the low, brutish man," lacked "moral courage [and] honor," and cursed everyone, from the lowest "recruit in his own ranks" to "the head of the General commanding the Russians."[44]

Martin could not tolerate the way Chaffee organized the march. "Instead of starting his little army with suitable transportation," Martin complained, "he loaded his enlisted men like pack animals and unlike his Japanese and Italian brothers the American is not a beast of burden." If making common soldiers carry too much showed disdain for enlisted men, Martin felt Chaffee's actions toward officers reflected base villainy. While the other allied officers appeared well groomed and well fed, Chaffee forced American officers "to live like farm hands and look like tramps." "All these things I say showed either ignorance or indifference little short of criminal," Captain Martin wrote accusingly.[45]

From August 7 through 13, the Japanese advance guard only occasionally glimpsed the retreating Chinese forces. The major resistance from the Chinese on the route to Beijing ended. The allied armies nonetheless laid waste to the Chinese countryside inflicting terrible suffering on the civilian population. As the forces advanced, they put "village after village to the torch and left a great swath of destruction in their wake." At Dong Zhou on August 12 the commanding generals agreed that the next day would be devoted to rest and reconnaissance. The generals also agreed that on August 14 the armies would consolidate their positions at the point of the Japanese advance guard to make their attack the following day on Beijing.[46]

Martin led Company M on a reconnaissance mission on August 13, moving the unit to within five miles of Beijing. As they paused, Martin could hear "heavy firing in Pekin which began at 9 last night." He did not know then that Russian General Linivitch had broken the agreed-upon allied attack plan. Martin could hear an exchange between Russian and Chinese troops at the Dongbian Mian, one of the massive gates to the city, which the Russians had managed to breach, trapping themselves.[47]

A dispatch rider broke Martin's concentration. General Chaffee ordered Martin to rejoin the main force. When the troops assembled, Chaffee moved them hastily toward Beijing to come to the aid of the trapped Russians. Later that morning, Martin moved his company within sight of Beijing.

The city presented a formidable target to capture. It consisted of several cities within a city, each surrounded by a monumental wall. The Tartar City and the Chinese City formed the two largest entities—each approximately a four-mile square. Within the Tartar City lay the Imperial City and the Forbidden City. One of Martin's colleagues described what U.S. forces saw as they gaped in awe at mighty Beijing:

> The wall surrounding the Tarter City is about 50 feet in height, 60 feet thick at the base, and 40 feet at the top; that of the Chinese City being 30 feet high and 15 feet thick at the top. The walls of the two cities, including that separating them, are pierced by sixteen gates [Mian], and over the gates and at the corners of the walls are tower-like structures

about 50 feet high, . . . for purposes of offense and defense. The Forbidden City is reached from the south thru the Imperial City thru a series of courts and gates, four or five in number, each gate being surmounted by a strong tower similar to those on the outer walls.

Martin pictured the city dialectically: "The imperial city is much like everything else in China," he said, "a varying mixture of wealth and squalor, cleanliness and filth, beauty and hideousness."[48]

Throughout the day, units of the Fourteenth Infantry led the siege at the walls and gates to gain entrance to the Chinese City. Having no ropes, ladders, or others means with which to climb, individual soldiers scaled the immense walls, unarmed, by "feeling for each new hold for hand or foot . . . [in the] many crevices in the face of the wall where bricks had fallen out." Late in the afternoon, Fourteenth Infantry soldiers finally unfurled a U.S. flag on top of the wall surrounding the Chinese City. "As its beautiful silken folds waved out over the wall," one soldier recalled, "American pride and patriotism voiced itself in a mighty shout of triumph and exultation . . . at the thought that ours was the first foreign flag to float over the walls of Peking in the China Relief Expedition."[49]

At about four that afternoon, Martin's company contacted a lone U.S. marine, a legation guard, who informed them that the way for their entry into the Tartar City lay clear. Within a very short time, meeting little further resistance, Martin and other members of the regiment entered the legation quarter where General Chaffee and his officers proceeded to the house of U.S. minister, Edwin Conger.

The legation hostages did not fare well under the siege. Of the 800 foreigners and 3,000 Chinese Christians who had taken refuge with the legations, sixty-six had been killed and eight, including several small children, died of disease. Hard pressed for food, much to the distress of British legation chief Sir Claude MacDonald, the survivors used what means they found at hand to feed themselves, eventually consuming MacDonald's prized race horses.

The hostage foreigners "decked themselves in their best attire" to receive the conquering armies. One of the British women resplendent in her finery took offense at her American rescuers, calling them "dirty." When the disheveled Americans stormed into the legation quarter they arrived "having been forced to live like farm hands and look like tramps," without "brush[ing] their hair or chang[ing] their linen(!)," Colonel Daggett said sarcastically. Dirty or not, most of the hostages accepted the ragged soldiers with open arms. Sir Claude MacDonald joined the scattered condemnation of the Americans' "disreputable condition." Thoroughly disagreeable,

MacDonald turned what should have been an occasion for unrestrained celebration into a reception decidedly less than cordial.[50]

That ordeal over and the drought having broken earlier in the evening, in softly falling rain Martin's regiment moved just outside the Tartar City and made their camp in the mud to await orders for the next day.

While the soldiers made their camp, U.S. missionaries who took refuge in the legations at the beginning of the siege drew up a resolution demanding reparations from the Chinese government. The missionaries made available copies of these resolutions to press correspondents later in the week. Having learned nothing from their recent experience, they imperiously demanded cash from the Chinese:

> 1. For loss of time caused by the Boxer disturbances. 2. For all travelling expenses, including those to and from foreign lands, necessitated by missionaries being peremptorily ordered to leave China. 3. For future rise of prices in building materials and labor. 4. For rent of premises until new ones can be built. 5. For literary work destroyed.[51]

For some missionaries, however, reparations would not suffice as warfare continued in some provinces. On the day that their brethren completed the resolutions, Eva and Charles Price and other missionary families departed Fenzhou for Beijing around nine in the morning, escorted by twenty Chinese soldiers provided by the district magistrate. Travelling ahead of the Prices, a second group of soldiers under the command of Lu Cheng San demanded a sizable tribute from each village through which they passed with the threat that if the villagers did not pay, the missionaries would be killed in the recalcitrant village. The inevitable occurred at the village of Nan'an, twenty miles from Fenzhou. When the missionaries arrived, Lu's soldiers, one of whom studied with Charles Price, attacked. They killed everyone, stripping the bodies and tossing them into a ditch.[52]

Meanwhile in Beijing, during the early morning hours of August 15 with Martin's unit bivouacked under the city walls, the Empress Dowager and the Emperor Ci Xi, both dressed in peasant clothing, made a precipitous retreat for their stronghold at Xian in Shaanxi Province, several hundred miles to the west, where they arrived ten days later.

Even though the royals had fled, the next morning General Chaffee ordered Martin's forces to assault and capture the Imperial City where "the armed and straggling remnants of the late proud and haughty Chinese army" held out. Guided by one of General Chaffee's staff, Martin marched Company M to the gates of the Imperial City, which they attempted to shatter with cannons. The massive wooden gates, "studded profusely with huge round nails and strengthening metal bars . . . [and] barred and heavily bolted," set in a wall ninety feet thick, finally yielded to the artillery.[53]

When the gates swung open, Martin gazed at a courtyard "about seven hundred yards long and ninety wide." At the farther end of the courtyard "stood an immense wall forty-five feet high, upon which rose a tower fifty feet higher," surrounded by a moat spanned by an intricately carved marble bridge. Following orders, Captain Martin deployed his second platoon under Lieutenant Murphy to advance.[54]

Lieutenant Murphy's platoon marched approximately fifty yards into the courtyard when they met "a withering fire from every kind of conceivable weapon that can be fired from the shoulder . . ." thus dispelling the incomprehensible illusion held by Martin's immediate superior, Major William Quinton, that they had entered the courtyard "without attracting observation." Caught in the open, with only weeds behind which to take cover, Murphy's men returned the fire. Colonel Daggett, his memory evidently dimmed by time, recalled later that the men "were nearly hidden by the weeds, and using smokeless powder . . . [thus were] not conspicuous target[s]." Daggett's memory notwithstanding, Martin's men met confusion and death.[55]

When the first shots rang out, and before Murphy's men could decipher their origin, several men of the platoon lay dead or dying. Discipline faltered in the confusion. The wounded "lay helpless" under the Chinese soldiers' "terrific fire." Reaching the wounded proved impossible so the Americans handed stretchers "to a number of Chinese prisoners, and with rifles pointed at their temples they were ordered to pick up the wounded." The prisoners did as ordered. Colonel Daggett decided to increase the fire directed at the citadel wall and ordered Martin to reinforce Lieutenant Murphy's position. Dodging a heavy rifle barrage, Martin led his company to Murphy's aid, "seemingly oblivious to the danger." Major Quinton later wrote that Captain Martin "kept such control of [his] men throughout the action that I never observed the American soldier, plucky fighter as he is, fight with more coolness and determined gallantry. It was a lovely sight to observe the men in action." Firing fiercely, Martin and his men quickly exhausted the one hundred rounds allotted each man. For several minutes, until more ammunition reached them, Martin and his men sat helpless as the Chinese poured fire down on them. Martin later wrote that "for a time it looked as though we might be practically annihilated."[56]

When more troops wielding Gatling guns and cannon poured into the courtyard and scaled the roofs of the buildings along its walls, the firing from the Chinese diminished, then ceased. When the Americans reached the far end of the courtyard they encountered the same kind of gate through which they had so recently come. Again they brought up artillery to blow open the gates. Inside, Martin and his men observed a courtyard about the same width as the last but less than half the length. At the farther end there stood yet another impressive wall and gate. Meeting no resistance, the troops advanced across this courtyard, blew open the gate, and entered into yet a third courtyard about as large as the first in length but significantly wider. At the far end was the first gate of the Forbidden City, a sight few non-Chinese had ever seen, where no Westerner had ever set foot.

As the Americans set up their cannon to repeat their actions yet a fourth time, one of General Chaffee's aides rushed up with an order to halt the attack and regroup back outside the Imperial City. Daggett could not have been more disappointed. "There was the Forbidden City," he said, "whose pavements . . . the foot of the white man had never pressed. The means were at hand. The skill and nerve to use them were there." But Chaffee denied him the goal, undoubtedly for "good diplomatic reasons."[57]

Once again Martin exploded at Chaffee's actions. Several of Martin's men lay dead in the courtyards and Chaffee "allowed the grand prize to be snatched" from his grasp. Martin proclaimed Chaffee a coward who "showed himself wanting in every attribute of a commander." The captain looked at the "many precious lives" snuffed out in a task "needlessly assumed" and declared that "history will record of General Chaffee that on a campaign made in the eyes of the world," he "was a small man, ignorant, drunken, brutal from the beginning to the end." He "repelled friend and foe alike," Martin wrote disgustedly to his wife.[58]

In fact Chaffee's order reflected a decision arrived at earlier in the day at a meeting attended by all the allied generals where they agreed that the Forbidden City would not be violated nor would the Imperial City be occupied. The next day, expressing their disapproval at the decision, the foreign ministers overruled the military commanders. General Chaffee stationed troops in the Imperial City and posted a guard on the Forbidden City with orders to allow no one in or out. With the exception of the Forbidden City, for the moment, Beijing, the capital city of the Chinese Empire, became occupied territory.

On August 16, the allied forces divided Beijing into occupation districts. U.S. troops began setting up camp expecting a long period of occupation. Two common threads tied together all the military districts—killing and looting. Of the killing, which at times proved indiscriminate and at others methodical, perhaps the best comment is that of General Chaffee. "It is safe to say," Chaffee remarked, "that where one real Boxer has been killed since the capture of Pekin, fifty harmless coolies or laborers on the farms, including not a few women and children, have been slain. The Boxer element is largely mixed with the mass of the population, and by slaying a lot one or more Boxers might be taken in."[59]

Singling Boxers out from other Chinese in a crowd proved a vexing problem for the allied armies—they looked just like ordinary peasants, which in fact they were. As the U.S. military discovered in its guerrilla war in the Philippines, then in China, and in a similar war sixty years later in Vietnam, the enemy could not be easily distinguished. As in Vietnam, allied forces ". . . regarded the peasantry as some sort of subspecies. They were not taking human life and destroying human homes. They were exterminating treacherous animals and stamping out their dens." Later, apologists, such as L.R. Marchant in his introduction to *The Siege of The Peking Legations: A Diary,* claimed that one need not "whole-heartedly condemn the activities of the forces."

> They were very much the creatures of their age, and what they did was very much comprehended by their contemporaries. . . . They believed that punishment was necessary and that it should be given firmly and on the spot. They felt that the best way to deal with children who misbehaved was to apply firm discipline at the scene of the crime, and their penal codes for adults were not known for their leniency. The Chinese were to be given similar treatment.

Ironically, during 1970, when Marchant made his comments on U.S. military action in China, the United States applied much the same logic and rationalization to another Asian people.[60]

Once the fighting concluded in Beijing, U.S. forces began a search for a suitable place to erect a permanent camp. Martin expected a long occupation, telling Louise not to expect him back in the Philippines until at least the spring. The need for shelter became particularly acute with regard to medical facilities for the wounded after U.S. Minister Conger refused them shelter at the U.S. legation. Having moved from exposure to the elements under the wall of the Tartar City, Martin's regiment settled in the Temple of Agriculture, "the first sensible camp which the poor American boys had so far had in the China Campaign." The temple furnished them with shade from the blistering sun, green grass on which to lounge, and two magnificent wells providing the first decent water the men had had since leaving Tianjin. Captain Martin dubbed the temple "a fairyland." It encompassed approximately 400 acres surrounded by a fifteen-foot-high brick wall. Every year the emperor came to the temple where he maintained a patch of land that he cultivated "with his own hands" as an example "to the farmers of the Celestial Empire."[61]

Martin wrote approvingly of the luxuries he found in the temple. He praised the beauty of "the golden horses, harrow, plows, harness, etc. etc, which were brought into the groves for the annual feast." His men commandeered silk tents, bronze candle sticks, and "beautiful tables and chairs" to use in their camp. He considered himself and the men lucky to have escaped "the filthy city districts . . . with their accumulation of filthy and dead bodies of both men and beasts which are still lying in the streets by the thousands festering in the sun."[62]

But things did not run as smoothly as he expected, which contributed to the growing resentment Martin held for General Chaffee. While camping under the Tartar City wall, his men slept in the open because they jettisoned their tents back in the corn fields. Now General Chaffee even refused the men permission to use tents abandoned by Imperial Chinese forces. He ordered dozens of enormous tents, able to shelter twenty or thirty men, left where the Chinese abandoned them, where they eventually rotted in the mud. Some of Chaffee's forces, suffering from sunstroke during the day and drenching storms at night, slept in the open. Many had no blankets and no change of clothing. "Imagine my condition," Martin lamented. "I am reduced to one pair of socks and two suits of under-clothing but I probably could never get my trunks up from Tianjin if I sent for them." Some soldiers took to wearing odds and ends of Chinese clothing they looted from shops and houses simply "to meet the demands of decency." During the first few days at the temple General Chaffee again refused permission to use the silk tents Martin found so beautiful but eventually, "by means of subterfuges and stratagems," his troops secured adequate cover but not before some soldiers "erected funny little shelters with umbrellas, rags, silks, and Chinese cloth or matting, and gradually collected furs, which they used as bedding," which gave the temple grounds an "interesting" appearance. "Such a patchwork camp was never before seen, certainly in an American camp," Colonel Daggett wrote later.[63]

In the division of Beijing into occupation zones, U.S. forces drew the west half of the Chinese City and a section of the Tartar City. When they took up their occupation duties, they forced the citizenry into "cleaning-up details." Attending to the rotting corpses of humans and animals being fed upon by dogs, hogs, and birds became their first priority. Slowly, Beijing residents who fled during the fighting returned to their homes and shops, lending an air of normality to the occupied city, a city that Colonel Daggett said "was filthy beyond description, and probably had been only a little less so for centuries."[64]

While the cleanup progressed, the foreign ministers called a conference to determine the disposition of the Forbidden City. With opinion divided, they eventually decided that the city must be entered "else the Chinese would believe the gods had intervened and prevented those sacred pavements from being polluted by the tread of the hated foreigner." The prevailing argument among the ministers called for breaking that particular superstition to "[teach] these people that they were at the mercy of the Allies."[65]

Not that the allies had not been providing that lesson already. Religious respect among the Westerners ended at the boundaries of Christianity. Western soldiers went out of their way to show contempt for Chinese priests and places of worship. They stabled horses in the temples, looted "art heirlooms of thousands of years of the nation's life to be found therein," and destroyed what they could not steal."[66]

The allied forces also carried out a "literary holocaust" with methodic ritual. They built a huge fire outside the city walls where, for more than a week, carts laden with thousands of books drew up to have their contents devoured by the flames.[67]

On the day appointed for the demonstration of allied power and suzerainty, August 28, 1900, representatives from the allied forces assembled before the Forbidden City's gates. Small detachments represented each country's army. General Chaffee warned the chief attendant at the gate of the Forbidden City that "if no resistance should be made, the city would be left intact; if resistance should be made, the city might be destroyed." When the troops arrived promptly at 9 a.m., the attendant submissively opened the gates.[68]

Contradictory sensations and aspirations gripped Martin as he led the 150 soldiers of the United States Army's detachment through the last of the six gates, the Imperial Gate, at the south entrance to the Chinese Imperial Palace. For the first time "in all the centuries," Martin wrote, the feet of white men were to profane "the holy-of-holies—the palace of the Emperor of China." Martin understood the historical significance. He felt himself an agent of history, participating in the chance of a lifetime, leading a grand military review in the Chinese Empire's sacred precincts. "It was the sight of a life time," he boasted. "Drawn up before the entrance gate were the chosen troops of Russia, Japan, England, America, France and Germany." Others agreed. Savage-Landor wrote glowingly:

> When one thought that for five centuries, since this Palace was built, these gates had barred the way to all civilizing influence, when one realized that, whatever had occurred outside in the way of intercourse with foreigners, no one had ever penetrated these sacred walls, it is excusable if one felt somewhat proud to be the first of one's race to set foot inside the Forbidden City. It was a memorable event in the history of China.[69]

"The present program," Martin wrote, majestically, "is simply to open the gates & march through the Imperial City & Palace—this done to come out & lock the place up again. Of the millions of loot in the place not an article will be permitted to be touched." U.S. soldiers, stationed along the route, would prevent any looting, Martin claimed.[70]

But Martin's conviction failed him. Captain Martin sacrificed what his commanding officer in the Philippines called a personal morality "beyond reproach" to the soldier's right to booty. Greed overcame good intentions. While Martin led the U.S. contingent through the Forbidden City, some of his colleagues looted the Emperor's palace. When he returned to camp, Martin could not resist the offers to share in the loot. "After the troops marched out," he wrote, "the grounds were cleared and the gates locked, but not until some precious loot had been secured by camp followers and your C. Harry is one of the few who was fortunate enough to have a friend to remember him on the occasion," he told Louise. With so much loot available

Martin, in dress uniform, poses with medals he earned in China. *Oregon Historical Society, 004897*

in Beijing, looters often showed "much good-nature," even generosity if the term can be applied to the giving away of stolen goods. "In a perfectly legitimate way," Martin boasted, "I have accumulated several treasures including two vases—one of jade and one of bronze—taken from beside the throne in the Emperor's palace and three perfectly bewitching pieces of gold embroidery taken from his private apartments. The three latter will make hangings of inestimable value. They are all quite large pieces."

He worried, though, about holding on to his booty, "for property rights now in China are not very sacred," he said with no hint of irony. Martin's colleagues even carried off the Emperor's throne. At their camp in the Temple of Agriculture they used the throne as a barber's chair until Major Quinton "came to its rescue and placed it for safe keeping outside his quarters." A photograph in Savage-Landor's book shows a cocky, relaxed Captain Martin standing next to Major Quinton seated on the throne beside his tent.[71]

In their eyes, the Chinese may have been "heathens," their society may have been corrupt, but foreigners coveted the beauties they beheld. Colonel Daggett recalled some instances of looting by U.S. forces, but claimed those caught looting "brought the blush of shame to the faces of their comrades."[72]

In fact, the Americans began their looting spree in Tianjin. Military commanders and popular press accounts claimed that "American soldiers in China were the only ones who did absolutely no looting." Their refusal to loot showed the "superiority of their morals," so the story went. But the truth is, U.S. soldiers joined their international comrades in stripping valuables from the Chinese. "They one and all were looters of the very first water." Some saw looting as the moral duty of Western soldiers. "In a war between civilized nations," Savage-Landor wrote, "looting is without doubt a crime to be severely condemned and punished, but in the case of a nation like the Chinese, who have no national pride, no respect for any government or law, nor for the life of others or of themselves, there seemed no way of punishing them except by touching their pocket. This the Allied soldiers certainly succeeded in doing extremely well."[73]

American soldiers lacked class and artistic taste as looters though, as far as the British were concerned, although they may never have seen Captain Martin's cache. Americans usually bypassed artistic embroideries, rare bronzes, and china ware for more utilitarian gold and silver, Savage-Landor claimed.[74]

Martin evidently acquired a penchant for looting. After that first taste he accumulated treasure that eventually filled several steamer trunks. He and Lieutenants Murphy and Bass worked as a team, sometimes staying up until the wee hours of the morning dividing up the day's finds. One night the three looters hit the "abandoned" house of "a rich old prince." How long

Martin expected the house to remain "abandoned" he does not say. His share of the plunder consisted of "three (3) handsome Russian sable cloaks, one cloak of ermine and astrakhan, one great coat of silver fox, four (4) bolts of silk, one hand painted fan and several other articles of lesser value." He promised Louise that she could dress in "handsome furs" for the rest of her life, "if I can get the stuff out of the Country before it is stolen." Louise though, had different standards and stuck to them. According to Martin's daughter, Jane Pyne, who inherited the twelve steamer trunks packed with the loot Martin eventually shipped back to the United States, Louise considered the precious contents to be stolen property: she never opened the trunks.[75]

As the occupation dragged on, Martin made himself as comfortable as possible. When the weather turned chilly in September, he slept under looted padded quilts. He eventually sent for his trunks in Tianjin to have more of his "things" around. "Whether we remain or not," he told Louise, " I have concluded to make myself comfortable."[76]

Throughout the fall, the allied forces conducted many punitive raids in the countryside in which they murdered hundreds of Chinese. In one "very pleasant little campaign," a joint British and American venture in which Martin participated, troops attacked "a Boxer stronghold" in the mountains twenty miles west of Beijing. When the allied forces trapped the Chinese in a pincer movement, "the Chinese threw away their guns as they ran so that the fight soon developed into a mere murder of them." Having subdued the Chinese, the allied soldiers proceeded to burn the village to the ground.[77]

As he travelled the countryside, Martin hardened his opinion of Chinese civilization. "The more I see of the Chinese," he wrote, repulsed, "the less I think of them." He compared them to his Chinese servants at Vancouver Barracks, claiming the latter to be the "best of the coolie class." Life in China remained difficult, Martin claimed, because "we find it impossible to get a clean, intelligent servant in Peking. All from high to low are base, filthy, ignorant, beasts," he moaned. His solution? "I should say," he wrote Louise, "that the world would be better off rid of the whole brood."[78]

By October the constant dinner parties at the legations and the thrill of chasing recalcitrant Boxers around the countryside lost their glamour. Martin eagerly anticipated a reunion with his wife and son. After several false starts, the president finally ordered the Fourteenth Regiment home in mid-October. Martin departed Beijing on October 21, retracing the route of the allied advance from Tianjin. The only incident of note to chroniclers of that return trip involved a confrontation between Captain Martin and a Russian officer. The story is amusing and best told by Martin himself.

On the return march from Peking and while approaching Ho-Hsi-Woo, the column of the regiment one evening was overtaken by a Russian officer of high rank in his three-horse, buckboard, driven by his orderly. At the time the rear battalion of the regiment, temporarily commanded by myself, was entering a defile, bordered on each side by low, swampy ground, the road being just wide enough to accommodate the column. I suddenly heard a loud shout, "Watch out, Captain! watch out!" but before I could even turn my head, I found my horse on his knees, with the Russian's horses on top of us. After extricating ourselves, I found that the Russian, seeing the narrow road before him, and not proposing to be delayed by our column, had deliberately plunged into us, regardless of consequences. The temporary check which he had received by my being in the way seemed to infuriate the officer, and, with violent gesticulations, he ordered his orderly to drive on. Equally determined that he should not break up our column in this manner, I ordered two enlisted men nearest us to take his horses' heads. This was too much. Taking the lines from his now helpless, bewildered driver, he forced his horses forward, but before he had completely gotten them away from the men holding them, I had ordered four more men to assist in stopping him and to keep him where he was until the rear of the column had passed. In spite of such a show of force, he persisted in violently urging his horses forward, and was only stopped by being knocked to the ground by the butt of a gun and having the horses unhitched from the conveyance. As he rose from the ground, he started to draw his revolver, when instantly several rifles were drawn on him. This seemed to bring him to a realizing sense of his impotency, and, putting up his revolver, he ran forward with tears in his eyes, and called out in French to the captain of the company then passing: "I am an officer, an officer! Look at my frightful condition, and the humiliation which has been heaped upon me! Can you not give me justice?" He received this consoling answer: "That's all right, old man; there's only room on this road for one of us, and we got here first." From a turn in the road we looked back to see the orderly getting the wreck together. His only witness was his commanding officer, standing off in abject despair.[79]

Martin boarded the U.S. ship *Warren* and sailed for Manila on November 3, arriving in the Philippines to the welcoming arms of his wife and child ten days later.

A considerable allied force remained in China, compelling the Chinese court to issue edicts banning the Boxers and instituting a strict suppression of the movement. As historian Joseph Esherick has noted, "it was this combination of imperial prohibition and enormous and frequently indiscriminate slaughter by foreign troops which finally brought the movement to an end."[80]

Notes

1. Marcus Aurelius, quoted in, Ward Just, *Military Men* (Avon Books, 1970), 13–14.
2. CHM to Ellis G. Hughes, typescript, July 22, 1900, CHMC, OHS.
3. Ibid.; the reference to "Brother John" comes from a derisive epithet current on the West Coast. Robert McClellan says in his book, *The Heathen Chinee*, that "'John Chinaman' (or even just 'john') . . . [indicated] the facelessness and anonymity attributed to [the Chinese immigrant] by his American hosts. 'Only John!' warned one author on the West Coast in 1896, 'yet in a few years he has overrun the coast.'"
4. Percy Maddux, *City on the Willamette: The Story of Portland, Oregon* (Portland: Binfords and Mort, 1952), 77–80. The material comes from a chapter entitled, "John Chinaman Moves In;" Robert McClellan, *The Heathen Chinee: A Study of American Attitudes toward China, 1890–1905* (Cincinnati: Ohio State University Press, 1971), 5, 6, 59, 60. Precise numbers even from the U.S. census were difficult to pin down as McClellan notes: "Estimates of the total Chinese population in the country varied widely and usually reflected the point of view of the analyst. . . . the point is that the Chinese did come in sufficient numbers to arouse the concern . . . of a large number of Americans." A.A. Roback, *A Dictionary of International Slurs* (Cambridge: Sci-Art Publishers, 1944), 153; *Seattle Post-Intelligencer,* July 10, 1900; *Los Angeles Times,* July 9, 1900.
5. William J. Duiker, *Cultures in Collision: The Boxer Rebellion* (San Rafael, California: Presidio Press, 1978), 9; I have opted to use, wherever possible, the modern-day "Pinyin Romanization" of Chinese place names, since the various sources used in this chapter all spell the place names differently. Thus "Fen Cho fu" becomes "Fenzhou," and "Tientsin" and "Pekin" in Charles Martin's letters become "Tianjin" and "Beijing" in the narrative's text.
6. McKinley, quoted in William Appleman Williams, *The Tragedy of American Diplomacy* (New York: Dell Publishing Co., Inc., 1962), 16–17; Denby, quoted in David Healy, *U.S. Expansionism: The Imperialist Urge in the 1890s* (Madison: University of Wisconsin Press, 1970), 180.
7. Williams, 45; Henry Steele Commager, *Documents of American History* (New York: Meredith Corporation, 1968), V.2, 10, 11; Williams, 43.
8. Herbert Hoover, *The Memoirs of Herbert Hoover: Years of Adventure, 1874–1920* (New York: The Macmillan Company, 1951), 47.
9. Harrison E. Salisbury in the foreword to, Virginia Phipps, Lucille Wilson, Arlene Caruth, eds., *China Journal 1889–1900: An American Missionary Family during the Boxer Rebellion* (New York: Charles Scribner's Sons), 1989.
10. Joseph Esherick, *The Origins of the Boxer Uprising* (Berkeley: University of California Press, 1987), 74.
11. Duiker, 13.
12. Esherick, xiii. Esherick goes on to say: "Although familiar to most people, the Boxer Uprising remains poorly understood. In the first place, the Boxers were not pugilists. Their 'boxing' was really a set of invulnerability rituals—to protect them from the powerful new weapons of the West.

   "A second common misunderstanding relates to the usual name for the Boxer movement: the Boxer Rebellion. The appellation is truly a misnomer, for the Boxers never rebelled against the Manchu rulers of China and their Qing dynasty. Indeed the most common Boxer slogan, throughout the history of the movement, was 'support the Qing, destroy the Foreign'—where 'foreign' clearly meant the foreign religion, Christianity, and its Chinese converts as much as the foreigners themselves. In the summer of 1900, threatened with a foreign military advance on the capital, the Qing court even declared its explicit support of the Boxers. . . . In order to save face for the Qing court and the Empress Dowager at its head, the fiction was created that the Boxers were really rebels, who happened to gain support from some Manchu princes who usurped power in Beijing. It was accordingly the Boxer Rebellion, and the Qing only had to be punished for not suppressing it earlier. Despite this purely political and opportunist origin of the term, the Boxer Rebellion has shown a remarkable ability to survive in texts on Chinese and world history." xiv

13. Esherick, 154, xiii; Robert M. Utley, *The Indian Frontier of the American West, 1846–1890* (Albuquerque: University of New Mexico Press, 1984), 251–52.
14. Duiker, 60, 56.
15. CHM to Ellis Hughes, July 31, 1900, CHMC, OHS; A. Henry Savage-Landor, *China and the Allies,* Vols. 1 and 2 (London: William Heinemann, 1901), 221.
16. Hoover, 48, 49.
17. Ibid., 49.
18. George Lynch, *The War of the Civilizations: Being the Record of a "Foreign Devil's" Experiences with the Allies in China* (London: Longmans, Green, and Co., 1901), 24; Savage-Landor, 133.
19. L.S. Sorley, *History of the Fourteenth United States Infantry: From January, 1890 to December, 1908* (Chicago: L.S. Sorley, 1909), 64, 65; CHM to LM, August 2, 1900, CHMC, OHS.
20. CHM to Ellis Hughes, July 31, 1900, CHMC, OHS.
21. CHM to LM, August 2, 1900, CHMC, OHS.
22. CHM to Ellis Hughes, July 31, 1900, CHMC, OHS.
23. Ibid.
24. Phipps, et al., 236.
25. Young, 165.
26. CHM to LM, August 2, 1900, CHMC, OHS; A.S. Daggett, *America in the China Relief Expedition* (Kansas City: Hudson-Kimberly Publishing Company, 1903), 55; Sorley, 68.
27. Sorley 69; Savage-Landor, 334, 335.
28. CHM to LM, August 2, 1900, CHMC, OHS; Lynch, 21, 26; Daggett, 56.
29. Daggett, 70; CHM to LM, August 5, 1900, CHMC, OHS.
30. Savage-Landor, 340.
31. Daggett, 60; CHM to LM, August 7, 1900, CHMC, OHS; Lynch, 32.
32. Savage-Landor, 358.
33. CHM to LM, August 7, 1900, CHMC, OHS; Daggett, 64.
34. Daggett, 69; Savage-Landor, 363.
35. CHM to Adjutant, Third Battalion, August 7, 1900, CHMC, OHS; Daggett, 67–68.
36. Savage-Landor, 364.
37. CHM to LM, August 7, 1900, CHMC, OHS.
38. J. Glenn Gray, *The Warriors: Reflections on Men in Battle* (New York: Harcourt, Brace and Company, 1959), 133; Savage-Landor, 364.
39. Savage-Landor, 364–65.
40. Ibid., 365; Daggett, 73; Sorley, 75; Lynch, 36.
41. CHM to LM, August 14 1900, CHMC, OHS; Daggett, 70; Savage-Landor, 373.
42. Lynch, 47; Daggett, 71.
43. Savage-Landor, 371–72, 373.
44. Ibid.
45. CHM to LM, August 17, 1900, CHMC, OHS.
46. Esherick, 310.

47. CHM to LM, August 14, 1900, CHMC, OHS.

48. Sorley, 78; CHM to LM, August 31, 1900, CHMC, OHS.

49. Sorley, 80, 81.

50. Ibid., 83; Daggett, 89; CHM to LM, August 14, 1900, CHMC, OHS; Sorley, 84, 85; Lynch, 77.

51. Savage-Landor, V.2, 193.

52. Felsing, in Phipps, et al., 238–42.

53. CHM to LM, August 17, 1900, CHMC, OHS; Major William Quinton to Captain Learnard, Adjutant, Fourteenth Infantry, August 17, 1900, CHMC, OHS; Daggett, 96; Savage-Landor, 196.

54. Daggett, 97–98.

55. William Quinton to Captain Learnard, August 17, 1900, CHMC, OHS; Daggett, 98.

56. Savage-Landor, 204; William Quinton to Captain Learnard, August 17, 1900; CHM to LM, August 17, 1900, CHMC, OHS.

57. Daggett, 99.

58. CHM to LM, August 17 and 27, 1900, CHMC, OHS.

59. Lynch, 84.

60. Neil Sheehan, *A Bright Shining Lie: John Paul Vann and America in Vietnam* (New York: Random House, 1988), 110; Marchant, 97.

61. CHM to LM, August 17, 1900, CHMC, OHS; Savage-Landor, 247; Daggett, 109; Savage-Landor, 266.

62. CHM to LM, August 27, 1900, CHMC, OHS.

63. Daggett, 109; Savage-Landor, 247–48; CHM to LM, August 20, 1900, CHMC, OHS; Sorley, 92; Savage-Landor, 248; Daggett, 111.

64. Daggett, 111.

65. Ibid., 106.

66. Lynch, 146.

67. Ibid., 146–47.

68. Daggett, 107.

69. CHM to LM, August 26, 27, and 29, 1900, CHMC, OHS; Savage-Landor, 375.

70. CHM to LM, August 27, 1900, CHMC, OHS.

71. Ibid.; Daggett, 108; Colonel A.S. Daggett to Adjutant General, U.S. Army, January 3, 1901, CHMC, OHS; Savage-Landor, V.1, 194; CHM to LM, August 29, 1900, CHMC, OHS; Savage-Landor, 268.

72. Daggett, 112, 113.

73. Savage-Landor, 200, 191, 194.

74. Ibid., 200, 201–02.

75. CHM to LM, August 20, 1900, CHMC, OHS; Jane Pyne, Martin's daughter, in a telephone conversation with the author, March 17, 1992. After that conversation, two of Martin's grandsons cautioned the author to be wary of claims made by Ms. Pyne because at the time of the phone conversation, they claim, she was in the advanced stages of Alzheimer's. She seemed remarkably lucid to this author, and remembered her mother's actions vividly.

76. CHM to LM, August 31, 1900, CHMC, OHS.

77. Ibid., September 19, 1900.

78. Ibid., September 6, 1900.

79. CHM as quoted in Daggett, 137.

80. Esherick, 310. The suppression of the Boxer movement somewhat parallels the treatment of the "Ghost Dance" that developed a decade earlier among Native Americans. To eradicate the movement, U.S. troops eventually slaughtered more than one hundred Sioux Indians in an unfortunate incident at Wounded Knee, South Dakota, in 1890.

Chapter Four

RISING THROUGH THE RANKS

We taught love of country, respect for constituted authority, submission to privation, fortitude in danger and hardship, and forgetfulness of self in loyalty to the higher ideal of the general welfare.
—Charles Henry Martin

Let him die. You all get to hell out of here and become soldiers again.
—Charles Henry Martin

BETWEEN HIS RETURN to the Philippines in November 1900 and his posting to Camp Grant when the United States entered World War I, Martin moved about a good deal, as is normal in the life of a soldier rising through the ranks. He ignored the advice of one of his superiors in China to "shake the army with its narrowing influences in peace times" and "go into the lumber business in the northwest where fortunes await men of business aptitude." The rest of that officer's advice, to "form the proper social and political ties," Martin had adopted long ago. He kept solid his ties to Portland's elite through Ellis Hughes, and continued, with Hughes's advice, to invest in Portland real estate.[1]

In July 1901, the army reassigned the Fourteenth Infantry. After their three-year-long stay in the Philippines, the army deliberately chose Fort Snelling, Minnesota, as a proper change of duty for the tropic-weary soldiers. Having acclimated to tropical weather, Martin's regiment "just hibernated" when the thermometer dropped to 46 degrees below zero in the frigid 1901 Minnesota winter. From Fort Snelling, the Martins moved to Fort Wayne, Indiana, for a year and then back to the Philippines for three more years (1903–06) where Martin took up supply duties again as chief quartermaster, Department of Visaya, Ilo Ilo. He reaped the benefits of studying with Ellis Hughes when he and several colleagues joined other Americans in profitable real estate speculation in the defeated islands.[2]

In December 1906, the Martins returned to the Pacific Northwest, where for the next five years, Captain Martin served once again at Vancouver

Barracks. Here, as constructing quartermaster, Martin supervised the building of new enlisted-men's barracks and officer quarters and then commanded two infantry regiments, the First and the Eighteenth.

After promotion to major in 1910, Martin spent two years on the General Staff in Washington, D.C., working for General Leonard Wood. His duties there included service on the military information committee in the Army War College, where he evaluated and reported on the advances in military technology made by other countries. General Wood used the information provided by this committee in shaping a model to reconstruct the U.S. Army and direct investments in weaponry.

While Martin evaluated the military capabilities of other countries, some units of the Organized Militia in Oregon (later called the Oregon National Guard) went through a period of disintegrating discipline among volunteers precipitated by inept leadership. So great had the problems become by 1909, that one battalion of the Third Oregon Infantry came perilously close to mutiny during field maneuvers. When the crisis could no longer be ignored, Oregon's political establishment began to look for someone to reorganize the militia. With his excellent military record and all the proper social and political ties having already been laid, Martin headed the list of prospective candidates. Governor Oswald West, who later played the role of advisor to Congressman and Governor Martin, led a group of prominent citizens and top militia officers in a letter-writing campaign requesting Martin's transfer to the Oregon Militia. Martin's confidant, Oregon militia Adjutant General W.E. Finzer, led the offensive through the military hierarchy. Twice during May 1910, General Finzer cabled the War Department chief of Division of Militia Affairs requesting that Martin be given a leave of absence to accept the colonelcy of the Third Oregon Infantry. Finzer knew of Martin's plans to retire in 1917 after thirty years of service and used those plans as a justification for Martin's reassignment. Captain S.L.A. Bowman of the Third Infantry, chairman of what seems to have been a "Draft Martin Committee," echoed Finzer's words in a May 17 telegram to Oregon Senator George Chamberlain. "Officers of the third infantry Oregon National Guard want Major C.H. Martin," Bowman cabled, adding, "they request you intercede with the War Department at once to obtain favorable action."[3]

Senator George Chamberlain, former member of the Oregon legislature, former Multnomah County District attorney, former governor, who moved in Martin and Hughes's Arlington Club circle, interceded two days later. Joining Oregon's other senator, Jonathan Bourne Jr., and "many prominent citizens of Portland," Chamberlain cajoled Major General F.C. Ainsworth, adjutant general, United States Army. "We desire to respectfully recommend that the application of Major C.H. Martin . . . for leave of absence . . . be approved," the senator wrote. The Oregon National Guard urgently needed Martin's expertise and assigning the major "will be in the best interests of the Government in developing the usefulness and efficiency of the National Guard in the State of Oregon."[4]

The pleading all received the same response. On May 21, 1910, Acting Secretary of War Robert Alison communicated to all the correspondents the same news—federal law prohibited an active duty officer from serving in a state militia.[5]

Somehow the Oregon National Guard limped along in its fractured condition for the next three years when the Third Infantry colonel resigned. The officers held an election to decide on a new colonel, and Martin received the unanimous endorsement of all qualified voters. After communicating this news to Martin and their political superiors, the supplicants took up Martin's cause once again, meeting this time with more success. When he learned of his election to the colonelcy of the Third Infantry in April, Martin wired General Finzer, thanking the general for "your faith in my ability." Nothing would "give me more pleasure," Martin said, "provided [it] can be arranged [for] Senator Chamberlain [to] take [the] question up with Secretary [Lindley M.] Garrison."[6]

During April 1913, as letters began circulating with the request that Major Martin be appointed to the Third Infantry, General Finzer and Governor West went to the top of the U.S. Army hierarchy with their requests, corresponding with the chief of staff, General Leonard Wood. Senator Chamberlain, responding to Martin's request, worked through the political bureaucracy. He wrote to the new secretary of war, Lindley M. Garrison, requesting favorable action on Martin's reassignment to the Oregon National Guard. Garrison demurred, claiming "that the Judge Advocate General of the Army is of the opinion that the Act of March 3, 1911, limits the power of the President to detach officers of the active list from their proper commands of duty with the National guard." Chamberlain could not accept the rebuff, however, because this time his prestige and power entered into the equation. He had already committed himself publicly when he told *The Oregonian* that Major Martin would be reassigned. Even though he "was one of the most genial, affable, companionable men" to represent Oregon in the Senate, Chamberlain nevertheless used his political sagacity to outmaneuver Secretary Garrison. As a senior member of the Senate Committee on Military Affairs, Chamberlain convinced committee chair Senator J.F. Johnston and Congressman James Hay, chairman of the House Committee on Military Affairs, to send a joint letter to Garrison. The legislators informed the secretary that in their opinion, "the intention of Congress was to extend and supplement the earlier legislation for the discipline and instruction of the Organized Militia."[7]

Forwarding the Johnston and Hay letter to Secretary Garrison, Senator Chamberlain, in his own cover letter, detailed at length his justification for Martin's reassignment. Chamberlain informed Garrison of Martin's election to the colonelcy, claiming the choice showed the resolute conviction of his supporting officers who felt that Martin "can, with his superior knowledge of military affairs, soon bring the regiment to the highest standard of military efficiency." Senator Chamberlain also pressed and expanded on the points made by Johnston and Hay.[8]

Congress had no intention of denying states the best possible leadership in military affairs, the senator claimed. "In time of peace," he wrote, "there is no better way to prepare for war than to properly train the National Guard of the several States, and every presumption ought to be indulged in favoring the detail of regular officers of the United States Army." Chamberlain chastised Garrison and the judge advocate general for misconstruing the intent of congress, claiming that the judge advocate general "has placed a wrong construction on the Acts in question in holding that there is anything in either of them which would prevent the detail of Major Martin for service and I trust you may be able to comply with the request."[9]

Martin meanwhile worked on General Wood who in turn also brought pressure to bear on Secretary Garrison. On June 7, succumbing to the pressure, Garrison recommended to General Wood that Major Martin be reassigned to the Oregon National Guard at the request of the governor of Oregon. Deeply satisfied, Major Martin accepted the assignment. Once again, maintaining the right political connections redounded to his benefit.[10]

Having achieved a reassignment to Oregon where he could monitor his real estate investments, please his wife who longed for home, and continue to build on his social and political relationships, Martin did not lose sight of the significant role Chamberlain played in the successful outcome. When Chamberlain gained the chairmanship of the Senate Military Committee, Martin used the opportunity to compliment his mentor. Martin congratulated the senator on his promotion to the chairmanship and told the Senator that the promotion boded well for the military because now it rested in Chamberlain's capable hands. The leading Democrat in Oregon responded affably. "[W]hile I may fail in the proper discharge of my duties," the senator wrote, "you can rest assured that it will not be from a lack of interest in the Army and its welfare." Chamberlain went on to praise Martin's "efficient leadership and instruction," noting that the Oregon

National Guard "will soon place itself in the first rank of . . . State organizations."[11]

For the next year, Martin set himself to reorganizing the Third Infantry. He removed most of the officers and replaced them with his own appointments. Working to return the trust shown by Chamberlain and to solidify his growing relationship with the senator, Martin convinced his Arlington Club circle and others within Oregon's political establishment to support an increase in the size of the U.S. Army and other measures dealing with military preparedness being pushed in Congress by Senator Chamberlain. "There is some military sentiment springing up here in Oregon," he wrote General Albert Mills of his success, "and the Senator's friends are using this to show him that, if he wishes to go down in history as a statesman, it must be from a military standpoint." At any rate, Martin reasoned, "pushing military policy will certainly bring him more credit than simply getting offices, and river and harbor improvements."[12]

Martin understood the usefulness of the press in his campaign to promote military preparedness while strengthening his links to editorial opinion makers. He used Captain George A. White, a Third Infantry officer and military affairs correspondent for the *Oregonian,* to publicize that paper's coverage of the campaign. "The military propaganda is certainly making headway in Oregon," Martin bragged in a letter to General Mills on December 16, 1914. "Every day a broadside . . . is being issued. The military editor of this leading paper is Captain White, inspector of rifle practice of my staff, and he understands the war department propaganda thoroughly." The campaign proved so successful that General Mills, on behalf of the War Department, commended Martin on December 29. "Congratulations are extended to you on your work with the Oregon Guard," Mills wrote. He especially commended Martin's influence and ability in directing the press "along proper military lines." The proper military position also carried the vote among Oregon's congressional delegation save one lone holdout, Representative Wallis Hawley of Salem, whom Martin sarcastically called "an ex-school teacher," claiming, "of course nothing else could be expected of him but opposition to anything military."[13]

Martin planned to retire in 1917 ending a thirty-year army career. By November 1914, with double urgency due to the expiration of his allotted time away from regular duty under the "Manchu Law," he began negotiating in earnest for a new posting. The so-called "Manchu Law," designed specifically for situations like Martin's reassignment with the Oregon Guard, which specified the length of time a regular army officer could be detached from active duty, required his reassignment before March 1915. Martin wrote to General Mills, requesting that his reassignment date be moved up to January 1915. Modestly, he claimed to have done "the military cause some good here in Oregon," while enjoying "my detail very much," but the Manchu Law required some haste. Martin wanted to stay in the Pacific Northwest though, and requested assignment to the Twenty-first Infantry at Vancouver Barracks. He rationalized the request by calling the short move a way for "both . . . myself and the Government" to "save trouble and expense." Besides, "packing up and leaving here in the dead of winter" could put "a very serious strain" on his wife's "state of health."[14]

While Martin prepared to move, Senator Chamberlain intervened once again, except this time Martin did not appreciate the meddling. Martin warned General Mills of impending trouble. Senator Chamberlain planned to amend the Manchu Law to allow Martin to serve longer in Oregon. "I am afraid my relief will cause some trouble," he wrote to General Mills. "There is going to be an effort . . . to keep me here." Martin asked that the general expedite the reassignment with haste before the information leaked out, causing Senator Chamberlain to put his plans into action.[15]

When trouble did eventually appear, Chamberlain was not the source. Martin's own creation, his Third Infantry propagandist Captain George White, became the chief agitator. White wrote to Secretary of War Garrison immediately on hearing of Martin's new assignment. "If true," he prophesied, "this will be a calamity to the Oregon National Guard." White placed himself "one with thousands here" who felt that Martin should stay in Oregon. The campaign led by White with the War Department became so intense that Martin officially disassociated himself from the efforts. In a brief message to the adjutant general U.S. Army, Martin disavowed the campaign, stating "I had no knowledge directly or indirectly concerning the . . . matter."[16]

Though Martin used George White for his own ends in the propaganda campaign, he had little taste for the man as a person or a military leader. Now White drew Martin's contempt. White wanted Martin to stay with the Third Infantry. He began a campaign ostensibly on Martin's behalf, that actually masked an attempt to tie his own political fortunes to the popular Martin in an internal power struggle between warring politicians. General Finzer, adjutant general of the Oregon National Guard, had supported George Chamberlain throughout his political career. Newly elected Oregon Governor James Withycombe, on the other hand, maintained a long-standing political battle with Senator Chamberlain, who had beaten Withycombe in the race for the governorship in 1908. Withycombe prepared to exact political revenge on Chamberlain by removing Finzer as adjutant general and selecting Captain George White as his replacement appointee.

Martin began moving behind the scenes with his political allies to thwart Withycombe's intentions. Martin tried to convince Finzer that legally the governor could not fire him. The law practically gave Finzer a lifetime tenure, Martin reminded Senator Chamberlain. However, Finzer wanted nothing to do with an expensive legal battle with the governor and agreed to a compromise that allowed him to remain in office until August 1915.[17]

Martin's opposition to White emboldened others in the guard who, "almost unanimously, [have] bitterly fought this appointment." Martin praised Finzer, as "one of the most kindly, lovable and loyal men I ever met, and these very qualities have caused him to consent to the resignation and thus save the guard from a bitter internal fight." He condemned White's meddling in political affairs and using undue influence on the new governor even before the election. Martin predicted White's failure at "reconciling the bitter feeling against him." White had "neither the temperament or the industry to make a success of the job," Martin wrote to Chamberlain.[18]

Martin's attempt to stay in the Northwest failed. As he took his leave for a new assignment with the Eighteenth Infantry in Texas, the *Oregonian,* in a brief editorial, lauded Martin's service with the Oregon National Guard and expressed hope that the army would reconsider its hasty action and return him to Oregon. He had turned a regiment in disarray "into one which was acceptable," the editors opined. Despite the hopes expressed in the newspaper, the army did not reconsider.

The Eighteenth Infantry took up positions near the Mexican border at Douglas, Arizona, during March 1915 as the United States moved ever closer to war with Mexico. As Martin's troops prepared fortifications, exasperation with U.S. foreign policy toward the five-year Mexican civil war threatened to bring Mexican revolutionaries over the border. Reformer Francisco I. Madero had overthrown Mexican dictator Porfirio Diaz in 1910. With the connivance of U.S. ambassador to Mexico, Henry Lane Wilson, Victoriano Huerta deposed then murdered Madero on February 18, 1913, one month before President Woodrow Wilson took office. President Wilson continued President Taft's policy of not recognizing the Huerta government. However, where Taft had acted to use recognition as a bargaining tool to settle disputes with Mexico, the moralistic Wilson continued nonrecognition as a first step to punish Huerta for what Wilson saw as Huerta's uncivilized behavior.

After a series of diplomatic failures with the Huerta regime in which the president's envoy attempted to bribe the Mexican leader, Wilson isolated

Huerta diplomatically and militarily from the rest of the world. The president then proceeded with the second step of his plan to depose Huerta by lending the support of the United States to Huerta's arch rivals, notably Venustiano Carranza. But Carranza proved to be an unwilling ally at best. Wilson became indignant when in mid-November 1913, Carranza rebuffed an envoy Wilson sent to offer U.S. cooperation. Carranza sent word to the U.S. president that he "did not want American support, would oppose the entry of American troops into Mexico with arms, and would proceed to establish [his] own government in [his] own way."[19]

The situation deteriorated even further after the invasion and occupation of Veracruz by the military forces of the United States in April 1914. Eventually Argentina, Brazil, and Chile offered to mediate the United States-Mexican dispute, an offer that President Wilson, Huerta, and eventually, Carranza accepted. But Carranza made it clear to the United States that he neither wanted nor needed help—either in conquering his country or in governing. While the delegates met in Niagara Falls, Canada, from May 20 until July 2, 1914, Huerta's power waned as Carranza's forces neared Mexico City. Huerta abdicated on July 15, 1914, and Carranza came to power.

Carranza implemented "one of the most momentous acts in the revolution." He "announced plans for agrarian reform . . . and for Mexico's claim to all its subsoil mineral rights." In his turn to the left, Carranza's attempt to claim sovereignty over his country's oil threatened U.S. oil companies. At the same time, Carranza's Constitutionalists split along factional lines, rivalries that plunged Mexico once again into civil war. Carranza's most successful general, Francisco "Pancho" Villa, led a revolt against the scholarly, idealistic, constitutional leader. President Wilson, still smarting from Carranza's rebuffs, decided to throw his support to Villa, to "depose Carranza, and obtain the establishment of a new provisional revolutionary government subject to American control."[20]

Carranza, his government and military strengthened through his sheer willpower, began a military campaign in January 1915 that pushed Villa and his forces northward. Thus it was in March 1915 that as Martin's troops dug in along the border at Douglas, Arizona, he kept a watchful eye out for attacks by both armies.

Standing in the Chiricahua Mountains with spring blooming all around him, looking through his field glasses at the Mexican trenches not far from his own, Martin reflected on other fighters "who caused our army so much trouble thirty years ago." Geronimo "surrendered at Slaughter's Ranch . . . just ten miles east of here," Martin wrote to his son, Ellis. Turning back to the present threat, Martin ridiculed the Mexican army. "The miserable outfit actually thinks that we are afraid of them," he scoffed. "Did you ever see Mexicans fight?" he asked. "The majority shut their eyes and let fly from the hip, or any old way at all. They seem to think that if the rifle goes off with a loud bang, they're fighting like fiends."[21]

In a reflective mood on his fifty-second birthday, Martin again took up pen and paper to offer fatherly personal and military advice to his son. Ellis had been participating in the "senior militia" at his high school for more than a year. Meanwhile, men from around the country were packing military camps that summer, responding to the calls Martin helped initiate for military preparedness, in what is known as the Plattsburg movement. But Martin's idea of preparedness did not include the Plattsburg Movement. Writing to Ellis, he criticized "the much heralded business men's camps held at Plattsburg & other places throughout the country this summer." He considered the Plattsburg training insufficient, lasting as it did for only a few weeks in the summer.

Martin praised Ellis for showing dedication to the year-long training in which he had participated. "In combat work I'd put you[r senior militia] up against many of our regular regiments," including his own Eighteenth Infantry which had, he said, "fallen far short of expectations." Because the family did not accompany him on this assignment, Martin had not seen his son for some time and remarked on the recent photographs supplied by Louise. "I noticed your wonderful physical development. Why you have the muscles of a prize fighter! That's Fine! Keep up your physical training and remember," Martin admonished, sounding like his own father, "that a strong, clear mind goes with a strong, healthy body." He reminded Ellis to write more often. "You must understand that just at present we are leading a too strenuous life here on the border . . . you must write me whenever you can for you have more time than I have." In closing, the major revealed his hopes for his teenage son, hopes that would, ultimately, never be realized. "I was glad to hear that you had taken up the five studies this year [and] at The Academy [West Point] you will, I know, continue to work hard to excel. I am 52 today. Pretty old, am I not? You'll soon have to take my place." In another contemporaneous letter, Martin again took up the question of his "old age," comparing himself to a colleague bitter at not being promoted. "How unlovely," he said to Louise, "to grow old at war with the whole world!"[22]

In fact, Ellis went on to become a deep disappointment to his family. He did not attend West Point, and made very poor marks at Princeton where he spent the war years. Ellis fought continual bouts with alcoholism that resulted in his inability to hold a job despite Martin's valiant efforts to use a lifetime of influence to keep Ellis afloat. Even after being defeated in his reelection bid for a second term as Oregon's Governor, the seventy-eight-year-old Martin battled for his son's soul. In 1941, while Ellis worked on a defense project in Argentia, Newfoundland, a job that the elder Martin procured through his contacts in Washington, D.C., the unmistakably anguished father's words indicate that Ellis was in grave danger of losing this job also, after recently having been fired by the National Parks Department and losing his civil service rating after yet another drinking episode. Martin itemized the history of his intervention on Ellis' behalf in obtaining this job and pleaded with his son. "You must stand by me," he wrote. "You must realize the desperate situation in which you are placed, and that you will have to make atonements for your past mistakes by going through a period of humiliation." He reminded Ellis that at forty-three years old, without recommendations from his employers, his situation for future employment would be hopeless. The son must adopt the military virtues, the father lamented. "I hope you realize that you have got to work hard, be loyal to your employer, correct in your conduct—in a word, go out of your way to get the approval of those under whom you are working. Your salvation depends upon it alone. . . . You only want to watch your step, cut out drinking, and all kinds of carousing. Otherwise you are a goner, I tell you frankly."[23]

The father's disappointments, however, lay years in the future. In July 1915, Martin had more pressing problems. As usual, he had strong opinions about the near-war situation between the United States and Mexico. His feelings came pouring forth in a letter to Louise on July 25, 1915. He blamed "the troubles" with Mexico on President Wilson's predecessor, President Taft and the U.S. ambassador to Mexico, Henry Lane Wilson, who, he said, was "either a knave or a fool. I suspect he was a little of both." Martin castigated Henry Wilson's lamentable performance. "Had we had a strong, able man in Mexico City at that time," he wrote, "all this later trouble could probably have been avoided." But in fact, both presidents had reacted with some determination with regard to the situation. President Taft had his secretary of state, Henry Knox, send a note to the Madero government demanding that Mexico "fulfill its international duties toward American citizens and their interests." Ambassador Wilson in turn recommended and then pursued drastic action. "These Latin-American countries," he wrote, "should be dealt with justly and calmly but severely and undeviatingly." To act otherwise would "bring disaster and forfeit to us, in the estimation of these peoples, the respect and awe with which they have been taught to regard us." When Madero failed to show the appropriate "respect and awe," Henry Lane Wilson then encouraged the plot which led to Madero's death."[24]

Martin accused Henry Wilson of committing a "great error in either impressing or actually misrepresenting things which had Mr. Taft known he would have saved the Madero government instead of undermining it as he did." In fact, quite apart from any advice from his ambassador, Taft had no intention of protecting Madero. Taft mobilized 100,000 troops in Texas and Secretary Knox, on Taft's instructions, hinted that if Madero failed to protect American interests, the United States would arm Madero's counter-revolutionary foes. Martin dismissed Henry Wilson as an "idealistic fool . . . with [his] head in the clouds." Wilson just did not understand Mexicans, Martin complained. Mexicans, like other foreigners, Martin explained, confirmed his belief "that the world is peopled to a great extent by the ignorant, the selfish and the knavish."[25]

As the confrontation with Mexico moved into a more militaristic phase through 1916 and into 1917, with Villa killing U.S. citizens in Mexico and New Mexico, Martin received a promotion to lieutenant colonel. When President Wilson had ordered Martin's old West Point comrade General John Pershing to invade Mexico in the spring of 1916, Martin's forces stayed in Douglas as reserves. Throughout 1916 and into January 1917, Carranza insistently demanded that Pershing's invasionary army withdraw from Mexico. Finally, President Wilson, being drawn inexorably into the war in Europe, capitulated. The withdrawal of forces began on January 27, 1917. In March, Wilson gave de jure recognition to Carranza's constitutional government.

Sitting on the sidelines while Pershing accrued all the glory irked Martin. He determined not to find himself there if the United States entered the war in Europe that had dragged on for three years. He began another concerted campaign urging Senator Chamberlain to act on his behalf. With his plans to retire put aside, Martin believed that U.S. participation in the war in Europe would follow the example set in previous wars: states would raise volunteer units with local sons as commanders. He begged Chamberlain to intercede. "If a large army is raised," he wrote the senator, "I hope that you will see that I am not forgotten by the War Department." Urging the senator to use whatever means available, Martin listed his leadership successes for the senator, arguing that when mobilization occurred, success and skill counted for little. "Usually volunteer troops are raised so hurriedly that the fitness of army officers detailed to duty with them and over them is never inquired into. It's hit or miss," Martin asserted. He had proven skills and now sat near the top of the promotion list for a full colonelcy, "by July 1st next at the very latest." Covering his bets, Martin also wrote to his "old friend," Senator Lewis of Martin's "native State—Illinois." "[I]n case volunteers are called if given a chance I know I could whip a brigade in shape as soon as anybody."[26]

Instead of using volunteers, the United States organized a massive professional army led by professional soldiers. On April 10, 1917, the War Department cancelled a program for civilian military training camps established earlier that year and substituted a professionally run training camp for civilian candidates seeking commission as officers. General Staff ordered Martin to take up duties as senior instructor for officer training at Leon Springs, Texas. As senior trainer, Martin made certain that his trainees would not fall short of anyone's expectations. For the next four months, he enforced rigorous discipline and training to raw recruits, turning them into soldiers. He drove the new soldiers relentlessly. He required physical stamina of his recruits. He instilled patriotism, insisting that the men would fight to fulfill President Wilson's pledge to "make the world safe for democracy." No man in his unit failed to understand and respect the authority of those over him. Martin demanded strict obedience. If he ordered men to suffer he expected them to suffer, to ignore their own suffering in pursuit of a higher cause. He instilled fear. He expected his men to fear him, but he also wanted them to know that fear in battle was a reaction to be overcome. He wanted to dispel any notion that when fired on, the troops would not feel fear. "If he is a normal human being," Martin told them, "He'll be badly frightened."[27]

Martin showed no mercy to young men who "were slow in catching on." He ridiculed slow starters as being men who lacked "something between the ears." In one training exercise Colonel Martin rode at the head of a retreating army. Attempting to regroup his men for attack, the colonel went back to see how the rear guard was functioning, but the rear guard could not be found. Galloping furiously over the four miles, Martin found the entire rear guard surrounding a prostrate companion under a tree. "He's dying," cried a lanky Texan. "Let him die," Martin bellowed. "You all get the hell out of here and become soldiers again." The rear guard fell in and departed. Only 1,500 of the original 3,500 recruits survived the rigors of training to graduate on August 11, 1917.[28]

Martin did not retire in 1917 as he had planned. President Wilson promoted him, temporarily, to brigadier general six days after the graduation ceremonies at Leon Springs. While the new officers scattered to training camps throughout the country, General Martin proceeded to Illinois where he would supervise the training of enlisted men for the war in Europe.

NOTES

1. CHM to LM, October 16, 1900, CHMC, OHS.
2. Duane Hennessy, "Straight from the Soldier—Martin," *Oregonian,* December 18, 1938; on real estate investments see several letters including among others Samuel Shay to CHM, May 1, 1901, and Albert Davis to CHM, October 19, 1901, CHMC, OHS.
3. Hennessy; Telegram, W.E. Finzer to Chief of Division of Militia Affairs, May 13, 1910, National Archives, Records Group 94, Box 1097; Telegram, S.L.A. Bowman to Senator George Chamberlain, May 17, 1910, National Archives.
4. Arthur H. Bone, *Oregon Cattleman/Governor Congressman: Memoirs and Times of Walter M. Pierce* (Portland: Oregon Historical Society, 1981), 47; George S. Turnbull, *Governors of Oregon* (Portland: Binfords and Mort, Publishers, 1959), 56–57; Jonathan Bourne Jr. and George Chamberlain, to Major General F.C. Ainsworth, Adjutant General, United States Army, May 19, 1910, National Archives.
5. Robert Alison to Senator George Chamberlain et al., May 21, 1910, National Archives.
6. CHM to W.E. Finzer, April 1, 1913, Report of the Adjutant General, 1915, CHMC, OHS.
7. Bone, 44; J.F. Johnston and James Hay to Lindley M. Garrison, May 22, 1913, National Archives.
8. W.E. Finzer to A.L. Mills, April 4, 1913, "Fourteenth Biennial Report of the Adjutant General of the State of Oregon to the Governor and Commander-in-Chief for the years 1913–1914," Twenty-eighth Legislative Assembly, State of Oregon Press, 1915, 38, CHMC, OHS; George Chamberlain to Lindley M. Garrison, May 22, 1913, National Archives.
9. Ibid.
10. Lindley M. Garrison to Chief of Staff, June 7, 1913, National Archives; CHM to W. E. Finzer, April 1, 1913, Report of the Adjutant General, 1915, CHMC, OHS.
11. George Chamberlain to CHM, August 21, 1913, CHMC, OHS.
12. CHM to General A.L. Mills, November 9, 1914, CHMC, OHS.
13. Ibid., November 16, 1914; A.L. Mills to CHM, December 29, 1914; CHM to Albert L. Mills, December 16, 1914, CHMC, OHS.
14. Ibid., November 9 and 16, December 1914, CHMC, OHS.
15. Ibid., November 9, 1914, CHMC, OHS.
16. George White to Lindley M. Garrison, January 4, 1915; CHM to Adjutant General, January 16, 1915, CHMC, OHS.
17. CHM to George E. Chamberlain, January 15, 1915, CHMC, OHS.
18. Ibid.
19. Arthur S. Link, *American Epoch* (New York: Alfred A. Knopf, 1955), 166.
20. Walter LaFeber, *The American Age: United States Foreign Policy at Home and Abroad, 1750 to the Present* (New York: W.W. Norton and Company, 1994), 280; Link, 168.
21. CHM to Ellis Martin, March 16, 1915; CHM quoted in a letter, George Pattullo to CHM, June 2, 1917, CHMC, OHS.
22. CHM to Ellis Martin, October 14, 1915; CHM to LM, July 25, 1915, CHMC, OHS.
23. CHM to Ellis Hughes Martin, August 20, 1941, CHMC, OHS.
24. CHM to LM, July 25, 1915, CHMC, OHS; Samuel Flagg Bemis, *A Diplomatic History of the United States* (New York: Henry Holt and Company, 1942), 545, 546.
25. CHM to LM, July 25, 1915, CHMC, OHS.

26. CHM to Senator George Chamberlain, March 22, 1917, CHMC, OHS.
27. George Pattullo to CHM, June 2, 1917, CHMC, OHS.
28. Hennessy, *Oregonian,* December 25, 1938.

Chapter Five

MAKING THE WORLD SAFE FOR DEMOCRACY

It is the tradition in the family that he was given charge of the Negro division because it was out of control. Evidently they were raping a lot of French women or something and the army felt that "Iron Pants"— that was the nickname he acquired at Camp Grant—they felt that my grandfather could bring some order back to the division.
—Charles Henry Martin II

I am beginning to wonder whether it will ever be possible for me to see an American (white) without wishing that he were in his Satanic Majesty's private domain. I must pray long and earnestly that hatred of my fellow man be removed from my heart and that I can truthfully lay claim to being a Christian.
—Unidentified black officer[1]

E VEN BEFORE THE WARRING POWERS agreed to establish peace in November 1918, many fearful white people, soldiers and civilians, in Europe and the United States launched a campaign to obliterate the collective reputation of black Americans who willingly served in World War I to secure the democracy for themselves that President Wilson promised to the rest of the world. That campaign had many motives and imbricated components. Many white officers, including General Martin, determined that blacks should never again be allowed to serve in leadership positions as military officers as they had during the war. President Wilson voiced the fears of many civilians when he told his personal physician, Rear Admiral Cary T. Grayson, that "black soldiers returning from abroad would be the greatest medium in conveying bolshevism to America; the French had put them on an equality with white men and 'It has gone to their heads.'" Racist whites reacted with disgust to the acceptance and recognition that black troops received from the French military and citizenry. Supporters of the status-quo ante vowed to reestablish and enforce the subordinate position of blacks in American society—to "eradicate any notions of equality they may have picked up in France." General Pershing assigned General Martin command of the segregated all-black Ninety-second Division at the end of the war, to see to it that black soldiers understood their place in the democratic society they had just helped to save.[2]

General Martin had experience with black soldiers. Assuming his command at Illinois' Camp Grant immediately after leaving Leon Springs, Texas, in August 1917, he turned his attention from training officers to training enlisted men. He enforced the same uncompromising severity in training on his new command, the 172d Infantry Brigade. "We have pounded you men as hard as we could," the general explained to the recruits. "We are pounding you now as hard as we know how and we are going to keep it up." When he considered the ideal relationship between himself and his men, Martin said, "I want 'em so when I walk down their company street they'll turn and look after me and say, 'There goes the old _____.'"[3]

Martin marched his brigade through rain, knee-deep mud, and waist-high snow as northern Illinois suffered through one of its harshest winters on record. Even when the temperature reached a record seventeen degrees below zero, the general sent the recruits on a twenty-one mile hike. "March 'em," he bellowed, "March 'em, make soldiers out of 'em." When the army reassigned General Thomas Barry in April 1918 due to a disability, Martin received another promotion, to major general, and became commander of the Eighty-sixth "Blackhawk" Division as well as commander of Camp Grant.[4]

As camp commander, General Martin again left no room for misunderstanding in his command. "There will be DISCIPLINE in this division," he told the thousands of soldiers. "Upon taking over the Eighty-sixth . . . General Martin instituted his 'thick-skinned-hard-as-nails' system of training . . . He was here, there and everywhere about the camp. No Lieutenant drilling his platoon or corporal instructing his squad could risk being off his guard for a moment." As he walked through the streets, soldiers did indeed turn and look after him. "There goes old Iron Pants," they said, a nickname that stayed with Martin for the rest of his life. No soldier at Camp Grant could long hide from the withering gaze of the ubiquitous General Martin, including African-American soldiers training in segregated units for duty with the all-black Ninety-second Division.[5]

When the United States entered World War I, African-Americans displayed enormous patriotic fervor. As moved as white Americans by President Wilson's pledge to make the world "safe for democracy," blacks thronged recruiting stations. Most of the black press supported President Wilson, arguing for patriotism; devotion to country now would surely lead to justice later. Black radical W.E.B. Du Bois set the tone for black support of Wilson's policies even though he considered Wilson a racist. In "Close Ranks," a controversial editorial in the National Association for the Advancement of Colored People (NAACP) house organ, the *Crisis,* sounding much like his accommodationist arch rival Booker T. Washington, Du Bois urged African-Americans to support the policy of the United States. "Let us, while this war lasts, forget our special grievances and close our ranks shoulder to shoulder with our own white fellow citizens and the allied nations that are fighting for democracy," Du Bois counseled.[6]

Du Bois's support of the war did not pass without criticism. "I am utterly astounded and confounded by the leading editorial of the July *Crisis,*" wrote William H. Wilson. "In no issue since our entrance into the war am I able to find so supine a surrender . . . of the rights of man . . . In God's name, what a reversal." Du Bois later deeply regretted his position in "Close Ranks," but at the time he "was caught up in the frenzy of mass patriotism" and the "thrilling vision of black troops fighting and dying across Flanders fields . . . [which] promised compensation for three centuries of appalling humiliations and brutality." Du Bois offered himself for service in the intelligence branch, embracing "the hope of full citizenship through carnage."[7]

When African-Americans offered their lives at recruiting stations for the great crusade during April 1917, they found that the U.S. military gladly accepted white volunteers, but blacks need not apply. The political and military establishment adopted the same policy for World War I that prevailed during the Civil War's first two years: this would be a white man's war. By July 1917, though, the situation changed; the army needed to recruit a massive force; they needed manpower—of any color. The War Department, carrying out the long-standing policy adopted during the Civil War, created two segregated all-black divisions, the Ninety-second and the Ninety-third, as well as designating Camp Des Moines in remote Iowa as the segregated facility where a few black officers would receive training. Originally military planners envisioned commissioning black officers to command all Ninety-second and Ninety-third division infantry, machine gun, and engineer companies, and assign black lieutenants to all light artillery regiments.

But as the scurrilous racist campaign vilifying black troops developed within the military, white officers replaced black officers in most instances.[8]

Almost immediately the prospect of all-black divisions training in the United States became a problem for the War Department. Southerners feared the probability that armed blacks would train beside whites in the south. To alleviate the problem, the War Department constructed separate cantonments for each army division with the provision that white troops must constitute a majority in each cantonment.

The Ninety-second Division took form late in November 1917 with headquarters at Camp Funston, Kansas, commanded by General Charles C. Ballou. Because of the provisions defining white to black ratios, the army broke the division into seven separate units, each attached to a separate training camp in widely separate parts of the country. The African-American soldiers at Camp Grant under General Martin's command constituted part of the dismemberment of the Ninety-second Division. "It was the only instance in which a division was never actually brought together until it reached the fighting front."[9]

The army enforced a policy of strict segregation throughout the training camps and compelled black soldiers to obey local segregation restrictions. As General Martin surveyed his camp on daily walks, he passed signs on camp buildings that reminded black soldiers, "This building is for white men only." At the Ninety-second Division headquarters in Kansas, General Ballou, whose reputation as an officer sympathetic to African-Americans preceded him, issued "Bulletin No. 35," when the manager of a movie theater refused to admit black soldiers.[10]

"Bulletin No. 35" destroyed black soldiers' confidence in Ballou—a confidence he never regained. In the document General Ballou cautioned black soldiers to remember that "no useful purpose is served" by acts that "cause the 'color question' to be raised." Legal rights had no place in the army, Ballou said. Army policy must be followed. Conflict over race in the army, he warned, is "prejudicial to the military interest of the 92d Division, and therefore prejudicial to an important interest of the colored race." Had he not continually warned "colored members of his command" to "refrain from going where their presence will be resented?" In spite of his warning, a black soldier had insulted white people by attempting to enter a movie theater. This sergeant "is guilty of the GREATER wrong," Ballou claimed, because no matter how legally correct, his actions provoked white animosity. If black soldiers persisted in going where "your presence is not desired," Ballou warned, the white men who "made the division" could just as easily break it "if it becomes a trouble maker."[11]

The black press bristled at Ballou's order, pronounced it a racial insult, and demanded the general's resignation. Ballou attempted, unsuccessfully, to refurbish his damaged credibility by explaining himself in the *Crisis.* "I have always believed," he wrote, "that the colored man's true policy is to win his way by forbearance rather than by force. . . . The colored candidates behaved very well, indeed; but a few were a bit inclined to make trouble at the least sign of race discrimination. . . . We were not going to lose sight of and jeopardize [our] mission by getting tangled up in social or political issues."[12]

The Ninety-second Division's separate units suffered under miserable conditions in the training camps. The army provided inadequate and dilapidated housing, kept rations at a bare minimum, and gave the black soldiers what clothing white troops did not need. Where other divisions forged an identity and unity through training, the Ninety-second, scattered throughout the country, remained fractured. Not until all the disparate components arrived in France in 1918 as part of the American Second Army did the division coalesce into an efficient fighting force. When other units went immediately into the fighting, the Ninety-second had to spend its first eight weeks in intensive training—together at last as a complete division.

Arrival in France did not alleviate the privations the Ninety-second suffered as separate units in the United States. Their troubles only increased when the Second Army commander, General Robert Lee Bullard, and General Ballou began to engage in a bitter feud. Despite "Bulletin No. 35," in which he demonstrated his conformity with the prevailing segregationist attitude, Ballou had nonetheless treated his black soldiers with reasonable fairness by prevailing standards. General Bullard, on the other hand, nourished an uncompromising racism. "Poor Negroes!" he wrote in his diary November 5, 1918. "They are hopelessly inferior." Bullard maintained that "our government seemed to expect the same of them as of white men," and forced the army to afford blacks "the same treatment as white men." Besides being "inferior soldiers," Bullard said, "the Negro is a more sensual man than the white man and at the same time he is far more offensive to white women than is a white man."[13]

General Bullard coupled his denigration of blacks with a contempt for General Ballou whom he viewed as a racial gadfly. "General [Ballou] who commands them," he wrote in his diaries, "can't make them fight. The general seemed to me also to have lost sight of military efficiency in the racial 'uplift' problem which seemed to fill his mind."[14]

Not only did Ballou contend with the opposition of his superiors, he suffered from lies and distortions from the officers under his command, particularly Lieutenant Colonel Allen Greer, chief of staff of the Ninety-second Division. Ballou lamented his situation, saying at a later date, "It was my misfortune to be handicapped by many white officers who were rabidly hostile to the idea of a colored officer, and who continually conveyed misinformation to the staffs of the superior units, and generally created much trouble and discontent. Such men will never give the negro the square deal that is his just due." Of his white officers, Ballou concluded, "[a]mong them all . . . I found every one of them would have given anything to be transferred to any other duty. It was the most pitiful case of discouragement that I have ever seen among soldiers."[15]

During the late summer and early fall of 1918 rumors, leaked from Congress and the War Department, began circulating through the press and public concerning the cowardly performance of black soldiers in France. Newspapers quoted unnamed sources who claimed that blacks failed as soldiers, and allegations surfaced that claimed black soldiers, "controlled by brutal instincts," roamed the French countryside raping white French women at random.[16]

At the beginning of their service in France, black soldiers did find a remarkable degree of social freedom and acceptance unlike anything they knew at home. They spent time in nearby towns and villages, drank wine and beer at a time when Prohibition ruled in the United States, and mingled with the French people. Indeed, the French welcomed the black soldiers and treated them with a warm respect that occasioned astonishment among the blacks themselves. One French woman wrote in a leading French newspaper: "Natives and foreigners smile at each other and try to understand each other. The next day we see the little children in the arms of the huge Negroes, confidently pressing their rosy cheeks to the cheeks of ebony." Her initial sense of apprehension, instilled by contacts with white Americans, dissipated, she reported.

> Very quickly it is seen they have nothing of the savage in them, but, on the other hand, one could not find a soldier more faultless in his bearing, and in his manners more affable, or more delicate than these children of the sun . . . We admire their forms—handsome, vigorous and athletic; their intelligent and loyal faces with their large gleaming eyes, at times dreamy, and with a bit of sadness in them. . . . Now one honors himself to have them at his table. He spends hours in long talks with them; . . . Soldiers, who arrived among us one clear June day, redolent with the scent of roses, you will always live in our hearts.[17]

White Americans, equally astonished, reacted with wonder. U.S. journalist E.W. Lightner wrote of his amazement at the equality shown black troops. "I, an American . . . was amazed to see the cordial mingling of all phases of the cosmopolitan population of the French capital . . . Everywhere and by all sorts and conditions of whites, they were treated as equals."[18]

Agitated whites in the U.S. Army reacted swiftly to quell any feeling of equality among black officers and soldiers. They posted French villages with signs reading "Niggers keep out!" One American officer from Virginia told some French men that "they had no use for 'niggers in the United States." Every black man "would rape a white woman if he was not held down by the whites," the southerner claimed. "He said that one of the first things that he wanted to do upon his return to the States was to join in a lynching bee; and he said to the Frenchmen, that he would 'send them a piece of a nigger as a souvenir.'" Prompted by their "neurotic terror of sex relations between black men and white women," white officers warned their black troops to have no contact with white women.[19]

General Ballou, supporting the fear among many whites that social equality would lead blacks to enjoy "this new and agreeable condition," drastically curtailed mobility for soldiers of the Ninety-second. As fictitious allegations of black rape circulated against his troops, Ballou cancelled passes, instituted an hourly roll-call for black soldiers, and began keeping a written record on all black troops.[20]

General Pershing took more direct action. On August 7, 1918, General Pershing's office issued an official order to the French Military Mission. That document, "Secret Information Concerning the Black American Troops," instructed the French in the "proper" or "American Way" to treat black soldiers. Responding to Pershing's instructions, the French Military Mission relayed an explanatory directive to French military authorities hoping to minimize contact between the French population and black soldiers. "It is important for French officers who have been called upon to exercise command over black American troops . . . to have an exact idea of the position occupied by Negroes in the United States," the directive began.

> American opinion is unanimous on the "color" question and does not admit of any discussion. The increasing number of Negroes in the United States . . . would create for the white race in the Republic a menace of degeneracy were it not that an impassable gulf has been made between them. . . . They are afraid that contact with the French will inspire in black Americans aspirations which to them (the whites) appear intolerable. . . . Although a citizen of the United States, the black man is regarded by the white American as an inferior being with whom relations of business or service only are possible. . . . The vices of the Negro are a

constant menace to the American who has to repress them sternly. . . . We must prevent the rise of any pronounced degree of intimacy between French officers and black officers. . . . We must not commend too highly the black American troops particularly in the presence of (white) Americans. . . . Make a point of keeping the . . . [French] population from "spoiling" the Negroes. (White) Americans become greatly incensed at any public expression of intimacy between white women with black men.[21]

Thus, by the time of the armistice, through rumor, lies, white paranoia and bigotry, and the personal battle being waged between General Ballou and General Bullard, the black soldiers of the Ninety-second Division occupied a precarious position. The "whispering gallery" so active in France and the United States effectively discredited black soldiers. Characterized as uncontrollable, degenerate, vicious rapists, black soldiers and the Ninety-second Division as a whole carried the stigma of utter criminal failure.[22]

General Martin spent the summer of 1918 honing the military skills of the recruits under his command at Camp Grant. Late in August the Eighty-sixth Division finally received orders to sail for France, departing the United States on September 8. They landed in Liverpool, England then traveled overland to Portsmouth. "While the troops were moving," General Martin and his staff made a stopover in London, where they "were entertained by Royalty," before joining the rest of the division for final training exercises at St. Andre-de-Cubzac near Bordeaux, France. While the Eighty-sixth underwent what General Pershing demanded of all newly arrived American forces before allowing them in battle—more training "in trench warfare and in offensive operations using the rifle and bayonet"—General Pershing, with most of the rest of the U.S. forces, had begun the concluding battle of the war in the Argonne Forest.[23]

When Marshal Foch conceived his final offensive along the entire Western Front, he intended to drive the Germans from France before winter and end the war in the spring of 1919. Pershing's position along the River Meuse and in the Argonne Forest was part of that overall offensive, which began on September 26. When the first phase of the Meuse-Argonne Offensive stalled early in October, Pershing broke the Eighty-sixth up into separate units and deployed them along the twenty-mile Meuse-Argonne front as reserves. General Martin joined General Hunter Liggett's First Army command. By the end of October, First Army had cleared the Germans from the Argonne "and First Army troops were through the German main positions." During the last ten days of the war, First Army units led the attacks on the fleeing Germans. When the armistice took effect on November 11, Martin found himself with units of the First Army at the German railhead at Buzancy.[24]

Eight days after the armistice, General Bullard relieved General Ballou of his command. Bullard wanted all black troops out of Europe and back in the United States where they could be controlled. "I recommended . . . that this division be sent home first of all the American troops," General Bullard recalled in his memoirs. He told General Pershing "that no man could be responsible for the acts of these Negroes toward French-women, . . ."[25]

On November 19, Martin reminisced years later, "word came that the 92d Negro division stationed around Marbach . . . was out of hand, roving in marauding bands and seeking night life." The general recalled that Pershing put him in command of the Ninety-second "for the purpose of disciplining the division for return to this country, the men having become demoralized from their contact with the French populace." General Martin asserted that he "quickly put an end to the trouble."[26]

Taking up his new command, Martin agreed wholeheartedly with General Bullard's views on the inferiority of the black race and the inefficacy of black troops as soldiers. Leaving aside physicality, Martin claimed that "the average negro is not by any means equal to the average white man." In general, Martin said, "the negro lacks the intelligence, education, common sense, initiative, determination, and pride of race" exhibited by white men. "He is by nature careless [and] thoughtless," the general reasoned, and black soldiers sought only their own "personal advantage and comfort." Martin made a compendium of racial characteristics for consumption by his superiors concluding that overall, the use of black soldiers had been a mistake. "He was not a success," Martin wrote.[27]

To break the black soldier's spirit, "Iron Pants" put the Ninety-second Division through a backbreaking "training" program, which might have proved useful prior to the armistice but now seemed vindictive to battle-hardened veterans. When not actually "training," Martin assigned black soldiers to manual labor gangs unlike that performed by any white divisions. Black troops constructed housing, salvaged equipment and materials, cleared barbed-wire from the battlefields, and coaled ships on which white troops sailed for home. The general requested the most loathsome duty imaginable for the Ninety-second, forcing black soldiers to retrieve decomposing bodies and body parts from the battlefields, then to dig the holes in which to bury them.[28]

Lieutenant Colonel Greer, General Ballou's second in command, remained as Martin's chief of staff. When General Martin ordered that black troops should have no leisure time, ensuring that no fraternization occurred between black troops and the French populace, Greer eagerly complied. Black troops received no passes, no days off. General Martin ordered military police to be ruthless with "our niggers."[29]

Colonel Greer busied himself in other spheres as well. On December 6, 1918, he sent a letter to U.S. Senator Kenneth D. McKellar. Sending the letter to Senator McKellar violated military law and regulations and could have subjected Colonel Greer to a court-martial if he did not first clear the letter with General Martin. Because no punitive action accrued to Greer when the letter's contents became public, coupled with Greer's consistent use of a plural pronoun, one must assume that General Martin approved Greer's actions. Whether Martin approved of or ever saw the letter is immaterial. He reiterated many of the charges himself. Greer attempted to solidify the rumors circulating in the United States about black soldiers. He characterized black troops as rapists, claiming thirty cases of rape at Camp Grant, "among which was one where twenty-two men . . . raped one woman." Holding that the spree continued in France, he told Senator McKellar that French women had reported fifteen cases of attempted rape and black troops had actually carried out eight assaults on French women. Greer claimed that "the Colored officers neither control nor care to control the men." In fact, the officers "themselves have been engaged very largely in the pursuit of French women, it being their first opportunity to meet white women who did not treat them as servants." Like General Martin, Greer continued to discredit black soldiers even after returning to the United States. "Taken as an average," General Martin wrote to army superiors developing a plan for future participation by blacks in the army, "their ignorance was colossal. . . . because it is an undoubted fact, shown by our experience during the war, and well known to all people familiar with Negroes that the average negro is naturally cowardly, and usually for him to display any courage it must be where he is properly led."[30]

Feeling they could no longer ignore the slanderous rumors about black troops circulating in the United States, black leaders prevailed on President Wilson to send a delegation to France to look into the charges. Robert Moton, successor to Booker T. Washington at Tuskegee Institute, headed the investigative team. As soon as he arrived in France, Moton went directly to Ninety-second Division headquarters. Sitting across from General Martin, Moton pointedly asked the General about the rape accusations. Oh yes, said Martin, rape "was very prevalent." Martin told Moton that "he was very disturbed" at the "great many cases." The general, referring to his command as "the rapist division" throughout the conversation, inflated the numbers even beyond Greer's fabrications telling Moton that "twenty-six cases of rape by black troops had been reported in recent months." Moton pressed the general for the pertinent records, which Martin grudgingly supplied. Moton reeled when he saw the actual numbers, but by that time General Martin had already transferred to the Ninetieth Division on occupation duty in Germany. The documents revealed that of the twelve thousand black soldiers in the Ninety-second Division, only two convictions for rape existed in the records and higher military headquarters overturned one of those two.[31]

Other even more ominous rumors also surfaced, both during the war and after the armistice, that white military commanders ordered illegal executions of black soldiers—a sort of military counterpart to the lynching and riot deaths prevalent in the United States during and after the war. Georgia's senator, Tom Watson, charged that without a trial, the military executed at least sixty-two men, many of whom were black. The army, and eventually a Senate committee, denied the charges. The Senate report bearing on Watson's charges dismissed the testimony of all black soldiers who claimed to have witnessed executions. It characterized their testimony variously as "the testimony of the very illiterate negro . . . just an ignorant negro's romance . . . [suffering from] serious mental deteriorations." Whether the executions actually took place will perhaps never be known, but the Senate report represented an essentially pointless exercise conducted simply as a convenient way to alleviate complaints directed at the army.[32]

General Martin relinquished command of the Ninety-second Division on December 30, 1918, after moving the division to Le Mans, where it eventually embarked for the United States. General Martin joined the Ninetieth Division as part of the Army of Occupation in Berncastel, Germany. He spent the next few months travelling around Europe as a tourist, visiting art galleries, museums, and famous cathedrals and being awed by the "glorious tulip fields" in Holland. In years to come, as a member of the Army General Staff, he helped formulate the postwar army's unwritten segregation policy: a policy never officially acknowledged; a policy designed to systematically exclude black officers from the military forces used to secure democracy for the world.

The Ninety-second Division languished near Le Mans for several months, becoming the last, rather than the first, division to leave France. The humiliation and degradation that the division's soldiers suffered at the hands of their military superiors during their service in France rewarded their loyalty and sacrifice. A black newspaper, the *Hot Springs Echo,* captured the

Martin with his 90th Division officers in Berncastel, Germany, 1919. *Oregon Historical Society, 017868*

essence of the tragedy awaiting black troops in the United States: "For valor displayed in the recent war, it seems that the Negro's particular decoration is to be the 'double-cross.'"[33]

NOTES

1. Unidentified African American officer, "Documents of the War," *Crisis,* May 1919, 20.
2. Robert H. Ferrell, *Woodrow Wilson and World War I, 1917–1921* (New York: Harper and Row, Publishers, 1985), 213; Jack D. Foner, *Blacks and the Military in American History* (New York: Praeger Publishers, 1974), 125.
3. *Chicago Examiner,* April 22, 1918.
4. Ibid., 1918; Duane Hennessy, *Oregonian,* December 25, 1938.
5. "Charles Henry Martin No. 19 Class of 1887," a typescript brief biography, CHMC, OHS.
6. Manning Marable, *W.E.B. Du Bois: Black Radical Democrat* (Boston: Twayne Publishers, 1986), 90; W.E.B. Du Bois, "Close Ranks," *Crisis,* July 1918.
7. William H. Wilson, "The Outer Pocket," *Crisis,* September 1918, 219; Marable, 96; David Levering Lewis, *When Harlem Was in Vogue* (New York: Vintage Books, 1982), 13.
8. The focus here will be on the Ninety-second Division. The Ninety-third was never brought up to full strength, and its various units were sent overseas at different times to join various units of the French Army.

9. John Hope Franklin, *From Slavery to Freedom: A History of Negro Americans* (New York: Alfred A. Knopf, 1980), 328.
10. Edward M. Coffman, *The War to End All Wars* (New York: Oxford University Press, 1968), 71.
11. General C.C. Ballou, quoted in Emmet J. Scott, *The American Negro in the World War* (Published by the author, 1919), 97–8.
12. General C.C. Ballou, "A Letter from General Ballou," *Crisis,* June 1918, 62.
13. Robert Lee Bullard, *Personalities and Reminiscences of the War* (New York: Doubleday, Page and Company, 1925), 291–98.
14. Ibid.
15. General C.C. Ballou quoted in, Arthur E. Barbeau and Florette Henri, *The Unknown Soldiers: Black American Troops in World War I* (Philadelphia: Temple University Press, 1974), 137.
16. Robert Russa Moton, *Finding a Way Out: An Autobiography* (College Park, Maryland: McGrath Publishing Company, 1920), 251.
17. Scott, 298–99.
18. Cited in Kelly Miller, *The World War for Human Rights* (New York: A. Jenkins, 1919), 511.
19. W.E.B. Du Bois, "The Black Man in the Revolution of 1914–1918," *Crisis,* March 1919, 222; W.E.B. Du Bois, "The Negro Soldier in Service Abroad during the First World War," *Journal of Negro Education,* V. 12, 1943, 327; Barbeau and Henri, 143.
20. Ibid.
21. Portions of this order are reproduced in many sources including Robert W. Mullen, *Blacks in America's Wars* (New York: Monad Press, 1973), 44; and John Hope Franklin and Isidore Starr, eds., *The Negro in 20th Century America* (New York: Vintage Books, 1967), 464–65.
22. Moton, 252.
23. Duane Hennessy, "From the Soldier . . . the End of War," *Oregonian,* December 18, 1938; James M. Morris, *America's Armed Forces: A History* (Upper Saddle River, New Jersey: Prentice Hall, 1996), 182.
24. "Named Campaigns-World War I," U.S. Army Military History Institute, www.army.mil/cmh-pg/reference/wicmp.htm; Hennessy.
25. Bullard, 297.
26. Hennessy, *Oregonian,* December 25, 1938; Samuel Holly Martin, typescript obituary, CHMC, OHS.
27. CHM, quoted in "Negro Manpower, Employment in Combatant Units," a study prepared by Lieutenant Colonel Harry B. Jordan for the Army War College, December 3, 1924, 5. The document is a typescript provided to the author by the Archives Branch, U.S. Army Military History Institute, Carlisle Barracks, Carlisle, Pennsylvania.
28. Barbeau and Henri, 164, 165.
29. Ibid., 167.
30. Lieutenant Colonel Allen Greer to Senator Kenneth D. McKellar, December 6, 1918, quoted in W.E.B. Du Bois, "Documents of the War," *Crisis,* May 1919; Scott, 438; Lieutenant Colonel Allen J. Freer to Assistant Commandant, General Staff College, April 13, 1920, Military History Institute.
31. Moton, 255, 256; Coffman, 232; Franklin, 336–37.
32. Senator Frank B. Brandegee, Chairman, "Report of the Committee on Alleged Executions without Trial in France" (Washington, D.C.: Government Printing Office, 1923), 1–15.
33. Barbeau and Henri, 174.

Martin sits for his portrait, 1919. He soon lost the Brigadier General's star. *Oregon Historical Society, 004887*

Chapter Six

RACISM IN THE RANKS OF A STANDING ARMY

As we have made the world safe for democracy, we now must make democracy safe for the world . . . to work or starve, to save or want, to play together or play hell, to be an American or to get out of here.
—Charles Henry Martin

The average negro is not by any means equal to the average white man.
—Charles Henry Martin

PRIOR TO GENERAL MARTIN'S ARRIVAL, the Ninetieth Division spent the latter part of November and most of December 1918 peacefully marching through Germany, dogging the path of the withdrawing German army. On December 21, division headquarters were established at Berncastel, Germany, an area "as interesting as that occupied by any troops of the Army of Occupation," one veteran recalled. "There is no lovelier portion of the Moselle Valley than in the region . . . made famous by the terraced vineyards which cover the hillsides lining the river banks."[1]

General Martin took charge of the division on December 30. Many divisional officers knew and admired Martin. He had built the division's officer corps in the officer training camp at Leon Springs, and most of the officers emulated Martin's style. The "spirit which he had inculcated in the young officers during the period of their candidacy became the spirit of the division," one division historian wrote. Officially the division guarded railroad stations, bridges, and "other sensitive points along the railways running through the divisional area." The Germans accepted defeat, so the division met no resistance.

General Pershing spent a good deal of time travelling through the occupied area holding inspections and reviewing troops. Martin wanted to make a favorable impression on Pershing, whose reputation as a no-nonsense, blunt commander not given to "gushing" Martin knew well. Martin pushed his troops through grueling training routines. Despite "the handicap caused by cold and snow in a mountainous country," Martin's troops performed "exact close-order drill, parades, and ceremonies." The precision displayed by his troops paid off. After one of his ubiquitous reviews, Pershing walked with Martin back to the headquarters building. Taking Martin's hand, the general of the army explained that though his position did not allow him to "make comparisons in the Divisions," he nonetheless wanted Martin to know "that there are none over here better than the 90th. It's just splendid, splendid . . . General you have an excellent Division." Martin and Pershing knew each other, of course, from their time at West Point, but Martin appreciated his superior's praise nonetheless.[2]

Martin's reunion with the officers of the Ninetieth Division, however, proved relatively short lived. By May 26, 1919, the Ninetieth Division sailed for home, signaling the dissolution of the division as a functioning whole. In fact, the United States demobilized quickly, dissolving the massive army created for World War I. During the war, many officers, including Martin, received temporary promotions while serving in Europe. As the army scattered, temporary promotions reverted to regular rank, so when General Martin returned to the United States, he reverted to a colonel in the regular army. Martin faced the situation sanguinely but held some bitterness. He felt that his service with the Eighty-sixth, Ninetieth, and Ninety-second divisions, and his late arrival in Europe kept him from receiving a regular army promotion to general. "I wish I could have had the 90th from the beginning," he lamented to Louise. "I would now be a General Officer in the regular army instead of having to go back to a Colonelcy." He would carry on though. "Well, it is alright," he wrote. "I am satisfied . . . that I did my damndest any way." Louise later recalled that "it was a discouraging experience to be so rewarded after duty well performed, but unlike so many others, he determined to stick to it—and refused to listen to the pressure brought to bear, urging him to resign or ask to be retired. . . . It was," she went on to say, "all in the line of duty, and he would say to me with a twinkle in his merry blue eyes: 'Why should the spirit of mortal be proud?' That has been his watchword."[3]

Colonel Martin spent the first few months back in the United States reunited with his wife as a recruiting officer in Portland. Then in October he took up recruiting duties in Chicago. His discontent at mid-Western banishment led him to contemplate retirement once again. Martin's army colleague, Henry Cabell, son of one prominent Portland family and married into the even more powerful Failing family, looked after his and Martin's burgeoning real estate investments. With those investments soundly placed, Martin could comfortably retire from the army and finally pursue his fortune among Portland's elite. "I feel that I must get out," he wrote to Cabell. "Both Louise and myself are living under conditions more trying than in any other period that I recall in our married life. I feel that I must . . . give her a settled home before it is too late." Adding to his domestic woes, Martin still bitterly resented his demotion. He felt slighted after all his hard work in Europe. Had he not whipped the Ninety-second and the Ninetieth divisions into shape? Had he not shown his worthiness for high command? Still, he languished in the mid-West "overshadowed . . . by inferiors," continuing "to serve ingrates." But events then coming to resolution in Washington, D.C., intervened once again to keep Martin in the army.[4]

During June 1920, Congress enacted a National Defense Act, "the most comprehensive and suitable legislation ever made for the military service of the United States," according to one military historian. The act settled a bitter intra-army feud, that spilled over into the political system, between Chief of Staff of the Army General Payton C. March and General of the Army John J. Pershing.[5]

General March represented the followers of Emory Upton—the "Uptonian" faction—within the ranks of officers who distrusted a volunteer citizen army, preferring instead to develop a professional standing army. They argued that "the regular army become the center of American military planning, the regulars to be reorganized into skeleton formations with full complements of professional officers." A war army, they said, would "be formed by filling the ranks with volunteers." The Uptonians, discarding the prohibitions against a standing army that prevailed since the Declaration of Independence, wanted a large force of regular soldiers on which to rely for rapid deployment should the United States go to war again.[6]

General Pershing objected to the "Uptonian Army" and through his surrogate, Colonel John McCauley Palmer, presented a substitute plan. After riveting testimony before Congress in October 1919, the Senate Military Affairs Committee made Palmer their military advisor. For ten months Palmer worked with the committee, framing a bill to create a citizen army. The consultations resulted in the 1920 National Defense Act.[7]

The most controversial element of the Pershing-Palmer plan did not make it into the 1920 act. Palmer, like many other military men, including Colonel Martin, advocated compulsory universal military training for all young men. The Pershing faction viewed compulsory army service as a socializing tool, to instill what the American Legion called 100 percent Americanism and thwart what they perceived as the rising threat of bolshevism in the United States. Military officers viewed the summer's events in 1919 with alarm, as the civilian government unleashed the "Red Scare," a purge directed at radicals espousing foreign "isms." General Merch B. Steward compared compulsory military training with compulsory public education. General Clarence R. Edwards believed compulsory service would root out bolshevism and instill respect for authority while preparing young men for the duties of citizenship.[8]

Martin also viewed the political, economic, and social dissension and loss of unity after the war as dangerous. In a speech at the Ninetieth Division's first reunion held in Dallas on October 20, 1919, he painted a grim picture for the veterans. What had happened to the United States, he wondered? Where had the wartime unity gone when just one year ago "the whole country was mobilized and ready for war." Now, he warned, in Europe and in the United States dangerous ideologies threatened Western Civilization. Workers who only one year ago put the country first now demanded benefits for themselves. There were no demands for "eight-hour" days during the war, Martin claimed erroneously. If the world could be saved, Martin predicted the veterans would have to do it. "As we have made the world safe for democracy, we now must make democracy safe for the world. It is up to us to do our part in preserving free government." During training the veterans had learned the great lessons, the lessons that should be instilled in all young men in the country: "Your courage, bravery and unselfishness," Martin prompted his audience. The foreign ideologies now threatening the country did not infect the training camps, he reminded them. "You learned to work or starve, to save or want, to play together or play hell, to be an American or to get out of here—those things that are so necessary to our government and to the hope of the world." Martin encouraged the veterans to take their lessons home, to return to their communities, to band together to stamp out the threats to civilization: "it is in your power through these associations to bring the world to rights." As the applause swelled over the colonel, he must have realized that he had hit a responsive chord. He would continue to emphasize variations on this theme for the rest of his life.[9]

While Congress debated and framed the defense bill, Pershing-faction staff officers advised General March that "unless something was done and done at once that we would have no army." Demobilization virtually gutted the ranks of the regular army, they warned. Indeed, the declaration adopted by Congress when the United States entered World War I stipulated that the national army would be disbanded at the end of the conflict, and General March presided over the mustering-out of almost three million officers and enlisted men. The regular army desperately needed troop replenishment for preparedness, the Pershing faction claimed, but the current recruiting campaign could only be considered a dismal failure. Already two general officers failed to bring any life to the effort, "giving the recruiting job up as hopeless." At the insistence of two staff officers from the operations section, General March agreed that Colonel Martin "was the man who could put it across." In this way General March delivered Colonel Martin from his banishment in Chicago, assigning him to the General Staff in Washington, D.C., and putting him in charge of the army's recruitment campaign.[10]

Leaving Louise in Chicago, Martin took up his new assignment as head of the Division for Procurement of Recruits, Adjutant General's Office. He threw himself into the recruiting drive with his usual determination and vigor. Increasing voluntary recruitment posed a formidable undertaking—the National Defense Act called for an army of 288,000 men as compared with 86,000 before the war. Martin developed the slogan "Earn, Learn and Travel," dangling the chance to study a trade, earn a living, and see the world as the bait to lure recruits. Spending one million dollars a month through April, May, and June, Colonel Martin crisscrossed the country traveling to each of the fifty-six district offices, firing any officer in charge of a district who failed to reach the monthly quota. When he took the job, approximately 1,350 recruits joined the army every week. By late May and early June 1920 that figure jumped to 2,274 per week. Martin's superiors took notice. "They all acknowledge around the War Department that I have by my driving methods put it over," he wrote. The colonel's drive and ambition left slower men, whom he called "duds," choking on his dust, as Martin forced himself to work even harder. While his superiors applauded his efforts, Martin wondered "whether it will get me anywhere." After thirty-three years of service he did not put much hope in the War Department to reward his diligence, especially after suffering the demotion from major general to colonel the previous year.[11]

His spirits picked up considerably, though, when the Board of General Officers that selected candidates for promotion finished its work and adjourned during June. For the twenty-two generalships available, the board recommended sixty colonels, so Martin reckoned his chances at "just one in three." Friends told Martin that the board forwarded his name, and one general on the board said "he did not see how I could miss it." The promotion announcement would not be made until after July 4, however, when General March returned from Europe.[12]

The wait for General March's return must have been excruciating for Martin. While he waited, he pressed ahead with the recruiting efforts, pleased that his superiors reported to General March "that I have worked a miracle." The recruitment branch had "more spirit and morale today . . . than in any other [branch] of the army," he wrote, adding sarcastically, "which for the greater part of it would not be saying much."[13]

Late in June, Martin complained to Louise about their separation, telling her that he would "try to arrange a trip later." Just then, as excitement built around the promotions, he wanted to "remain around the War Department." By this time Martin felt fairly confident that his success would result in his promotion to brigadier general. He had his superiors "all agog" at the "climb in recruiting." His accomplishments looked impressive indeed. He recorded "the biggest week in months and the height of a steady climb" when recruitment reached almost 2,500 for one week. When news reached him that Secretary of War Newton D. Baker had received a letter recommending Martin for promotion, the colonel appreciated the writer's effort but remarked pessimistically that "of course [it] will do me no good." Anyway, at least his superiors had to take notice of his work. One remarked that he "was putting some 'pep'" in the army at last. "I have breathed the breath of life into a dead body," Martin rightly claimed.[14]

When General March finally published the promotion list in July, Colonel Martin's name did not appear on it. From Portland Henry Cabell attempted to console his old friend. "I was sorry to see the list of General officers just promoted without your name on it," he wrote Martin. "The best thing for you to do is to retire," Cabell said. "You have a right to feel that you have not been given your due," he went on, "but there is no use troubling about these things, forget them." Martin's future lay in Portland, Cabell prophesied. "You should get out soon . . . You will in the next few years make much more in money [in real estate] than you will possibly be able to get from your active army pay."[15]

But Martin showed the same determination now that saw him through his dismissal from West Point. He determined to carry on, to make the army recognize his worth. He redoubled his passionate efforts in the recruitment drive. By November Martin reported that "we are now getting a thousand recruits a day." For the month of November, Martin wrote, "we will get as many recruits as composed the authorized strength of the Regular Army from the Civil War to the breaking out of the Spanish-American War."[16]

As it had at West Point, indeed, throughout his military career, Martin's determination paid off. The army received enormous benefits. By the end of the year, the army bulged at the seams with new recruits. For Martin the benefits became apparent when his name finally appeared on the promotions list. On October 10, 1921, Colonel Martin became Brigadier General Martin, regular army.

Ironically, Martin performed his recruiting duties too successfully. By 1922, after having built enlistments up through Colonel Martin's energetic leadership in the recruitment campaign, Congress compelled the General Staff to reduce the standing army's strength from 280,000 to 125,000.[17]

For the next year, General Martin moved from position to position within the General Staff. Following a brief stint as commander of the Sixteenth Infantry Brigade at Fort Meade, Maryland, from July 1 to September 10, 1922, he took up duties as assistant chief of staff, Office of Personnel Policies, G-1. As General Pershing's assistant, Martin seized the opportunity to champion the policy he had earlier advocated regarding African-Americans in the U.S. Army.

Immediately after World War I, spurred by the discontent produced at having blacks serve in the armed forces, various military leaders began studying the actions of blacks during the war with an eye to the future role of blacks in the military—that is, should African Americans have any role at all. During April 1920, while Martin accumulated recruits, the General Staff College in Washington sent out inquiries to various white officers who served with blacks during the war. Within days of each other, Martin and his former Ninety-second Division chief of staff, Lieutenant Colonel Allen Greer, responded to the inquiries. Greer's response reiterated his previously published opinions. For three plus pages Colonel Greer, in what he called "a statement of my opinion based upon bitter experience," poured forth venomous condemnation of black soldiers and officers. "Their principal idea was not that they were in the service to fight for their country," Greer reported, "but that they were there for the advancement of their racial interests." Greer maintained that disaster would follow from capitulation to black political pressure to have "negro officers command negro troops in the future. . . . Not only will those troops fail in war," he warned, "but the seed of racial ferment will be sown and we will have to reap the consequences thereafter."[18]

If the army could "resist political pressure," keeping blacks out of command positions, Greer stated, then the only place in the army for blacks lay in "service, labor or pioneer troops." In fact, he wrote, "negroes make excellent teamsters, better in fact than white soldiers do. They also make good chauffeurs." On one point Greer remained unyielding: "care must be exercised that they shall always be kept under the supervision of white officers. Otherwise," he wrote mendaciously, "we may expect just as it happened in our division numerous cases of rape." He could not produce evidence of the rapes he told the General Staff College, because "the perpetrators, in [the] vast majority of [cases] were either undetected or else escaped punishment."[19]

Martin's response, though more politic than Greer's, oozed poisonous defamation. On several points Martin's and Greer's comments agree so completely that they could have consulted prior to composing them, although no evidence exists that they did. Martin made his reply to the inquiry, he said, "as a result of five months' observation of negroes running in number at times as high as 25,000 at Camp Grant, Ill., (where I commanded) and later from a service after the armistice of over a month in command of the 92d Division in France."[20]

Part of the inquiry requested "a resume of the past use made of negroes in the United States Army, with particular reference to their officering, organization, training and performance during the World War." Martin broke this "problem" down into "two sides"—ethical and practical. Ethically, Martin reasoned, the Constitution of the United States required the president to listen and respond to blacks who petitioned for inclusion in the military forces. "He cannot totally ignore their demands," Martin wrote. The practical considerations he broke down into two further considerations—political and military. Politically, Martin deduced, blacks were almost impotent, because "the negro is of very little importance except in certain sections of the country, namely, certain large cities, such as Boston, Chicago, etc." Militarily, he went on to say, these considerations must be broken down yet further into two more subcategories—"one is his general fitness as a soldier, the other a matter of the extent to which you can mix white and colored men without affecting the morale and efficiency of each." Martin held little hope for blacks' fitness as soldiers. As previously noted, in this report to the General Staff College, he characterized the average black man as being inferior to the average white man "except from a physical standpoint," writing that blacks in general "lack intelligence, education, common sense, initiative, determination, and pride of race. He is by nature careless, thoughtless, his mind is more likely to be on his personal advantage and comfort than on his business." If black soldiers had "proper" leadership, General Martin went on, "he has the necessary courage to be a good soldier, but not equal to white men who have had the same amount of training." Martin viewed black participation in future wars as inevitable though. In the future he said, "in all wars that may arise in this country, it will be necessary to organize some combatant units of negroes. This is for political reasons and because white people will not be willing for their sons to go to the front and be killed, while negroes simply stay back and perform labor without danger."

The general included a short list of black officers' failures in the recently concluded war:

1. Racial characteristics—Inferior intelligence, meager education, carelessness, false pride, lack of stamina, easily discouraged.

2. He was greatly elevated socially (especially in France), making life very sweet—in fact, too sweet to lose.

3. The men did not have real confidence in their negro officers. Knowledge of this fact weakened the limited faith the officers had in themselves.

4. Most of them fraternized with the enlisted men.

5. Because of their natural carelessness they did not attempt to maintain discipline in their organizations.

Grudgingly, Martin granted exceptional cases among a few blacks where "some of them possess the necessary qualifications to become good officers." But black officers and enlisted men all suffered from a debilitating problem in Martin's mind. "The desire for social equality is the average negro's chief ambition in life," he said. "He may appear loyal or even servile," Martin went on to say, "but in his heart of hearts he longs for that one thing—social equality. Most of them are very ungrateful and easily discouraged."

In his determination that white soldiers not be commanded by black officers Martin remained obdurate: "[y]ou cannot have white enlisted men about where they must serve under colored officers." Even where blacks served under white officers, the prevailing mode of operation, Martin cautioned some restrictions. "Before officers (white) are assigned to colored organizations their attitude toward negroes should be known." He maintained that "no officer who has a violent prejudice against negroes and who has no faith in their courage or ability should be assigned to duty with colored troops," ruling out most of the officer corps and thereby diminishing the chances for blacks to serve in the army at all. "Neither is it believed," he wrote, warning of the dangers of fraternization between the races, "that officers who would fraternize socially with negroes should be assigned to colored organizations. Except in very few places in the United States whites do not associate with negroes therefore for white officers to fraternize with colored officers introduces a situation entirely out of the ordinary." A system of perceived racial equality in the army would prove very dangerous to the system of racial domination, Martin warned. If white officers socialized with black officers, "there are very few negroes who will not have their 'heads turned' or take advantage of this situation."

Finally, with regard to the formation of black units in case of war, Martin recommended that "no units higher than regiments of Infantry and Cavalry" be formed and that there be "no original commissions for negroes in these regiments above that of 1st lieutenant."

While the General Staff continued to study the future of black soldiers, instructors excerpted Martin's recommendations for use in officer training courses at the Army War College.[21]

As assistant chief of staff, G1, Martin ordered a secret study undertaken to define the duties of African-Americans in the army. The study did not reach the general prior to his reassignment in Panama, but it eventually landed on his successor's desk on November 10, 1925, as a report titled "Employment of Negro Man Power in War," classified as a "Secret Study AWC [Army War College] 127-25."[22]

In a preface to the study, "Notes on Proposed Plan for the Use of Negro Manpower," the authors deliver some rationalizations for the plan's conclusions. Though Martin is not quoted by name, his words appear throughout the study, which asserts that blacks' subordinate position in society and in the army results not from white racism but from their own innate racial inferiority. First and foremost, the document says, the plan is based on the assumption that "military considerations alone should govern in war."

> The negro issues should be met squarely. The War Department had no predetermined and sound plan for the use of negro troops at the beginning of the World War. It had no adequate defense against political and racial pressure and was forced to organize negro combat divisions and commission unqualified negro officers. The results are well known. . . . The War Department when occasion demands should be able to present this matter frankly to those who make demands or should know the facts. The negro, particularly the officer, failed in the World War. . . . The negro does not perform his share of civil duties in time of peace in proportion to his population. He has no leaders in industrial or commercial life. He takes no part in government. Compared to the white man he is admittedly of inferior mentality. He is inherently weak in character. . . . The Mobilization Plan provides for approximately 140,000 negroes for non-combatant duty. This would leave approximately 30,000 for the experiment of combat duty. The majority of negroes left at home will be in the southern states where they will be needed for labor and where they can best be handled by competent whites.[23]

The body of the study is composed of six sections. Throughout—whether or not Martin's position as head of G1 influenced the compilers of the report to include his analysis and recommendations—his contribution, though unacknowledged, is evident. His recommendations—restricting unit size, original commissioning of black officers only at the grade of first lieutenant, assignment of black and white troops (no whites under black officers), assigning the majority of blacks to manual labor rather than combat units, and contingencies to thwart black political pressure on the legislative and executive branches—the study adopted wholesale. Although never officially acknowledged nor publicized, this study, which the army implemented, formed the basis of U.S. Army policy with regard to African-Americans from the mid-twenties through the early years of World War II.

Black Americans, from the Revolutionary War to World War I, misjudged the depths to which white racism drove American society. They assumed, wrongly, that proving their devotion to the United States would end the oppression under which they lived. Surely, they reasoned, white racism would end when white Americans saw the sacrifice blacks would endure. Even after World War I, as white racism reinvigorated the Ku Klux Klan, blacks still hoped, still imagined, that service in the military would open the door to full citizenship.[24]

General Martin spent much of his tenure as head of G1 serving as Pershing's representative at various functions around the country designed to cement better relations between the National Guard and the army, service that Martin found exceedingly pleasant. As "the great man's" stand-in, audiences paid him "unusual honors." At one such gathering at Fort Meade, Maryland, Martin warned student soldiers that "the enemies of right living, democracy and our dearly bought institutions of liberty continue their assaults upon the individual and the nation alike." While naming the uniform that they shared, "a symbol of democracy," Martin did not mention the militarized Jim Crow under which black soldiers lived. Calling the assembled students the hope of the future, the general continued, "We are here as Americans to play our part as best we can in the development of those qualities that will enable each and every one of us to contribute most effectively to national and individual defense against the enemies of our country and ourselves." Those enemies could arrive as "marching armies," the general told them, or "faithless and disloyal citizens unworthy of the name." He warned the students not to fall into the "national or individual apathy" being shown by the rest of the citizenry. Stay vigilant to avoid disaster, the general said, "for the preservation of the glorious heritage handed down to us" showed the way to act. Train well, he concluded, to "become invincible defenders of right and justice which represent the only causes for which this nation will ever rise in arms."[25]

On September 13, 1924, Martin spent an exhausting day participating in the "events in connection with the retirement of General Pershing." That day, in a letter to his old friend Cabell, Martin revealed that his service on the General Staff also neared an end. "I am to be relieved from my detail on the General Staff . . . Monday, September 15th. I am first on the roster for foreign service, and I am to succeed General Fox Conner in command of an Infantry Brigade in Panama." Once relieved, Martin spent six weeks on leave with Louise. On December 1, 1924, he set off on the final assignment of his military career.[26]

NOTES

1. George Wythe, *A History of the 90th Division* (N.P.: The 90th Division Association, 1920), 187.
2. Ibid., 189, 192; CHM to LM, April 27, 1919, CHMC, OHS.
3. CHM to LM, April 20, 1919; LM to Harry E. Dutton, September 19, 1934, CHMC, OHS.
4. CHM to Henry C. Cabell, April 5, 1920, CHMC, OHS; CHM to LM, June 30, 1920, CHMC, OHS.
5. William Addleman Ganoe, *The History of the United States Army* (New York: D. Appleton-Century Company, 1942), 479.
6. Russell F. Weigley, *Towards an American Army Military: Thought from Washington to Marshall* (New York: Columbia University Press, 1962), 106.
7. Ibid., 230.
8. Richard C. Brown, *The Social Attitudes of American Generals, 1898–1940* (New York: Arno Press, 1979), 129.
9. CHM quoted in Ibid., 131.
10. CHM to LM, June 30, 1920, CHMC, OHS; Duane Hennessy, "Straight from the Soldier—The End of War," *Oregonian,* December 25, 1938, 5.
11. Ibid.; CHM to LM, undated, probably sometime in late May or early June, 1920, CHMC, OHS.
12. CHM to LM, undated, 1920, CHMC, OHS.
13. CHM to ?, undated letter fragment, probably June 1920, CHMC, OHS.
14. CHM to LM, June 30, 1920, CHMC, OHS.
15. Henry Cabell to CHM, July 20 and 28, 1920, CHMC, OHS.
16. CHM to William C. Alvord, November 26, 1920, CHMC, OHS.
17. Weigley, 240; Ganoe, 484.
18. Woodrow Wilson quoted in, Robert H. Ferrell, *Woodrow Wilson and World War I, 1917–1921* (New York: Harper and Row, Publishers, 1985), 213; Allen J. Greer to Assistant Commandant, General Staff College, April 13, 1920, U.S. Army Military History Institute, Carlisle Barracks, Carlisle, Pennsylvania.
19. Ibid.
20. CHM to Colonel H.A. Smith, April 6, 1920, Military History Institute, Carlisle Barracks, Carlisle, Pennsylvania.
21. Ibid.

22. Lieutenant Colonel Harry B. Jordan, "Course at the Army War College," memorandum for the Director, G-3 Division, Army War College, December 3, 1924; Army War College, "Employment of Negro Man Power in War," November 10, 1925, file 127-25, U.S. Army Military History Institute.

23. Ibid., 127-25, preface.

24. Ulysses Lee, *The Employment of Negro Troops* (Washington, D.C.: U.S. Government Printing Office, 1966), 3–36.

25. CHM to William C. Alvord, February 8, 1923; unidentified newspaper article, 1923, CHMC, OHS.

26. CHM to Henry C. Cabell, September 13, 1924, CHMC, OHS.

With Vice President Dawes at the Panama Canal, 1925. *Oregon Historical Society, 004883*

Chapter Seven

GOVERNING THE PANAMA CANAL

Communists congregated [in Panama to] fish in troubled waters.
—Charles Henry Martin

THE U.S. ARMY had three choice commands reserved to reward its most senior officers, commands where the military and foreign policy of the United States intersected—Hawaii, the Philippines, and Panama. Military commanders serving in any of these places oversaw large numbers of troops prepared for any eventuality and needed diplomatic as well as military acumen. Military planners considered newly promoted Major General Charles Henry Martin, at the pinnacle of his military career, perfectly suited for assignment to the difficult task of administering U.S. interests in Panama.

As divisional commander, with headquarters in Balboa, now the Canal Zone's main city, Martin commanded more than 14,000 troops. In the final analysis, the United States' "Panama Policy" rested on these troops. By 1925, when Martin assumed command, the Panama Canal occupied "a fundamental [place] in the foreign policy of the United States." Militarily and economically, the canal allowed the expanding and increasingly important U.S. Navy to sail easily from the Atlantic Ocean to the Pacific Ocean, while also putting"the gigantic industrial complex in the Northeast thousands of miles closer to the mineral wealth of South America's western coast and the supposedly bottomless markets of Asia." The United States had to ensure the navigability of the Panama Canal at all costs. The War Department made protection of the canal one of its top strategic priorities, receiving significant congressional appropriations to meet that goal.[1]

General Martin inherited a volatile and sensitive situation—militarily and politically, internally and externally. Externally, the United States and Panama sparred verbally over sovereignty issues while internally, political tensions mounted between the small Panamanian oligarchy that controlled wealth and politics and the mass of the population who lived in abject poverty. The army also expected Martin to restore its damaged credibility.

Early in 1924, prior to Martin's arrival, the War Department invited representatives from newspapers across the United States to witness the spring maneuvers. The move proved to be a public relations disaster when reporters generally agreed on the inadequacy of existing canal defenses. Editorial writers demanded that "Congress forget politics and take action adequately to safeguard the canal itself," it being accepted as fact that "the fate of the United States may yet rest on that waterway." Faced with the need to reorganize in Panama, the War Department drafted its proven miracle worker, General Martin.[2]

The general's training and experience prepared him well for the assignment. Iron Pants moved into action reorganizing the soldiers under his command. Predictably, exhausting physical training accompanied by strict discipline constituted the essence of his program. When the troops met his standards, he effectively erased the army's black eye by conducting public military exercises demonstrating that his forces could effectively protect the canal from enemy attack.

Not that there were no diversions to the constant military obligations. The other component of his office, the diplomatic responsibilities, he carried out with considerable delight. He demonstrated his diplomatic acumen by hosting an endless round of official dinner parties and greeting dignitaries passing through the canal.

During Martin's first year in Panama, internal political tensions remained just under the surface. Though the primary military mission of the United States revolved around defending access to the canal, providing acceptable protection for the canal also required a stable political situation in Panama. To ensure stability, the U.S. government used military forces as a colonial police force. They maintained stability by making Panama safe for the dominating oligarchy and the economic interests of U.S. corporations and banks.

The foundation for U.S. police power resided in the 1903 Hay-Bunau-Varilla Treaty between the United States and Panama, and Article 136 of the Panamanian Constitution that gave the United States not only full sovereignty over the Canal Zone (the ten-mile-wide swath bisecting Panama with the canal at its center) but further stipulated that the United States guaranteed the preservation of Panamanian "independence." Should unrest occur in the cities at either end of the waterway—Colon and Panama City— by treaty, the United States could step in to restore order. In time of war or internal disorder, moreover, the United States could occupy lands outside the canal zone.[3]

By the end of World War I, many Panamanians began to question those provisions. They argued that Washington could only intervene when

Panamanians requested assistance. But the United States continued, as it had since at least 1912, to intervene in intra-Panamanian disputes at its own discretion. That year U.S. troops responded with force to riots in the red light district of Cocoa Grove and again in 1915 in the same area. In response to the latter disturbances, the United States demanded that the Panamanian police surrender their high-powered rifles. After some diplomatic maneuvering, the police did surrender the rifles and were left with pistols only. The U.S. government shipped the rifles to the United States and sold them on the open market.

In 1918 another large-scale uprising occurred centered in Chiriqui Province, home of the United Fruit Company's banana plantations. The Panamanian police, armed only with their pistols, proved impotent in protecting the assets of the United Fruit Company when agrarian rebels killed one of its American employees. U.S. forces then descended on the area, killing indiscriminately. Once again, the U.S. military had difficulty discerning poor farmers from agrarian rebels—as with the Boxers and other Chinese peasants, they all looked much the same.

For the next two years, the U.S. forces occupied the province to protect United Fruit employees and property. The troops left Chiriqui in 1921, but peasant unrest did not end. In 1924, just prior to Martin's arrival, Panamanian President Porras requested protection from U.S. troops when mobs besieged the presidential palace. The U.S. military quickly routed rebels but could not wipe away the reality that lay at the heart of the contradiction between the oligarchy and the poor.

By 1925 the United States had a well deserved reputation in Central America as "Yankee Imperialists." Citing Theodore Roosevelt's Corollary to the Monroe Doctrine, the United States had, during the first two decades of the twentieth century, intervened in Cuba, Haiti, Santo Domingo, Mexico, Nicaragua, and Panama to protect U.S. economic interests. Crusty Marine general, Smedley Darlington Butler, explained the imperialist nature of U.S. foreign policy aptly:

> I spent thirty-three years and four months in active service as a member of our country's most agile military force—the Marine corps. I served in all commissioned ranks from a second lieutenant to major-general. And during that period I spent most of my time being a high-class muscle man for Big Business, for Wall street and, for the bankers. In short, I was a racketeer for capitalism . . . Thus I helped make Mexico and especially Tampico safe for American oil interests in 1914. I helped make Haiti and Cuba a decent place for the National City Bank to collect revenues in . . . I helped purify Nicaragua for the international banking house of Brown Brothers in 1909–1912. I brought light to the Dominican

Republic for American sugar interests in 1916. I helped make Hondu-
ras "right" for American fruit companies in 1903.[4]

One U.S. visitor to Panama in the 1920s remarked on the mutual animosity evident between the majority of the Panamanian population and the
soldiers and civilians of the United States. Panamanians disliked North
Americans because of "their resentment at our hardly concealed contempt
for them. . . . [As] for the casual clerk or mechanic we Americans call him
'spiggoty' with frank contempt for his undersize, his lack of education, and
for his large proportion of Negro blood. He responds by calling North
Americans 'gringos' and hating us with a deep, malevolent rancor that needs
only a fit occasion to blaze forth in riot and in massacre."[5]

Panamanian radicals threw an added ingredient into this inflammatory
mixture when they created a new political party, Accion Communal. Both
General Martin and U.S. Ambassador Roy T. Davis attributed the party's
origins to the worldwide Communist conspiracy. Martin complained that
Communists had congregated in Panama to "fish in troubled waters." Though
the waters were indeed troubled, the radical movement had its origins not
in Moscow but in the deep frustrations felt by the indigenous and poor in
Panama. They did not need foreign provocateurs to point out the appalling conditions under which they lived. Indigenous radicals developed the
Panamanian Communist Party to carry on a two-front political war to end
the continued occupation of Panama by the United States and to evict the
oligarchy from power.[6]

One of the most significant uprisings prior to the 1931 Panamanian
Revolution occurred during October 1925 while Martin commanded U.S.
forces. Known as the "revolt of the renters," the uprising's organizers attempted to end the exorbitantly high rents demanded by the oligarchy, in
particular by the man the United States had just made Panama's first vice
president, Ricardo Arias Calderon. The uprising began innocently enough
with renters gathering and marching in Panama City, gatherings that went
unmolested by the police. Martin later claimed that instead of taking stern
measures early on, which they should have done, the Panamanian government permitted the unrest to grow. Finally Panamanian President Arosemena
informed General Martin that the situation went beyond his ability to
maintain control. He said that he could not count on his police and fire
departments because they "were infected with disloyalty."[7]

When the renters appeared in the streets, workers out on a general strike
joined the march, broke into saloons to fortify themselves, and set off false
fire alarms. President Arosemena called on Martin to put down the rebels.
Martin, cognizant of the discontent over previous U.S. intervention in

Panamanian internal affairs, refused to supply troops until the president put the request in writing. The general agreed to intervene but only if the Panamanian president allowed a countrywide declaration of martial law. Further, the general said, the president must make the request in writing to allow Martin to be in compliance with army regulations. Imperiously, General Martin gave President Arosemena one hour to make up his mind.

Leaving the president in the unenviable position of having to request formal intervention by the U.S. Army, Martin drove the five miles to the infantry target practice range where he ordered 1,500 troops into transport trucks and sent them off in the direction of Panama City. As he expected, General Martin found the formal written request for U.S. intervention waiting on his desk when he returned to his headquarters.

Martin followed the troop convoy moving into Panama City in his car. He set the troops, bayonets fixed, in the streets in a solid mass stretching from building line to building line. As the troops advanced into the city they swept everything and everyone out of their line of march. The action appalled some members of the U.S. diplomatic community. The American charge d'affaires ran out of the University Club as Martin passed and stormed at the general. "You're ruining what has taken 50 years to build up—good will." Martin turned threateningly toward the shocked diplomat and bellowed, "The city is under martial law. About face and go back into your club at a run. If you don't I'll have you put into the trucks with the . . . mob."[8]

By late afternoon Martin's forces crushed the unorganized uprising. He rounded up and jailed dozens of peasants whom he labeled the riot's instigators. The general received accolades from his military superiors for the decisive action. When the general withdrew his troops from Panama City, General William Lassiter sent Martin congratulations. "I desire to express my strong appreciation of the manner in which the troops deported themselves," Lassiter wrote. "All ranks co-operated in carrying out this duty in a manner to reflect credit upon themselves and upon their country." Martin's use of force did not crush the aspirations of poor Panamanians: it did secure their abiding enmity. Later that year, when retired General John Pershing visited Panama City, angry crowds displayed their hatred of the U.S. military by hurling rocks at Pershing's car. [9]

In December the War Department promoted General Martin to commander of the Canal Zone, the highest U.S. military position in Panama. While radical Panamanians plotted clandestinely during the remainder of Martin's service in Panama, they did not surface again. General Martin brought Louise to live in the lavish estate the army provided for its top officer. There, she hosted parties and entertained visiting dignitaries. In addition to Vice President of the United States Charles Dawes, who accepted the Martins' hospitality for six days, they played host to members of the British royal family, heads of state, and assorted dignitaries from the United States.

Though General Martin welcomed all visitors to the Canal Zone, he allowed only certain dignitaries to visit the military fortifications. When a delegation of thirty-two Congressmen arrived for an inspection tour, Martin welcomed them extravagantly but with conditions. The congressmen could tour the military fortifications under his command, the general said, but "the policy of these headquarters is not to permit anybody to go into the fortifications . . . except high officials of the government." Therefore, he said, "this policy, of course, would exclude the women . . . of the party going with the congressmen into the fortifications."[10]

The general sometimes used his position to publicly chastise or scold Panamanian officials when he decided their actions warranted an official rebuke. At a banquet given in his honor on November 6, 1926, he openly criticized the Panamanian government for erecting a monument to Ferdinand De Lesseps and the French for their early work in pressing for a Panama Canal, thus slighting what Martin considered the vital role played by Theodore Roosevelt and the United States. He scolded the Panamanian officials, pointing out that of the ten tablets on the French monument, only the last one made passing allusion to the group primarily responsible for the "birth of [Panamanian] nationality and the accomplishment of the prodigious work."[11]

On October 1, 1927, Martin circulated General Order 42 to troops stationed with the Panama Canal Department. "After 45 years service in the United States Army, I am today passing to the retired list. Of all this service, none has been more pleasant than that in the Panama Canal Department."[12]

So ended Charles Henry Martin's military career. His years of service coincided with momentous events in the history of the United States. As he graduated from West Point in 1887, the United States entered the final decade of the nineteenth century suffering through upheaval and uncertainty. Recurring economic depressions, labor unrest, the closing of the frontier, and the process of industrialization combined to lead many people to the conclusion that modern civilization itself was threatened with destruction. To many citizens, chaos and revolution seemed inevitable.

Martin witnessed the last impediment to complete continental empire vanish with final defeat of the Indians. He saw a country torn apart in the 1890s by depression and want. In 1892 the agrarian radical Ignatius Donnelly described a country on the brink of collapse: "We meet in the midst of a nation brought to the verge of moral, political and material ruin. . . . The people are demoralized."[13]

As Martin joined U.S. forces in the Philippines and China, the United States entered into a "great debate" that developed around the ways to solve the immediate problems and prevent future crises. Politicians, military professionals, intellectuals, businessmen, and the mass of the citizenry reached the same conclusion about goals but differed over the means. The solution that developed, for "all but an infinitesimal segment" of those pondering the crisis, rested in the pursuit of an expansionist foreign policy, an assertion of a doctrine of free trade articulated by the government of the United States as the "Open Door Notes."

> The issue . . . concerned not whether such expansion should be pursued, but rather what kind of expansion should be undertaken. . . . A strong majority agreed that foreign policy could and should play an important—if not crucial—part in recovering from the depression of the 1890's and in forestalling future difficulties.[14]

When the internal battle faded into the background, the United States used its military forces to uphold the doctrine of free trade and exert its great international influence. Charles Henry Martin played a role in the evolution of twentieth century foreign policy. Soldiers became the instrument of government policy, and some soldiers also, in certain circumstances, became formulators of government policy. The enlisted soldiers and junior officers were always the instruments; some in the officer corps became formulators. Martin played both roles. As U.S. foreign policy evolved over time, as the sphere of influence expanded, as the nation grew more powerful, so Charles Henry Martin rose through the ranks, evolving, transforming, feeling his own power and sphere of influence grow.

Martin liked wielding power. He treasured it. He revered it. He nurtured it. He used it. He did not want to give it up.

NOTES

1. Samuel Flagg Bemis, *A Diplomatic History of the United States* (New York: Henry Holt and Company, 1942; Walter LaFeber, *The Panama Canal: The Crisis in Historical Perspective* (New York: Oxford University Press, 1978), 61.
2. Unidentified newspaper article that quotes editorial opinion from around the country, National Archives, Records Group 165, Records of the War Department General and Special Staffs, War Plans Division, General Correspondence 1920–1942, Box 10, 73.
3. Edward F. Dolan, *Panama and the United States: Their Canal, Their Stormy Years* (New York: Franklin Watts, 1990), 103.
4. Smedley D. Butler, quoted in Jenny Pearce, *Under the Eagle* (Boston: South End Press, 1982), 20.
5. LaFeber, 79.
6. CHM quoted in the *Oregonian*, December 25, 1938; LaFeber, 80–81.
7. *Oregonian*, December 25, 1938.

8. Ibid., December 25, 1938.
9. General William Lassiter to CHM, National Archives, Records Group 98, Box 3, Panama Canal Department, 1915–1939.
10. CHM to Governor of the Canal Zone, National Archives, Records Group 98, Box 42.
11. President R. Chiari to CHM, November 13, 1926, National Archives, Records Group 98, Box 3.
12. CHM, General Orders No. 42, October 1, 1927, National Archives, Records Group 98, Box 3.
13. Ignatius Donnelly quoted in Lawrence Goodwyn, *The Populist Moment: A Short History of the Agrarian Revolt in America* (Oxford: Oxford University Press, 1978), 167–68.
14. William Appleman Williams, *The Tragedy of American Diplomacy* (New York: Dell Publishing Co., Inc., 1962), 22.

Chapter Eight

LAND SPECULATOR TURNS POLITICIAN

The world is peopled to a great extent by the ignorant, the selfish and the knavish.
—Charles Henry Martin

WHEN A SOMEWHAT OVER-EAGER Colonel John T. Geary asked Martin for advice about venturing into a political career after retiring from the army, Martin told the colonel he could not just jump from the army to politics without a "buildup." Using himself as an example, Martin explained, "you must understand that I came to Oregon fifty years ago, mixed with the people here and got acquainted with all the old timers. Later I married the daughter of an exceedingly well known, progressive citizen." Wealthy and powerful too, he could have added. Martin married well indeed. When Louise eventually inherited the Hughes Investment Company after her parents' death, that wealth passed into Martin's hands.[1]

From his arrival in Oregon in 1873, Ellis G. Hughes, Louise's father, built a reputation and acquired wealth and power in Portland as a leading figure in the law, banking, railroad, and real estate investment communities. He maintained that position for more than thirty years. An indefatigable Portland booster, Hughes once helped finance and organize the fitting-out of a railroad car that toured the east coast promoting opportunities in the Pacific Northwest, Portland especially. Many Portlanders considered him the father of the Port of Portland after he drafted the Port of Portland Commission legislation in 1891. He served as one of the original commission's members, "an honor reserved for the city's business and community leaders." Though his law practice established his power base among Portland's elite, Hughes increasingly relegated his actions at the bar to a subordinate position when his career as an investor and land speculator held out more promise for financial advancement. Early on he became a member of the exclusive Arlington Club, the social gathering place for Portland's ruling class males. Situated at the seat of power, Hughes founded the Irvington Investment Company and eventually became the leading real estate developer in Northeast Portland. He owned more than 400 lots in the Irvington Addition, valued on his 1895 tax bill at over $90,000. He intended to use the Irvington property as a way to cash in on the population increase brought about by his Portland boosterism. Hughes and the other prominent Portland land speculators envisioned Irvington as a "self-contained middle to upper class residential district."[2]

When Ellis Hughes died on August 27, 1909, his speculation paid enormous dividends to his widow Maria Louisa and their only child Louise Martin. The two women divided the estate equally as Hughes's will directed. Martin, by then a U.S. Army captain, thoroughly enmeshed in land speculation himself with Hughes's tutoring, acted as the women's advisor. When they filed to probate the will, Maria Louisa, as administrator, appraised the value of Hughes's estate at $256,996. According to their estimate, the personal property amounted to $34,968 and the real estate holdings composed the other $222,028. After a protracted argument with the state treasurer, who claimed that the estimate on the value of the real estate was too low, the estate entered into a compromise, raising the real estate's value to $291,350. That brought the assessed value of the total estate to $326,318, almost $100,000 over the original appraisal. In today's dollars, the difference amounted to approximately $1,000,000.[3]

Ellis Hughes's influence on Martin began even before Martin married Louise. Early on in their courtship, at Hughes's urging, Martin began putting his savings into Oregon real estate. Unfortunately his early investment in timber land produced unsatisfactory results. During Martin's service in the Philippines, thieves cut down and carried off all the timber, leaving the investment worthless. While thieves cut down his timber in Oregon, Martin, Cabell, and other officers managed to turn speculation in Philippine property to more profitable ends.

Upon Ellis Hughes's death, Maria Louisa and Louise dissolved the Irvington Investment Company, founding in its stead the Hughes Investment Company. From that beginning in 1910 until Maria Louisa's death on February 18, 1923, Martin combined his military service with his position as company secretary, overseeing the company's affairs through a series of surrogate business managers. Maria Hughes became company president though Martin actually made most of the important decisions. Martin kept in contact with the company business managers by phone and letter as he and Louise moved around the world. When he necessarily had to seek the company president's agreement for major decisions, Mrs. Hughes exasperated Martin because she did not exhibit a firm grasp of the family business nor, according to Martin, did she understand the intricacies inherent in building a successful speculative business at all. At one point, from Chicago where he was then serving, Martin sent an urgent letter to Maria Hughes's attorney seeking support for denying her permission to withdraw capital from the company. "We must be perfectly frank with her," he told Attorney William S. Nash, "she must understand what a plight she would be in if the monthly income from the Hughes Investment Company were cut off." They needed to present a united front, Martin claimed. "It is necessary to be very firm with her and to insist for her own good that she should follow yours and my advice." Mrs. Hughes did as they suggested. The capital stayed with the company.[4]

Throughout the period 1909 to 1920, Hughes Investment struggled to compete for residential lot sales with the Rose City Park and Laurelhurst developments. Martin managed to keep Hughes's vision concerning Irvington's residential uniformity intact, but he had to constantly badger and cajole his Portland realtor, Ritter, Lowe and Company, to improve sales. "I was the boy who in 1910 and 1911 pegged these lots up to $2500 apiece and could I have remained on the ground, I believe even in spite of the war they would not have met the terrible slump which they did," Martin reminded E.J. Lowe. "I succeeded in getting the people enthusiastic in this tract because I, myself, became enthusiastic." Now Lowe needed enthusiasm, Martin said. "Make a market at [the right] psychological time which is June, the month of roses," he counseled Lowe at one point. "Why should California agents come to Portland to show you realtors how to sell real estate? . . . Telegraph me collect every Saturday night weekly sales," he demanded. Lowe, in numerous letters, attempted to assuage Martin's ire. "We are continuously working and advertising . . . leaving nothing undone to make sales, but the vacant lot market is still very slow," he said in one variation on a recurring theme.[5]

During the post–World War I recession, Hughes Investment suffered from some financial uncertainties, especially during the period from 1920 to 1923. The company was land rich but cash poor. At one point, thinking that only Martin's presence could bring company land sales out of the doldrums, Henry Cabell urged that Martin retire from the army and come home to take charge. "We believe the best thing for you to do is to retire," Cabell wrote. "There is no doubt in our minds that you should get out soon . . . you [could] make much more money handling the Hughes estate." But this occurred at just the point that the colonel redoubled his recruiting efforts to get his general's star, so Martin stayed in the army. Besides, the company, even though cash poor, had increased in value from 1909 by over $200,000. The July 31, 1920, balance sheet shows that Hughes Investment had, in cash, Liberty Bonds, and real estate, $536,964.[6]

The Martins took very little money out of the company during these years. What few dividends Louise received always went right back into company investments or toward paying city assessments. Mrs. Hughes's yearly withdrawals from company assets, on which she lived, Martin credited as loans from the company, which would later be deducted from her estate. Martin used whatever he could from his $8,000 yearly salary to offset the payments to Mrs. Hughes, which forced him and Louise to maintain a careful watch on their finances. Martin constantly complained about tight budgets during these years. They lived in Washington, D.C., while he served on the General Staff, which Martin called "pretty expensive," and also paid for Ellis's Princeton education. "It certainly takes a lot of money to put a boy through one of these universities," Martin wrote about Princeton. "But," he continued, "as he graduates in June we hope to be relieved of it." Ellis's graduation that summer did indeed relieve them financially, but the alcoholism Ellis developed during his Princeton years brought suffering and torment to his parents. His life after Princeton consisted of one prolonged spiral down as parents and child struggled with the disease.[7]

Eventually even General Martin's determination could not keep Ellis Hughes's vision for Irvington alive. Residential lots moved very slowly, especially after Ralph B. Lloyd's diversified development encroached as close as three blocks from Irvington. Early in 1921, Martin moved to diversify Hughes Investment to take advantage of a boom in downtown property development. He entered into negotiations with the owners of the Blake McFall Building at S.W. Fifth Avenue, offering to trade eighty percent of the remaining Irvington lots for the downtown property. Eventually, adding $100,000 cash borrowed from the Metropolitan Life Insurance Company to sweeten the deal, Hughes Investment completed the sale. That left the company with 117½ lots in the Irvington district in December 1921. Predictably, the company renamed the downtown structure the Hughes Building where it "enjoyed a prominent commercial existence until it was destroyed by fire in February 1977."[8]

The company experienced a rather grim financial year in 1922, losing more than $13,000. Early the next year, February 18, 1923, Mrs. Hughes died, casting a momentary shadow over Martin's expectation that the national economy would improve. "On all sides," he wrote, "the opinion is general that we are on the eve of the most prosperous times the country has ever seen." At her mother's death, Louise became the owner of all outstanding stock in the Hughes Investment Company. With some creative bookkeeping centered on all the "loans" the company had provided for Mrs. Hughes's support since 1909, Martin and company attorney William S. Nash managed to transfer the bulk of Mrs. Hughes's estate to the company's ledger.[9]

Martin's early optimism concerning the economic outlook for 1923 proved somewhat premature with regard to Irvington real estate. Throughout the year, he buried business manager William Alvord and attorney Nash under a barrage of letters fired off from his office in the War Department urging action. Because Portland continued to improve amenities in Irvington financed through property tax liens, Martin thought the company profits in those lots would vanish, especially considering he could not foresee anyone buying the lots if the company raised the asking prices. Martin made a practice of paying city liens on the Irvington property improvements at the last minute, and in 1923 the city threatened to auction some company lots in Irvington to satisfy the debt. As the foreclosures approached, Martin sought to use his social contacts to forestall the city's action. He asked his old friend and chairman of the city planning commission, John C. Ainsworth of the U.S. National Bank, to intercede with the city on his behalf and urged action on Nash. "Could you not go to [the city]," he queried Nash, "and argue [them] out of putting these lots up for sale for the present." Finally, William Alvord found a solution. Alvord informed Martin in June that "it requires three years for a person to foreclose a certificate of delinquency for . . . taxes and if they do not change their system, they cannot begin to buy in and get title to any of our Irvington property until three years have passed after October next." While the Hughes Investment Company's Irvington lots escaped the auction block, the city continued to auction off other property that had been taken for tax delinquencies at rates that cut deeply into any sales Hughes Investment anticipated from its Irvington lots. Martin fumed for years about property taxes being used to finance government operations. When the opportunity arose, he took actions as governor to alleviate taxes on real estate speculation.[10]

In 1924, as Martin's tenure at G1 neared an end, the company again needed a cash infusion to carry it through, even though 1923 had turned out to be a record year. Martin sent every cent he could spare from his salary to tide the company over, dipping often into his savings. That year his troubles multiplied when Louise balked at sustaining company operations with additional cash from her inheritance. "I have been advising her right along," Martin complained, "to let us have some of her money to help pay our debts but she has not seen it that way and has strenuously objected."

In June when she refused Martin's request to put $2,000 into the company, he raised the money himself and loaned it interest free to the company behind her back. "I feel that Mrs. Martin would be embarrassed by knowing that out of my slender means that I let the Company have money without charge," he wrote the new business manager G.G. Jones. Unfortunately she doesn't understand as you and I the makeshifts which a successful business has to undergo to get along."[11]

But "get along" the company did under Jones's capable management overseen by Martin's ubiquitous letters. The real estate market gyrated wildly in 1925, up during the first part of the year, then falling off, then up again, and finally moving down as the year closed. "Conditions here, particularly in the downtown business section, have changed wonderfully in the past few months," Jones wrote to Martin in Panama during January. "It has become a regular 'bull' market." But by August, Martin railed at Ritter Lowe agents to get moving on selling lots in Irvington and Forest Glen where Martin and Cabell had investments separate from the company. "Our equity in these lots is reaching the vanishing point," Martin pointed out to Lowe. "When that time comes, of course, our interest in the property as well as your commissions is gone." Turning harsher, Martin urged, then demanded that Lowe "sell all the remaining lots, without concession of price, this fall." Martin reminded Lowe that his "campaign has now been going on for six years." Lowe's commissions stayed secure, Martin said, so "it makes little or no difference to you when the lots are sold, but it does to us." Using his best general's commanding tone, Martin concluded, "I want you to start in an intensive campaign right now to do what you have been promising to do every one of the six years you have had control of that property, namely: clean it up for us. Now the time for talking has passed, and the time has arrived for you to either put up or shut up."[12]

Slowly, steadily, gradually, the company paid off its debts throughout the period Martin served in Panama. The arrival of Californian Ralph Lloyd in Portland boosted Irvington sales considerably when Lloyd paid more than $2 million for an adjacent tract of land that he announced plans to develop.

In 1927, when the Martins retired to Portland, the general assumed personal command over the company business. He applied the same vigor to real estate speculation that proved so successful in the early twenties during his drive to bring recruits into the army. He sold lots, paid off the city liens against company property, and speculated in other sections of Portland, notably the Mount Scott and the Guilds Lake districts. He expanded the company's interests into financing home construction and mortgage lending. But Martin felt Portland development lacked control, it moved too chaotically, without planning. He moved but the city did not follow. He complained that Portland businessmen lacked foresight and drive. He bluntly told the Portland Realty Board that "we are the most backward community on the Pacific Coast." Thinking small would never put Portland in the position it deserved, he claimed. "We have little groups who are doing little things. They confine their energies to two-bit wrangles on tinhorn enterprises. . . . What this city needs is leadership," the general demanded.[13]

The general in Martin then sought to create order where he found chaos. He would bend the city to his vision through the force of his will. He set out to develop what he considered Portland held inchoate—the potential for enormous riches if only men with determination would take drastic action. He wanted Portland's businessmen to develop vision and practice discipline. He built on his own protests stretching back to as early as 1922 when he complained that while in the United States generally "we are on the eve of the most prosperous times the country has ever seen," Portland lagged behind. "I can not think that a great fine city like Portland will allow a few pessimists to keep it out of the procession," he said in 1922. "I think the chief trouble with Portland is the psychology of its leaders, such as they are. The trouble is one of the little crowd of uplifters running things, whose only idea is to sob and to spend the people's money."[14]

During the early months of 1930 with Hughes Investment Company finally on a secure financial foundation with close to $500,000 (approximately $5.2 million in today's dollars) in assets, Martin turned his frustration with Oregon's shortsighted leaders into a run for political office. Having "cast his net widely" after retirement, he parlayed his active participation in the Red Cross, the Chamber of Commerce, and other civic affairs, his place in Portland's ruling elite, and his glowing military reputation into a nomination for the United States House of Representatives.[15]

When Martin moved back to Portland permanently he asked an Arlington Club friend for political advice. He did not "want to sit before the fireplace dwelling on happy memories." The friend suggested volunteering as a way to build political contacts throughout the community. And as Oregon was a staunch Republican state, "register as a republican." Martin followed the advice although he later claimed, vociferously and adamantly, that he had never deserted the Democratic Party, his father's party. Then in 1930, with the nation mired in a "Republican depression," Democrats approached Martin, urging him to run for Congress. They "assured him that his candidacy would bring about a complete reunion and harmony in the party." He allowed Democratic Party activists to wage a write-in campaign on his behalf during the May primary for Oregon's Third Congressional District seat.[16]

According to historian Robert Burton, over the years Oregon voters showed a basic political loyalty to the Republican Party, "a political loyalty abandoned only temporarily and on certain occasions under stress of political change during the progressive era," early in the twentieth century. With the Republican Party ascendant nationally in the 1920s, Oregon voters only occasionally favored Democratic candidates with their votes—notably in 1922 when the Ku Klux Klan became an active political player, endorsing prominent Democrats, to elect a Democratic governor and congressman. Riven by factional power struggles, though the Oregon Democratic Party remained virtually powerless between 1920 and 1930.[17]

The 1929 economic collapse, however, prompted a dramatic shift in party identification in Oregon and the nation. Voters reacted to the economic disaster by switching loyalties. Martin followed the trend. Oregon Democrats perceived an unprecedented opportunity. Using the Republicans' unpopularity as a catalyst, they attempted to ensure that the Democratic Party became a viable competitor in the two-party system or, with any luck, to win total control of state politics. As part of a precinct-by-precinct reorganization, party activists seized on Martin's popularity within the business community to propel him toward the nomination for the House through a write-in campaign during the primaries.

Having easily won the May 1930 Democratic primary, Martin prepared himself in earnest for the general election. His Republican opponent, incumbent Franklin F. Korell, came to prominence in Republican political circles during the 1922 election as the Ku Klux Klan-sponsored candidate in the Republican primary for the Third Congressional District seat, narrowly losing the nomination to incumbent Clifton N. McArthur. Korell's problems in the 1930 election against Martin did not center around his Klan endorsement. Martin never made an issue of the Klan endorsement, an endorsement he would have undoubtedly sought himself had he been running in the same election because the Klan had, he said later, "the highest motives behind it." Korell's major problem centered on his identification as a Hoover Republican. He contended that the only real issue in the campaign was "the welfare and progress of the people of the United States, and more particularly the prosperity and progress of the people of Oregon." Unfortunately, he also claimed that the way to prosperity led through President Hoover. "The administration at Washington under the leadership of President Hoover," he stated in his platform, "started immediately the work of business construction and as a result we are once more on the upgrade in a business way, with a fair assurance that before long we will be traveling along the high road of prosperity at the usual pace."[18]

Korell's identification with Hoover proved an easy target for Martin. Oregon Democrats generally formed a cohesive unity in their opposition to President Hoover, blaming the economic collapse on Hoover's unwavering support for unethical businessmen and unscrupulous Wall Street investors. Two other decade-old factionalizing issues, though, continued to plague the party's fragile unity: the repeal of prohibition and the party's position regarding whether public money should be used to develop the Columbia River's hydroelectric potential.

The 1928 presidential election shattered the official, if not unanimous, Democratic party commitment to prohibition when the party's presidential candidate, Alfred E. Smith, proposed prohibition's repeal. Oswald West, former Oregon governor, longtime party activist, and Democratic National Committeeman, should have vigorously supported the party's candidate in the Oregon campaign. Instead, West considered Smith's nomination a disaster for the party and organized the opposition to the repeal movement among Oregon Democrats. However, Walter Pierce, another former Oregon governor and Democratic Party leader, supported Smith's call for prohibition's repeal. The bitter public feud between the party's wet and dry factions relegated the Republican primary campaign to the sidelines. Though West did not actively campaign against Smith in the fall, his inactivity helped ensure a clean sweep by Republicans in the November election. After the election, West and Pierce buried the hatchet and called for the party's revitalization. When the economy collapsed a year later, the Depression provided the unifying issue for party revitalization and propelled a massive shift in voter loyalty to the Democratic Party, locally and nationally, bringing in farmers, industrial workers, and more problematically, racial and ethnic minorities. After a decade of intra-party strife, Oregon Democrats united, jubilantly relishing a battle with Republicans over economic issues.

The other concern that animated the factional split in both the Republican and Democratic parties centered around the issue of public power, which eludes solution to the present day. The state grange initiated the fight over public power and hydroelectric development during the late nineteenth century. Since that time, candidates' political aspirations often depended on their stance concerning public power. The 1930 election proved not to be an exception.

George W. Joseph won the Republican gubernatorial primary. Joseph had long supported state and municipal public power development and ownership. He promised if elected to bring that vision to a reality. Old guard Republican conservatives who headed the Republican State Central Committee opposed Joseph's position and attempted to promote wealthy former state senator Henry L. Corbett in opposition to Joseph. When Joseph died suddenly in June, the old guard did not lose its opportunity to appoint a candidate more in tune with its ideas, settling on Phil Metschan, chair of the Republican State Committee and owner of the Imperial Hotel in Portland. A safe conservative, Metschan repudiated Joseph's platform while showing sympathies decidedly in favor of private utilities. Progressive Republicans, outraged at Metschan's anointing, bolted the Republican state convention. They held their own convention, choosing wealthy department store owner Julius L. Meier as an independent candidate. Meier had previously offered to provide $50,000 to any candidate who would carry the public power banner. He now picked up the Joseph torch himself, endorsing the Joseph platform literally word for word, earning endorsement by the Oregon Grange and the State Federation of Labor.

The Democrats' fragmentation over the power question rivaled that of the Republicans. As with prohibition, the factions again centered around Oswald West and Walter Pierce—West opposing public power and Pierce supporting Joseph's stand. Ed Bailey, West's candidate, eventually garnered the nomination but sidestepped the public power question during the primaries. In the general election, Republican Metschan and the Democrat Bailey assumed similar positions, supporting federal rather than state hydroelectric development, while Meier maintained his wholehearted support for Joseph's platform positions.

The impetus for Bailey's and Metschan's eventual support for federal development centered on a statewide ballot initiative appearing on the November ballot. If passed, the initiative provided for the creation of public or people's utility districts (PUDs). Pacific Power and Light Company, for which West worked as a paid lobbyist for over a decade, and the other private power companies perceived a chance to defeat Meier and the ballot initiative at the same time. They poured vast sums of money into the campaign. For months, with Democrat Ed Bailey virtually lost on the sidelines, Metschan and Meier waged an ideological battle between "free market" versus control by "the people." In the November election, Meier received more votes than his two opponents combined.

The public utility district initiative passed with a 33,000 vote margin while a similar PUD measure also passed in neighboring Washington State. The Washington law allowed PUDs to be formed and granted authority to issue revenue bonds by a single vote of the people in the proposed districts. Oregon's law, however, allowed utility companies the potential to twice defeat PUD formation or financing because PUD formation and financing through general obligation or revenue bonds occurred in two separate votes. Private utility companies in Oregon have used this two-stage process to great advantage in the decades following the 1930 vote. If well-financed campaigns to defeat PUD formation did not prove efficacious, campaigns to defeat bonding proposals usually did. At the end of the twentieth century, while eighty percent of Washington residents enjoyed power rates well below the national average by virtue of being served by PUDs, eighty percent of Oregonians received electricity from private utilities at significantly higher rates than those in Washington.

Martin "unqualifiedly" endorsed harnessing the Columbia River's potential through government financed development but not on the Joseph model. "The Columbia River must no longer be permitted to flow unvexed to the sea," Martin claimed in the campaign. "It must be canalized and reharnessed for barge transportation, hydro-electric power and irrigation." However, neither private enterprise nor the state could undertake the work. Sounding much like a nineteenth-century railroad capitalist, Martin claimed that "[t]oo vast and far reaching for private exploitation, this must all be a public development. Especially the Government must always hold its hand on the switch" in developing hydroelectric potential. To accomplish this goal, "it is necessary that Oregon have in congress someone who will see that this plan is carried out, not by creation of unnecessary commissions for surveying and wasting time, but by immediate action . . . and I pledge myself, if elected, to prosecute the general plan to its ultimate fulfillment."[19]

Understandably, Martin made no mention of the PUD ballot initiative that would undercut the private utilities' position. While Martin obviously favored federal development of Columbia River potential, he certainly did not want to undermine the rights of private profit derived from that development. The federal government would finance development and private companies would sell electricity to homes and industry. While Martin needed no convincing to support free-market positions, he did have an added incentive to work for and support the power interests' positions. Martin's campaign finance report to the clerk of the House of Representatives for the 1930 campaign shows that his old comrade in arms and friend Henry Cabell, a large investor in Portland General Electric, contributed thirty-five percent of the total dollars spent on the campaign.[20]

Martin's ambiguous position on public power and big business in general is evident in a radio speech ostensibly devoted to the power issue. Martin invoked his hero Theodore Roosevelt's "trust-busting" reputation, calling Roosevelt "the last Republican who worked consistently and continually for the welfare of all the people." The speech oscillated somewhat confusingly between the current Democratic economic populism and "the fundamental

precepts upon which this great nation was founded . . . that private enterprise . . . should be encouraged," attempting to tie the two together. While
he eventually arrived at his discussion of public power, he first dealt with
"the trend toward monopolistic control of our business and commercial life,"
one of the "gravest problems confronting the American people." Martin had
no problem with Pacific Power and Light or Portland General Electric selling power to Portland residents, but he did perceive a danger when trusts
held the major control over these companies. He likened that control to the
growth of department store chains. "Monopolistic control of chain organizations," he claimed, resulted in "inefficient efficiency . . . spreading
throughout the nation." Unchallenged monopolistic action throttled private initiative and enterprise, Martin cautioned. He laid the blame for the
stock market crash and resulting unemployment and economic "disturbance"
on this trend toward monopoly. Condemning President Hoover, he warned
that the "formation of trusts more gigantic and powerful than any that threatened our economic welfare in the days of T.R." now threatened the country's
future. Hydroelectric development in Oregon too suffered from "thimble
rigging in financing and ownership of utility companies that makes the tales
of the Arabian Nights seem like puerile twaddle." Martin wanted control
over utility companies put back in the hands of local shareholders who knew
best what interests animated Portland.[21]

If "thimble rigging" meant control by trusts, Martin accurately analyzed
the situation. Sixteen giant holding companies controlled seventy-five percent of private power output in the United States. "Portland's electric and
gas utilities were integral parts of the interstate holding company networks.
The utilities' officers and directors were front men, or puppets, whose decisions and actions were ordered from above—from the financial centers of
New York and Chicago." Unlike the local utilities such as Portland General Electric and Pacific Power and Light which came under minimal state
regulations governing their operations, the national holding companies faced
no such monitoring. In this situation, Martin said, "is the nubbin of the
power problem we face."[22]

In keeping with the trust-busting image of Theodore Roosevelt, Martin wanted the giant holding companies and trusts broken up to foster local ownership and competition. "Competition," he claimed, "would bring
lower rates and more efficient operation by the producing companies." He
urged voters to "encourage private enterprise and initiative and competition,"
which he claimed "will create a condition where men are employed and where
the purchasing power of the people will be restored by having work. This
principle I will fight for in Congress."[23]

Aside from Cabell's financial aid, infusions of cash from the Democratic National Committee, and significant contributions by the candidate himself, the largest donations to Martin's campaign came from the Association Against the Prohibition Amendment, headquartered in New York. The association itself and individual association donors gave the campaign more than twenty-five percent of the total dollars raised. The prohibition question did not appear in the first uncirculated "confidential" platform document, but eventually Martin incorporated his stance for repeal into the campaign. In Martin's last enunciation of his platform, he claimed that in addition to ridding the country of gangsters profiteering from prohibition "the discussion and settlement of great economic questions of national importance are either neglected or diverted by the constant intrusion of an essentially local sumptuary law. . . . I favor a repeal of the eighteenth amendment, with the return of the whole question to the separate states with such help from the National Government as any state may wish."[24]

Franklin Korell, Martin's general election Republican opponent, made the general's campaign relatively easy. Korell claimed that prosperity would return before long. President Hoover's actions thus far, by being patient and efficient through wise and temperate legislation helpful to business, promised a return to progress and prosperity. Korell incessantly repeated this, as he attempted to blunt Martin's onslaught. One of Martin's advisors, newspaperman Wallace S. (Buck) Wharton, who later became Governor Martin's budget director and executive secretary and whom Martin appointed as a state tax commissioner, offered a point-by-point refutation of Korell's platform, which Martin used throughout the campaign to attack Korell. As Korell focused on his service in Congress, Wharton dryly commented, "if we judge the future by the past Lord have mercy on us. The past has been rather tough and in nothing particular to brag about."[25]

Adopting Wharton's suggestions, Martin zeroed in on Korell's status as a nonentity in the seventy-first Congress. Martin said that the republican government established by the constitution depended on the character of the men chosen as representatives. Korell, a "cheap and designing" politician, had no character, Martin claimed; he simply used his office as a meal ticket. While "we hear" about issues in Idaho and Nebraska because "they are represented by such able men as Borah and Norris—men who take their public duties seriously, and see to it that the voice of their constituents is heard in Washington and that their interests are not overlooked or neglected. . . . [W]e hear nothing of Oregon in our governmental affairs." Why? Because Korell "comes before his constituents unfortunately with a clean record—a clean record for non-accomplishment of anything in the interest of the people of Oregon." Mocking Korell's service on the House Foreign Relations Committee, Martin wondered if it was "perhaps while dressed in his spats and long tail coat and attending some social gathering of the underlings of the Diplomatic Service . . . [or at] social opportunities with foreign diplomats . . . [or] trips abroad at government expense . . . that Mr. Korell permitted the opponents of our proposed lumber tariff to put over their program." Martin pledged that "if elected this fall, I will not sleep on the job as my opponent has done but will put forth every effort to bring about the early adjustment of all questions now standing open."[26]

Throughout the campaign, when discussing economic issues, Martin used populist language developed as part of the Democratic Party's overall strategy. Like other Democrats, he played on people's genuine fears and popular resentment against power elites to promote himself as a would-be savior. At one point Martin gave a long speech detailing the threat to local retail merchants and capitalism itself if outsiders gained control over the local economy. Again he used the "chain store" concept as the metaphor. Retail merchants, the church, hospitals, fraternal organizations, service and social clubs, and "all other charitable activities . . . the Boy Scouts, Red Cross, YMCA and other activities that stand for community betterment," all stood a real chance of destruction if chain stores succeeded in taking over the United States. "Something must be done," Martin said, to "save American community life in many of its most desirable and historic phases." Martin argued for capitalism's continuation, but he promised a better capitalism when, as Theodore Roosevelt claimed before him, the "bad trusts" are broken up.

In his rise to political power, Martin played on popular resentment against powerful elites over whom the public had little control. The general, however, did not mention his own standing among Oregon's elite. He wanted to destroy the power of what he called unscrupulous elites, so that men like himself, men who knew what was best for the people, could pursue the nation's business. Thus, in this early phase of his political life, Martin blamed the country's economic woes on these unscrupulous elites. However, once he felt that the economic stranglehold held by these elites was destroyed and when the capitalist economy still languished, he turned his focus to other forces, other outsiders.[27]

The independent Julius Meier won the gubernatorial election in the fall. Reflecting back on the election some years later, Martin wrote to an aspirant for office, "When I ran for Congress in 1930, it looked pretty black until about the middle of October. I was so sick at heart that I could not sleep, but I had the approval of my conscience in what I was doing and succeeded in convincing the people that I was right in the stand which I had taken." He had indeed convinced the voters. Martin was the only major Oregon Democrat elected to office in the 1930 election. He smashed Korell 55.1 percent (49,316) to 39.7 percent (35,483) with the remaining five percent of the vote going to the Independent Peter Streiff Jr. Joining such illustrious predecessors as Andrew Jackson and William Henry Harrison, Martin was only the fourth major general in U.S. history to be elected to Congress.[28]

NOTES

1. CHM to Colonel John T. Geary, January 18, 1937, CHMC, OHS.
2. E. Kimbark MacColl, *The Growth of a City: Power and Politics in Portland, Oregon, 1915 to 1950* (Georgian Press Company, 1979), 292, 326.
3. Copy of court order, no date, CHMC, OHS.
4. CHM to Mr. William S. Nash, Chicago, May 10, 1920, CHMC, OHS.
5. CHM to Ritter Lowe Company, telegram, undated; CHM to E.J. Lowe, May 17, 1922; E.J. Lowe to CHM, May 15, 1920, CHMC, OHS.
6. Henry Cabell to CHM, Portland, November 26, 1920, CHMC, OHS.
7. CHM to William G. Alvord, Washington, May 3, 1921, CHMC, OHS.
8. CHM to E.J. Lowe, Washington, D.C., May 17, 1922; CHMC, OHS; MacColl, 328, Walter Stablerer to CHM, December 22, 1921, CHMC, OHS.
9. CHM to G.G. Jones, Washington, March 21, 1923; William S. Nash to CHM, July 10, August 9, September 6, December 24, 1923; G.G. Jones to CHM, August 2, 1923, CHMC, OHS.
10. CHM to William S. Nash, Washington, D.C., May 29, 1923; William Alvord to CHM, June 18, 1923, CHMC, OHS.
11. CHM to G.G. Jones, June 24, 1924, CHMC, OHS.
12. G.G. Jones to CHM, January 29, 1925; CHM to E.J. Lowe, August 22, 1925, CHMC, OHS.
13. Undated, unidentified newspaper clipping, found in one of five scrapbooks, CHMC, OHS.
14. CHM to W.C. Alvord, May 25, 1922, CHMC, OHS.
15. Hughes Investment Company Records, 1930 balance sheet, CHMC, OHS.
16. CHM to Colonel John T. Geary, January 18, 1937; CHM to William C. Alvord, May 25, 1922, CHMC, OHS; Arthur H. Bone, *Oregon Cattleman/Governor Congressman: Memoirs and Times of Walter M. Pierce* (Portland: Oregon Historical Society, 1981), 386–87; *Spectator,* editorial, undated but probably 1930, CHMC, OHS.
17. Robert E. Burton, *Democrats of Oregon: The Pattern of Minority Politics, 1900–1956* (Eugene: University of Oregon, 1970), 39.
18. On the Ku Klux Klan see CHM to Major General Eli A. Helmick, January 4, 1937 and CHM to Brig. General C.C. Herron, January 6, 1937, CHMC, OHS; "Korell Issues Platform Citing Prosperity Note," *Oregonian,* September 21, 1930.
19. Two typescript platform documents, CHMC, OHS.
20. CHM to Clerk, House of Representatives, November 21, 1930, CHMC, OHS.
21. Undated typescript of a radio address, CHMC, OHS.
22. Ibid., and MacColl, 411–12.
23. Undated typescript of a radio address, CHMC, OHS.
24. Typescript platform document, CHMC, OHS.

25. Wallace S. Wharton to CHM, undated, CHMC, OHS.
26. Undated typescript of a radio address delivered during the campaign probably late in October, CHMC, OHS.
27. Typescript of a speech, March 16, 1930, and undated typescript of a speech, CHMC, OHS.
28. CHM to Colonel C.A. Robertson, July 25, 1940, CHMC, OHS. A typescript brief biography of Martin at OHS mentions that Martin was one of four major generals to be elected to Congress. Including Martin, I located the names of three but have been unable to locate the name of the fourth general.

Chapter Nine

CONGRESSMAN MARTIN

I went along with the New Deal at first but with its objections and leadership development, I am through with it. I am going to stand by the old Party as it was, and not follow this crowd who are not Democrats and whom I am satisfied if continued in power, will do irreparable damage to our country and its time-honored institutions. I am a Democrat, but not a New Dealer.
—Charles Henry Martin

FOR THIRTEEN MONTHS after winning the election, from November 1930 until December 1931, Martin waited to take his seat in Congress. For a man who craved order and action, the time must have passed excruciatingly slowly. The lame-duck Republican Seventy-first Congress adjourned on March 4, 1931, and the regular session of the Seventy-second Congress, Martin's Congress, did not begin to sit until December 7 of that year. With Democrats in control of both houses, Martin joined ninety new representatives in the House, seventy-four of whom, like Martin, occupied seats for the first time. Intraparty conflicts kept most serious legislation designed to alleviate the Depression bottled up in committees. Especially acute among the majority Democrats, factional battles ensured that neither Speaker of the House John Nance Garner nor the majority leader in the Senate could mold the Democratic majority into an effective voting bloc on which they could depend or control. Martin quickly became identified with insurgent Democratic conservatives who acted as an independent voting bloc. He served on six committees, notably Rivers and Harbors, which provided him the arena to press several pieces of legislation beneficial to Oregonians.

President Hoover recognized that his reliance on volunteerism to bring the country out of the Depression was not working. Slowly, he concluded that the federal government must step in to provide the necessary means. This did not mean governmental assistance to individuals. To intervene at the individual level meant instituting a variety of socialism that Hoover found abhorrent. The president believed economic recovery required a balanced federal budget, so he demanded that any Congressional actions with regard to economic recovery meet that criterion. When progressive Democrats sponsored a bill for expanded public works programs and unemployment relief that introduced deficit spending, Hoover successfully blocked the legislation. While Hoover opposed direct relief to individuals, he championed relief for corporations. He proposed creating a Reconstruction Finance Corporation (RFC) through which to provide low cost loans to banks and agricultural and commercial interests. The president pressed Congress to take up the bill for the RFC in December, but Congress disbanded for the Christmas holidays. When the enabling bill finally passed on January 15, 1932, Representative Martin did not cast a vote. He did vote for a bill that passed four days later, putting a five percent interest cap on all RFC loans. Then, twice, he cast affirmative votes for measures that allowed emergency highway construction appropriations to find their way to Oregon's coffers.

On two important relief bills that would have provided direct aid to individuals, Martin joined minority Republicans voting against the legislation, opposing the Democratic leadership. House Resolution 12445, on which Martin voted nay with the majority, would have provided destitution relief, direct loans, or advances until June 30, 1933, to states, counties, and cities. Martin and the conservative southern Democratic bloc believed direct aid would undermine individual initiative and worse, in all probability, deficit spending would exacerbate the ravages of the Depression.

On March 29, President Hoover warned in a press conference that "another bonus bill . . . was on the way." In fact a "Bonus Army," led by a Portlander, would soon descend on the capital to demand immediate payment of the bonus for wartime service passed by Congress in 1924. The American Legion began pressuring Congress for just such a bill in 1920 as "adjusted compensation" for time spent by soldiers in World War I whose pay, at $1.00 per day, fell well below the pay earned by civilians. The bill that eventually passed, the 1924 World War Adjusted Compensation Act, provided for payment in 1945 to WWI veterans "twenty-year paid-up endowment policies on the basis of $1.00 a day for home and $1.25 a day for overseas service."[1]

Walter W. Waters, an unemployed cannery worker, organized Portland World War I veterans, who called themselves the Bonus Expeditionary Force (BEF). Much like their 1894 predecessors in Coxey's Army, the BEF jumped trains heading east toward Washington, D.C., to petition Congress for economic relief. Their actions inspired other veterans around the country to join in the movement toward Washington. After the Illinois National Guard briefly dispersed the BEF in East St. Louis, Waters arrived in Washington with more than a thousand men. Over the next few weeks—in dilapidated cars and trucks, hitchhiking, stealing rides on trains, bringing their wives and children with them—BEF contingents from across the country converged on the Capitol. By June, 20,000 bonus marchers sat in their camps on the mall and across the Potomac River from Washington on Anacostia Flats waiting for Congress to act—the most massive protest ever assembled in the nation's Capitol. Though their actions remained peaceful, many politicians and military leaders felt the very presence of the BEF, so different from the usual lobbyists who swarmed around the Congressional hive, presented a threat.

While the BEF gathered, Congress debated Representative Wright Patman's bill for immediate payment of the bonus. On June 15 Representative Martin again joined the Republican minority voting against bonus payments. As Martin waited for his turn to speak that day, Representative Thomas L. Blanton of Texas castigated General James G. Harbord who had said that the bonus marchers had no right to come to Washington. Martin jumped from his seat and interrupted Blanton, shouting, "I resent this attack on General Harbord." Blanton shot right back, "My colleague from Oregon and General Harbord are in the same box," he said. "They each draw $6,000 a year retired pay in addition to their big salaries [referring to Martin's Congressional salary of $10,000 and Harbord's reputed $100,000 pay from Radio Corporation of America]." When Martin again tried to shout him down, Blanton screamed across the floor, "You sit down. I am going to give you orders now. Sit Down! This is one time that you, a big major general are going to take orders from a private. You sit Down!" When the speaker of the House ruled his outbursts out of order, Martin resumed his seat and did not interrupt Blanton further.[2]

Later, when he launched into his prepared speech, Martin spoke "insistently and vehemently against the measure on the House Floor," but the Patman bill passed the House anyway. Reiterating the arguments of his Republican colleagues, Martin said he believed in enactment of what he called "adequate relief measures . . . as a means of assisting our people in this grave economic emergency," but he refused to "support any measure restricted to benefits for special groups or interests." Martin's general theme revolved around economy in government and balancing the federal budget. "This is nothing but a raid upon the Treasury," he claimed. Turning to the bonus army, Martin flatly rejected the demands of the unemployed veterans claiming, "the ex-soldiers in this country should send their lobby home and should never again allow political or other forces to lead them to strive for further payment from our government." Martin told his House colleagues that he would oppose "this attack on our general welfare." He found the bonus army particularly "odious because, among its self-constituted leaders are some men who . . . by no stretch of the imagination experienced any more risk during the war than though they had never volunteered or been drafted; some men who served a little while and were rejected as unfit; some men who appeal to greed in their own personal political interest . . . There are leaders even who had no part in the World War, who have persuaded [American Legion members] to desert to a new standard, which should bear the strange devise, not 'excelsior,' but 'grab.'" These corrupt leaders had built "membership rapidly from the disaffected and easily led, prostituting patriotism."[3]

Later, deriding, "the antics of the World War Veterans," Martin castigated enlisted veterans for making it difficult if not impossible "to make any differentiation between the needs of an officer's widow and an enlisted man's widow." Evoking the "freaks and rats" who composed Coxey's Army so many years ago, he claimed the BEF "overplayed their hand." Martin's ideological associates tagged the BEF as "Communists and hoodlums—not veterans at all," while the general claimed that the bonus would bankrupt the country. "The big pension was all right in the fat years, but when the government started running behind so badly and everybody was suffering, it was just too much. The knife had to be put into the appropriations to save the credit of the country." The day after the vote, S.M. Mears telegraphed Martin from Portland. "Feel additionally honored to know you after reading your . . . speech against payment of the bonus at this inopportune time. . . . [Y]ou have shown your ability and mettle as a statesman." Two days later, the Senate defeated its version of the Patman bill.[4]

Walter Waters, the other Portlander in Washington, viewed events differently. Though the bonus payments appeared dead legislatively, Waters and the BEF decided to "Stay till 1945." On the last day of the congressional session BEF members crowded into the Capitol. "'Comrades' . . . Waters shouted to them from the portico, 'you've got to keep a lane open for the white collar birds inside so they won't rub into us lousy rats.'"[5]

Eventually, in late July, President Hoover ordered "troops [to] clear the area in the business district and return the rioters to . . . Anacostia flats where they could be placed under guard. General Douglas MacArthur, chief of staff of the U.S. Army, assisted by Majors Dwight Eisenhower and George S. Patton, took personal command of the forces. MacArthur called out "Four troops of cavalry . . . with drawn sabers," six tanks, four infantry companies, and a machine gun squadron to carry out the president's orders. When the force first appeared on the mall, "the Marchers cheered . . . and called, 'Here come our buddies.'" Eventually the veterans began "moving back under the pressure of the soldiers toward the Anacostia Bride." The president ordered MacArthur not to follow the retreating veterans, but MacArthur ignored the command, spurred his troops across the bridge and attacked the veterans camp. As their makeshift village, made out of cardboard boxes, packing crates, old newspapers, and other scraps taken from the city dump burned, the veterans panicked, "thousands of veterans, wives, children, began to run" to escape soldiers, smoke, and tear gas. "When it was all over, two veterans had been shot to death, an eleven-week-old baby had died, an eight-year-old boy was partially blinded by gas, two police had fractured skulls, and a thousand veterans were injured by gas." Of the army's assault on the bonus marchers Representative Martin said not a word.[6]

Having accomplished virtually nothing to assist a desperate nation, Congress adjourned on July 16, 1932. The country would elect a president in November and Congressman Martin's campaign for re-election was well under way by the adjournment date.

During June, while Congress still sat, the Democratic Convention met in Chicago. Delegates chose Franklin D. Roosevelt as their presidential standard-bearer. The party platform, apart from its balanced budget proposal, alienated conservative Democrats. It "called for repeal of the Eighteenth Amendment, a 25 percent reduction in government expenses . . . and an enlarged program of public works and unemployment relief, state unemployment and old-age pension laws, banking reform, control of farm crop surpluses, reciprocal trade agreements, and Philippine independence."[7]

Representative Martin's platform, like that of every Democrat running for office in Oregon, mirrored the national party platform. Martin's rhetoric duplicated FDR's populist appeals to voters almost word-for-word:

> Roosevelt: "Even if billions could be raised and useful works could be found, public works could only be a stopgap. A real economic cure must go to the killing of the bacteria in the system rather than to the treatment of external symptoms."

> Martin: "To provide for our people enduring this grave emergency it may be necessary to provide additional money. That we must do. Government must not be in league with the monied interests, aiding and abetting them to exploit and loot the common people in any manner."

> Roosevelt: [Government should] "provide at least as much assistance to the little fellow as it is now giving to the large banks and corporations."

> Martin: "I contend it is a woeful breach of trust to provide for the financial welfare for corporations made sick by mismanagement of their blood sucking money barons while the common people are forgotten. It is

wrong to aid distressed banks and forget about the distressed owner of homes."

Roosevelt: "As a result of our blindness, of our failure to regulate, and of our failure to say that if private capital will not operate for a reasonable profit Government will have to operate itself . . . [Americans must pay] vastly more for that very necessary part of our modern life—electricity—than they should be paying."

Martin: "In the matter of public utilities the government should stand by ready to take over the operation as a government monopoly in the event private ownership fails in its obligations to the public."

Roosevelt: "We cannot allow our economic life to be controlled by that small group of men whose chief outlook upon the social welfare is tinctured by the fact that they can make huge profits from the lending of money and the marketing of securities."

Martin: "We have seen small well organized groups seeking private gain at public expense operate as great financiers."

Roosevelt, Martin, and most Democrats throughout the country provided voters with a sense that programs could be devised, giving citizens hope as opposed to the inaction and drift of President Hoover's administration. Roosevelt carried the Democrats to overwhelming victory in November. But Franklin Roosevelt and Charles Henry Martin, even though they both ran as Democrats, could not have been more different. FDR was an internationalist—urbane, worldly, and long used to the subtleties of political power. FDR proved to be reasonably adaptable, innovative in his philosophy, and willing to discard some of what did not work. Martin was parochial, in many ways a holdover from nineteenth-century America. Martin's was a straightforward and simple personality. He maintained a rousing Fourth of July patriotism with a storybook, myopic view of U.S. history. He viewed contests as clearly defined and dealt little in abstractions. His personality and his background were more suited to success in military than political life. Later, as governor of Oregon, Martin repudiated his Rooseveltian stances, condemned those around the president who promoted new ideas in a world shaded with gray, and eventually leveled his guns on Roosevelt himself.[8]

In Congress during the interval between the November 1932 election and the new president's inauguration in March 1933, short tempers and frayed nerves coupled with nonexistent party discipline created a void. Hoover and the old regime attempted to nullify the election's results by putting forward legislation that would head off any FDR initiatives prior to inauguration. Roosevelt worked behind the scenes with Democratic senators and representatives to blunt Hoover's actions. As the economic situation continued to deteriorate, the second session of the Seventy-second Congress remained stalemated.

Franklin Roosevelt assumed the presidency on March 4, 1933. On March 5, he called the Seventy-third Congress into special session to provide the action for which the electorate clamored. The marathon "hundred days" congressional special session opened on March 9. From then until May 15, the House elected a speaker and passed a variety of legislation: agricultural relief; farm mortgage relief creating the Federal Emergency Relief Administration (FERA); funding for the Muscle Shoals and Tennessee Valley development project (later the Tennessee Valley Authority or TVA); relief of home mortgage indebtedness; currency regulations; provisions for Economy in Government, which gave the president powers to cut the salaries of federal employees by as much as fifteen percent and to reduce pensions and allowances of war veterans; establishment of the Civilian Conservation Corps (CCC); new appropriations for the Reconstruction Finance Corporation (RFC); and passage of the National Industrial Recovery Act (NIRA) and creation of the Public Works Administration (PWA). Inexplicably, Martin did not cast a vote on many of the bills adopted during the "hundred days" legislative marathon. Though he publicly opposed his own party colleagues during the Hoover administration, perhaps he felt that opposition to FDR and the overwhelmingly progressive Democratic Congress so early in Roosevelt's term presented too many political dangers. Martin later claimed that he supported every Roosevelt proposal. Clearly though, Martin did support some measures proposed by the president. FDR "called for budget cuts aimed at saving $500 million," believing "that progressing toward a balanced budget was essential." "In addition to aiding bankers . . . [and] cutting budgets . . . the new President called for reorganization of the federal government to bring about greater efficiency, reduce waste, cut bureaucracy, and eliminate duplication." These initiatives certainly reflected Martin's campaign rhetoric and conservative ideology. Martin's official voting card, the card stamped by the congressional clerk "yea, nay, or not voting," recording each member's vote, is blank for the "hundred days" period. But according to the Congressional Record, in addition to being recorded as "not voting" on several important pieces of legislation such as unemployment relief, Martin did vote for the farm relief bill and opposed industrial recovery legislation, which also included money intended for state highway projects. When Martin's voting card again reflected his consistent presence in the House beginning on May 15, most of the important legislation had already cleared the House floor. Martin's absence during one of the most important periods in the long history of the U.S. Congress seems excessive. What is to be made of the void in his voting record? There is no indication of an illness keeping him away from his congressional duties. No mention is made in the *Oregonian* of Congressman Martin's prolonged absence. One is left with the distinct impression, speculative in the absence of evidence, that despite his rhetorical support for Roosevelt's election and his declarations of loyalty, the general could not induce himself to ratify what he perceived as dangerously "Socialistic" New Deal legislation. On June 16, the special session adjourned.[9]

Five days later, Martin initiated correspondence with the White House that resulted in his most lasting contribution to Oregon and the Pacific Northwest—persuading FDR to authorize construction of Bonneville Dam, for which he has not been given due credit. Grand Coulee and Bonneville dams eventually became "the cornerstones for the world's largest hydroelectric power system, which today includes 29 major federal dams and 124 other federal and non-federal hydroelectric projects." In his "My dear Mr. President" letter, Martin began "May I not ask, and in the most urgent terms at my command, that you exercise the needful authority under the national recovery administration to bring about at the earliest possible date the construction of a dam for navigation and power in the Columbia river between Oregon and Washington below the mouth of the Snake river?" The congressman intended to hold the president to the promise he had made to Oregonians. During the presidential campaign at a stop in Oregon, Roosevelt made pointed reference to Columbia River development and laid out proposals for the federal government's role in seeing that massive project funded and completed. Roosevelt pledged "that the next great hydroelectric development to be undertaken by the Federal government must be that on the Columbia river." Not only should the federal government undertake the building of dams and the generation of cheap power, it had a duty to encourage the formation of public utility districts, Roosevelt said.

> Where a community—a city or county or a district—is not satisfied with the service rendered or the rates charged by the private utility, it has the undeniable basic right, as one of its functions of Government, one of the functions of home rule, to set up, after a fair referendum of its voters has been had, its own governmentally owned and operated service. . . . the very fact that a community can, by vote of the electorate, create a yardstick of its own will, in most cases, guarantee good service and low rates to its population.

Martin later renounced Roosevelt's "yardstick principle" when Congress codified it in the 1937 act that established the Bonneville Power

Administration. This first letter, though, presented no conflict with the president's wishes. Martin reminded the president of at least part of his promise: "The people of my district and of Oregon have reposed implicit confidence in your good offices concerning the construction of a dam . . . since your statement in Portland in September, 1932, that the Columbia must be the object of the next large hydroelectric development undertaken by the United States." Martin urged the president's answer. "Mr. President," he wrote, "I consider this request the most important and far-reaching that I can make of you and the administration of which I have the honor to be a part. Your immediate response will be hailed with the most cordial gratification."[10]

Both public and private interests had long recognized the hydroelectric potential of the Columbia River. According to Martin, "agitation prompted the Oregon legislature of 1913 to name a committee with power, but limited funds, to investigate and report on the power possibilities on the Lower Columbia." In that same year, the United States Reclamation Service and the Portland Electric Power Company explored the possibilities for a dam near Warrendale, thirty-five miles east of Portland. None of the explorations initiated action because both private utilities and the state lacked sufficient funds to cover the costs.[11]

During Hoover's presidency, principally through the efforts of Oregon's senior senator Charles L. McNary, who usually receives credit for seeing Bonneville Dam to fruition (although that claim now seems overblown), the U.S. Army Corps of Engineers undertook a $600,000 engineering study concerning the feasibility for power development along the Columbia River. McNary became convinced that the federal government must develop the river's potential when he read the corps' report in 1931. The report concluded that "The Columbia River offers the greatest opportunities in the United States for the development of hydroelectric power. . . . The enormous power potentialities when fully realized would change the economic aspect of the whole Pacific Northwest."[12]

Legislation adopted during the hundred days committed $3.9 billion for emergency public works. Martin and McNary, who "worked in perfect harmony," decided "the time had come to push the project" for development of a Columbia River dam "from the President's large appropriation and not wait for action on the part of Congress." Both men presumed that they would have great "difficulty in inducing Congress to appropriate money" for the dam, "but if we could talk the President into allotting or earmarking the funds necessary for that purpose, we would be riding high." Following Martin's letter to the president, and a similar letter from McNary late in

August, two months after Martin's communication with Roosevelt, Martin and McNary went to the White House to urge the president to take action. "He seemed sympathetic," Martin wrote a short time later, "and directed that we assemble all the papers in the matter and put them aboard the yacht in which he made his Sunday cruises on the Potomac River, that he might make a thorough study of the whole subject."[13]

When they again called on the president, Roosevelt expressed some irritation at the bulk of the material, which filled several boxes, that they wanted him to read. The president told the two that "he could not possibly find the time to go through all the papers." FDR evidently spent enough time with the correspondence, though, to ascertain some serious misgivings on the part of the Army Corps of Engineers. The corps would not recommend a dam at Warrendale because, lacking a rock foundation, the dam would have to be built on gravel, which would leave it vulnerable to destruction in a flood. Roosevelt did, however, promise that if a suitable foundation could be found somewhere nearby, he might be willing to set aside as much as $25 million to cover the cost of construction. In any case, the president said, "he would not approve the construction of a dam at Warrendale."[14]

Martin scurried back to the House Rivers and Harbors Committee, of which he was a member, to secure a $25,000 appropriation to make a geological survey on the Columbia River between Bonneville and Warrendale. On July 18, "much to our delight," the corps reported "that a . . . suitable . . . rock foundation for a dam had been found at Bonneville where the swift current of the river had washed out to the rock foundation all the sand and gravel that lay there," Martin recalled. With Congress adjourning for the summer vacation, Martin and McNary brought the "good news" to the president at the White House. In the course of that meeting, McNary "expressed the opinion that Secretary [of the Interior, Harold] Ickes would oppose the construction holding that the authorization which the President had made for the Grand Coulee Dam of sixty-two million dollars, was all the Northwest could urge." "The President replied," according to Martin's account of the conversation, "You Gentlemen go home on your vacation, and I will take care of brother Ickes." Roosevelt had placed Ickes in charge of the Public Works Administration where, with a $3.3 billion congressional appropriation to spend on federally sponsored public works projects to provide employment and stimulate the economy, Ickes became the administration's primary weapon fighting the Depression. In what sparked a bitter feud between the two men, Ickes did attempt to scuttle the project, believing that the Northwest did not have the population to consume the energy produced by two massive dams. Martin perceived this as a personal attack, and developed a burning hatred for Ickes. He even claimed that Ickes's later attempts to thwart his reelection as governor were political payback for Martin's success in altering the president's mind on Bonneville.[15]

Convinced that they had prevailed with the president, Martin and McNary left Washington, McNary to his home at Fir Cone near Salem and Martin to the Gearhart Hotel on the Oregon coast. Throughout the summer, newspapers announced awards of large sums of money to various projects across the country "by a Board presided over by the Secretary of War and of which Mr. Ickes was a member," but no announcement came about Bonneville Dam. In early September, Martin became "alarmed over the delay," so he drove to Fir Cone to sound out McNary. Martin expressed his misgivings to McNary, who asked Martin if they could depend on the president's word or not. "I only know what [New York state] Senator [now U.S. Representative James W.] Wadsworth told me," Martin replied. "Wadsworth told me that in New York state, they had no faith or confidence in Roosevelt's word and always went to see him in pairs so there would be a witness to what was agreed upon." McNary's response was equally gloomy. "I am not only worried," McNary replied, "I am alarmed; the delay is ominous. You and I have talked too much, and if we fail to get that dam, we will lose face and have to leave Oregon. One of us must go to Washington at once, to see what the trouble is."[16]

McNary begged off, claiming to be "far from well" and still recuperating from a serious illness. He urged the trip on Martin who reluctantly consented. Arriving in Washington, Martin went immediately to the White House after consulting with some House colleagues. To his dismay, he found that Roosevelt's interest in Bonneville "had apparently waned." Harold Ickes persuaded the president that in giving his tentative approval to Bonneville, "a mistake had been made." As the meeting concluded, the president told Martin "there were some matters concerning Bonneville he had to look up and that if I would come back within a few days he would let me know how the matter stood." With McNary's dire warnings still fresh in his memory, Martin refused to let the issue drop. He decided to make a visit to his old friend General Brown, chief of the Army Corps of Engineers, with whom he had served in the Office of the Provost Marshal General during the military occupation of Manila. General Brown maintained that the corps stood ready to build the dam if authorized but informed Martin that his mission had failed. "Well Martin," Brown said, "you have lost your Bonneville Dam. There is a crowd around here that have succeeded in what they say is pulling the President out of a hole. He promised you and McNary too much." Brown did, however, hold out a glimmer of hope. "I just got word that a memorandum on the subject is to be sent down here, and I will inform you as to its nature when I receive it."[17]

When Martin again called on General Brown, Brown relayed the memorandum's contents. The White House asked the corps two questions: "what would the cost and feasibility be of building a 25-foot dam at Bonneville . . . [and what] was the cost of building a 72-foot dam for navigation only." Brown sent the questions to Colonel Thomas M. Robins at San Francisco, the engineer in charge of the district, for a response. "They always do that," Martin said of the corps, "for the Army engineers detest cheap politicians and get information from the source, where it should be obtained. They do not bend to political influence or pressure."[18]

When the report finally arrived, Colonel Robins concluded "that a 25-foot dam would be an utter waste of money, and that a 72-foot dam without power production would be even worse." He proposed "that a dam be built with ten power units at a cost of $42,000,000 and suggested that it would be advisable to install only two units at first with a cost of $31,000,000." When General Brown handed Martin the report, he told him that "it was being sent to the White House." Martin now considered the whole exercise akin to a poker game, so he decided to withhold his knowledge of the report's contents from FDR but considered himself fortunate to have seen "the cards in the other fellow's hand without his knowing it." He would raise the ante with the president at the appropriate moment.[19]

In one version compiled in 1936, Martin claimed the next word of events came from the president's secretary, who told Martin "the president was approving an allocation of $250,000 for additional exploration and research for the location of the dam." In a more contemporaneous version, the congressman claimed to have noticed an item in the *Evening Star* authorizing $250,000 "to uncover a site for a dam on the Columbia River near Bonneville." Whichever version is correct is beside the point; either way, Martin felt betrayed by the president. He knew, he said later, exhibiting his growing distaste for Roosevelt, "exactly what the game was."

> It was the old game of kissing them off. All of the exploratory work had been done; the engineers had tested the foundation. The game simply was to make this allocation of money to satisfy those of us from Oregon and to get us to go home, while the president and the rest of them simply forgot about Bonneville proper, despite the president's promise to have it built. . . . I also found out that Ickes was doing his utmost to devise some way in which the president could withdraw his offers and proposals on Bonneville completely.[20]

As events unfolded, Martin stayed in touch with McNary by phone. McNary said he still did not feel up to the trip but he would come if Martin thought it advisable. Weighing the options, Martin reasoned that as one of 435 congressmen who "are not given free access to the president because it is felt that if they have a substantial majority in the House, it does not make much difference what any one man wants," the president could tell him "to go to hell." Martin considered McNary's chances at securing a positive response from the president greater than his own because "there is the well established practice of admitting Senators to see the president at any time they desire due to the fact that the Senate has the power of confirmation on presidential appointees, and hence the executive does not want to antagonize members of the Senate." Acting on his analysis, Martin phoned McNary. "Now is the time to come," Martin told the senator. Still reluctant, McNary said he would only come if Martin commanded. Telling McNary that "the door was blocked, the situation grave," Martin commanded the senator's presence in Washington. McNary grudgingly acquiesced. While he headed to Washington, Martin went to the White House on Saturday morning to arrange a meeting with the president. FDR's secretary told Martin that a meeting was out of the question because FDR had a full schedule on Monday and would be leaving for Hyde Park on Tuesday. Martin insisted, making a veiled threat that by turning them away FDR risked losing McNary's support in any close Senate vote. "There is no use," the secretary said. "You're not going to see the president, nor is Senator McNary. It cannot be done."[21]

Meeting McNary's train Sunday night, Martin told the senator that the matter "was in its most critical state." McNary asked Martin's advice. What should they do? Martin suggested that they go to the White House on Monday morning when the doors opened and sit down in the president's reception room and remain there until FDR spoke to them. If Roosevelt did not see them on Monday they would repeat the action on Tuesday and every day until Roosevelt relented. McNary concurred and even suggested that if they were unsuccessful on Monday, he would hire a chauffeur to drive his car and follow the president up to Hyde Park if necessary.[22]

On Monday morning, the two men met at the White House. Roosevelt's secretary's office teemed with people who wished to see the president. As they sat there, Marvin McIntyre, originally an Oregonian and now a Roosevelt aide, passed through the office. Serendipitously, Martin knew McIntyre through his work with the Oregon Democratic Party, and he impulsively pulled McIntyre aside to solicit his help. McIntyre went into the president's office and when he returned a few minutes later he told the two relieved fellow Oregonians that the president would see them in an hour or so.

McNary and Martin walked around the block "in the blistering hot sun" while they waited for FDR, feeling "like a couple of fellows who were in a poker game and had everything to get or our shirts to lose."[23]

Roosevelt greeted them effusively as the two men sat down in his office. Using all the famous "Roosevelt charm," he told them that "he had Bonneville all fixed up, that [we] were going to [get] $250,000 to continue . . . exploration and research work to determine where the dam should be located."

"Why, Mr. President," Martin replied employing his best poker face, "all that work has been done and the Army engineers have fixed the site." Roosevelt, who evidently had not read the engineers' most recent report, seemed surprised. Martin slowly pulled from his pocket his ace in the hole, his copy of Colonel Robins's engineering report, which General Brown had provided. As FDR glanced at the report, Martin told him that an additional $250,000 would be wasted money. Taking the document back from the president, Martin then read the report's relevant conclusions aloud. The president explained that he had not seen the report, that the original "must have gone to Ickes' office." When Martin finished reading, FDR laid his head back in his chair, raised his arms in the air, and roared with laughter. Then, "waving his long finger at us, he said, 'I'll go for $36,000,000 [or $31,000,000 depending on which of Martin's versions one reads].'" Martin, caught off guard and totally surprised by Roosevelt's immediate response, rushed around the president's desk, shook FDR's hand, and gushed that Roosevelt "was following the footsteps of our great leader, Thomas Jefferson and that by approving the Bonneville Dam he was sending a second Lewis and Clark expedition to rediscover the Oregon Country." McNary approached Roosevelt's capitulation more warily. "Mr. President," McNary urged, "can't you give us a little writing confirming this action?" Roosevelt swirled around in his chair, threw out his arms again and said to McNary, "Senator, I will notify you later today of my action, but there will be no note."[24]

As it had throughout his life, Martin's determination and doggedness proved to be very effective in this showdown with FDR. Unfortunately, proving again his ill-suitedness for politics, Martin moved quickly to take public credit for the triumph for himself, negating McNary's role altogether. The *Salem Capital Journal* erupted with enthusiasm over the congressman's achievements and later attributed to him "a greater influence than any other Oregon Congressman of the present generation." Disgusted at Martin's self aggrandizement, Walter Pierce suggested to Senator McNary that the nation's capital be moved from Washington, D.C. to Oregon. "All it requires is the sort of effort which our friend the General could very easily put forth these last few days of Congress," Pierce wrote. "It would not require any activity on the part of Oregon senators. If you will merely acquiesce, I feel sure that the Paul Bunyan of Oregon democracy could accomplish this with great ease." After all, Pierce concluded, had not Martin's statements in Oregon's newspapers shown "what Paul has really accomplished, single-handed in Congress?"[25]

Letters and congratulatory telegrams poured in from Oregon citizens for Martin's triumph. One correspondent, Rosemary Schenck, vice-chair-man of the Democratic State Central Committee, congratulated Martin on his work and said his success proved what she had long said, "that we need men like you in Washington, that we must have men like you there." What would we have done, she asked, if Martin had been a politician at the state level only? "This evening at a meeting," she went on, "I heard mention made of 'Gen. Martin for Governor,' . . . and I was so grieved that I am writing to you now—midnight—to say that while you could of course have that place . . . in Oregon . . . that we would all be proud to have you lead us in our work, we must have you in Washington. All Oregon needs you there. Think what would happen to us if you throw us to the wolves."[26]

The smoldering embers of the volatile political situation in Oregon surrounding the issue of public versus private control of energy produced at the dam burst into open flame with FDR's approval of the Bonneville project. The Oregon Grange and the State Federation of Labor demanded that the power produced at Bonneville be allocated principally to homes and farms at the cheapest possible rate through a federal program, the Columbia Valley Authority (CVA), modeled after the Tennessee Valley Authority. The private utility companies, industrial interests, and the Portland Chamber of Commerce maintained that though they supported federal development of the Columbia River, the power generated by the dam should serve both public and private uses. But, as Chamber of Commerce spokesman Walter W.R. May said, "It is vital that we remember that Bonneville . . . [is not] a subsidy for public-ownership agitation. It will produce more power than we can now use in the state and the quickest way to put it to use is to attract industries to use it in large blocks."[27]

Congressman Martin set in motion his plan to thwart any attempt by the president to encourage the development of public utility districts (PUDs) along with the dam's construction. Martin especially opposed the "yardstick principle," enunciated by FDR during the campaign. He stepped out warily in his first public disagreement with the president. In a speech to the Portland Realty Board not long after gaining FDR's authorization to proceed with the Bonneville project, Martin steadfastly supported the private utilities and chamber's position claiming that "[t]he power which the government will develop at Bonneville is not intended to force down the rates of existing power companies. This power is intended for the great chemical and metallurgical reduction plants whose first consideration is cheap power and an inexhaustible supply."[28]

Martin probably did not intend to fracture the Oregon Democratic Party with his speech, but the controversy the speech aroused reopened all the old wounds. However, the factional infighting that developed redounded to Martin's political benefit. Many Democrats optimistically had predicted that Roosevelt's election in 1932 heralded a renaissance for the state party. They had urged Martin to run for Congress, feeling that his election would also signal "a complete reunion and harmony in the Party." They envisioned a coalition of farmers and industrial workers represented by the grange and the State Federation of Labor, and set about to cement those bonds. After Roosevelt's decision on the Bonneville project, Rosemary Schenck's concern that Martin would leave Congress for the governorship proved well founded. Conservative Democrats from across the state encouraged Martin to run for governor throughout the fall of 1933.

By January 3, 1934, the day before the Seventy-third Congress convened, someone in Martin's office sought out the advice of Ralph Watson at the *Oregon Journal.* "Could you advise me," the writer queried, "for my confidential use, the answer to these questions: First—Does Bert Haney want the Democratic nomination for governor? Second—What is your impression as to whether he would be a candidate if General Martin were to run?" Watson responded on January 6, convinced that Haney would not run "if Martin beat him to the punch as an avowed candidate. "I say this," Watson went on, "because it is the general belief among republicans and democrats alike, generally speaking, that Martin could clean any democrat in the primaries, and any republican candidate now [being] talked [about] as a possibility." Two days later, Donald J. Sterling, managing editor of the *Oregon Journal,* bluntly stated the case to Martin. "I want to know from you, frankly and confidentially, whether you contemplate being a candidate for Governor . . . In my opinion, Martin, [Henry] Van Duzer, and [Bert] Haney are the most available [candidates] in order named." Martin coyly responded to Sterling several days later. "Since receipt of your letter," Martin claimed, "I have been like the preacher who received a call from another church— 'praying for light.' I appreciate more than I can tell your loyal steadfast devotion to me," Martin went on, "but . . . if I must make a decision at this time, I will say that I am not to be considered for the Democratic nomination for governor."[29]

Sterling and the *Oregon Journal* came under scathing criticism from progressives in Oregon, none more incensed than Democrat Richard L. Neuberger, who eventually represented Oregon in the U.S. Senate. "The newspapers of the Pacific Northwest are predominantly reactionary," Neuberger wrote in 1938. "The Oregon Journal, . . . [whose] managing editor, Donald Sterling, hinted to his friends that he was the 'political boss of the Oregon Country,' . . . sets the tempo of this tune." Political boss or not, Sterling frequently advised Martin, and his cajoling in early January 1934 seems to have carried significant weight in Martin's eventual decision to enter the primaries, although Oswald West claimed credit for inducing Martin to enter the race. Sterling would not take Martin's no for an answer. "I would feel remiss," Sterling wrote on January 24, "if I did not advise you, as you doubtless already know, that it is conceded upon all hands that you could be elected Governor, . . . It is not necessary for you to make up your mind this minute," he said, "but please do not close the door on the suggestion."[30]

As late as January 30, Martin had still not made a decision, but he finally did announce his candidacy in the first week of February 1934. Newspapers throughout the state responded positively to Martin's announcement and conservative Republicans saw in Martin a chance to repudiate Julius Meier and the party's public power wing. Sterling and other Democrats quickly signed on to the campaign as unofficial advisors. "We are in this thing to win," Sterling confirmed.[31]

Not all of the newspaper coverage proved quite so supportive. Walter Pierce's wife, Cornelia, published a letter severely chastising Martin's support for the private utilities. "I look upon this [race] as the most critical . . . in the history of Oregon, because of the power fight, and the coming opportunity to save the power for the people or sell them out permanently. I fear the latter," she wrote. She saw the situation as dangerous, she said, because "Martin . . . [does not have] the slightest comprehension of the situation, or if [he has, he is] not to be trusted." Turning her attentions ad hominem she concluded, "I cannot, in any other manner, excuse the utterances of Martin. It does not seem possible that anyone could be such a fool, but I suppose it is possible for anyone who has spent his life in the army. That does not require much intellect. The old boy is just befuddled. I do not believe he is willingly a tool, but he is certainly unwittingly a tool."[32]

Though Martin's stand on public power infuriated the Walter Pierce wing of the party, no one in the public power bloc stepped forward to challenge Martin in the primary until Willis Mahoney, mayor of Klamath Falls, entered the race. Martin understood that his opposition to FDR's "yardstick principle" threatened his support among Democrats. He cautioned campaign leaders to choose speakers carefully. When the campaign staff proposed attorney A.A. Smith of Baker as a speaker, Martin wondered at the advisability. "I am told he is a wonderful speaker and an able man in every respect," Martin wrote, "but he is openly aligned with the power companies before the legislature and the people. Would not this agitate the question that the power companies are backing me?" The question was already being agitated. The *Oregon Statesman* claimed, with some accuracy as it turns out, that Oswald West pulled the strings on Martin's puppet, and the *Salem Capital Press* went further, claiming that the utility companies, for whom West lobbied, "ordered West to induce Martin to run for governor." To head off speculation about his support among the power interests, Martin cautioned his campaign staff to make their own judgment about fund-raising but "be discreet as to its source."[33]

Martin effectively exploited a rift within the public power bloc over Mahoney's candidacy. Mahoney's support for Senator Huey P. Long's "Share-Our-Wealth" program and Francis Townsend's "Old Age Revolving Pension Plan" made Mahoney an opportunist and a dangerous demagogue to many progressive Democrats. Bert Haney eventually signed on with the Martin campaign because he found Mahoney a "crafty, plausible demagogue." The Martin campaign also successfully recruited Republicans, although some Republicans preferred to keep their support under cover. "Though I am anxious to see general Martin elected," Dorothy Lawson McCall wrote to a volunteer in the Martin campaign's Women's Division, "I am registered as a Republican, which might be embarrassing if I took any active part in the primary campaign." Mahoney evidently scared other Democrats too: on election day, Martin won the closed Democratic primary with fifty-eight percent of the vote.[34]

Martin laid out a campaign in the general election that focused on the New Deal's popularity and accomplishments—he would become Oregon's FDR. Oregonians viewed the New Deal favorably indeed, with good reason. "Government payments under crop adjustment and production control contracts increased from $71,000 in 1933 to $4,685,000 in 1934 and, in the long run, helped to push Oregon's total cash income in agriculture from $49,777,000 in 1933 to $120,621,000 in 1937." In addition to agricultural support and the Bonneville Dam project, the Farm Credit Administration, the Civil Works Administration, the Public Works Administration, and the Civilian Conservation Corps all made significant investments that benefitted Oregon considerably.[35]

As Martin developed the campaign's themes, he relied on strategy papers from several advisors. Oswald West clandestinely provided Martin with "confidential" briefing papers on a variety of subjects, which, had they been known, would have confirmed Martin's close relationship to the private utilities. D.O. Hood, of Hood Brothers Stocks and Bonds, provided several lengthy papers, the essence of which made their way into Martin's campaign rhetoric. "The strong point of the campaign, I think," Hood wrote, "should be support of the national administration in its endeavor to restore our economic stability. Admit freely that mistakes have been made, and others are certain to be made, but this administration is doing things . . . [It] proposed to find a practical way of distributing our great wealth so that all will have their just share . . . [while] endeavoring in every way possible to preserve private property rights." Bert Haney, not knowing Oswald West covertly advised Martin's campaign, offered his own unsolicited comments, cautioning the general about selecting speakers. "My advice," Haney confided, "is to be very wary . . . It seems to me you should use every effort to avoid giving endorsement to any . . . [person] who is directly or indirectly connected with the larger public utilities, for your campaign in the primary was injured by support from those notoriously known by reason of their utility connections, and their past record as lobbyists. . . . Lastly, may I suggest the necessity of avoiding too much ultra conservative management in your campaign. Frankly, I think it reacted to your disadvantage in the primary." As always, Martin listened carefully to Donald Sterling. "Van [Duzer] has an idea, and it is sound as a nut," Sterling counseled, "that while economy in government is a threadbare political battle cry, in this instance you can well afford to declare for and go through with, when elected, . . . a program of economy in the operation of the state government." Sterling also counseled Martin to keep his association with West under wraps.[36]

In addition to planks supporting "strict and impartial enforcement of all laws," development of Bonneville power (with no mention of the "yardstick principle"), reduction of taxes and "retrenchment in state expenditures," and a "scientific program of unemployment insurance," Martin promoted "enactment of an adequate and uniform system of old age pensions designed to abolish poverty among the aged and dependent and to eliminate our present antiquated system of caring for the poor." Martin never fleshed out the details of his old age pension plan, but he had to address the issue in the campaign and to tread very carefully around any commitment.

Doctor Francis E. Townsend in California posed unique problems for Martin and FDR. In September 1933, Townsend published a letter to the *Long Beach Press-Telegram* outlining his Townsend Old Age Revolving Pension

Plan. He promoted the plan as "a solution both to the problems of the elderly and the crisis of the Depression." According to historian Alan Brinkley:

> The federal government, he proposed, should provide everyone over sixty with a pension of $150 a month (the figure soon jumped to $200), "on condition that they spend the money as they get it." The result would be to pump new money into the economy, open up jobs for younger people, and ultimately put an end to the blight of hard times. A nationwide transactions tax (a tax on all sales, wholesale and retail) would finance the system.[37]

FDR led the scramble among Democratic politicians to propose legislation to counter Townsend's proposal. An Old Age Pension bill waited for approval in Congress. When Martin came out strongly against the Townsend plan, his campaign spokesman in Hood River, E.R. Lafferty, wrote him apologetically, "I am very sorry to have you come out against such a popular plan. . . . Jeff Carson Sr. and myself were very embarrassed for any explanation." A few days later an obviously agitated Martin responded. He warned Lafferty that the *Oregonian* twisted his words. "Our President is strong for [an Old Age plan]," Martin said, "I came out strongly for the Old Age Pension . . . in Congress, I supported the Old Age Pension." The country could not afford the Townsend plan rate, Martin said, implying that a plan with lower payments might be acceptable. The candidate reserved special ire for what he saw as the worst effects of the Townsend plan. "Such a law would have to apply to all citizens of the country," Martin exploded, "and would especially disrupt the South where the colored people are so improvident. Think what would happen in the South—an old colored fellow and his wife getting $400.00 per month. All the people in the neighborhood would live off them and all work would stop." Lafferty promptly responded, thanking Martin for his "frank statements" but complained that "there are many who have read your speeches of late in regards to Old Age Pensions, who would like to hear an out right view from you," a complaint that dogged Martin throughout the general election. "As to your suggestion of the Colored people, I am in accord with your line of thought," Lafferty said agreeably, "however you know the Colored People sure can put on the DOG and I expect they would spend their pension faster than the white." No doubt Congressman Martin nodded in agreement as he read the letter.[38]

The public power controversy also split the Republican Party. When Governor Meier announced that he would not run for reelection, two candidates from the Republican public power bloc announced for the primary, Sam H. Brown and State Treasurer Rufus Holman. Both Brown and Holman supported and championed public ownership, and both supported an initiative sponsored by the grange that would provide public financing to build electric transmission lines from Bonneville. Another Republican, Joe E. Dunne, entered the primary with a position on public power as evasive as Martin's. He supported "cheap power," for whom he never said, and opposed the initiative for state construction of electric transmission lines. Neither Brown nor Holman felt obliged to step down to give public power supporters a single candidate to run against the ambiguous Dunne, which allowed Dunne to win the primary with a plurality vote of thirty percent to twenty percent each for Brown and Holman, with two other candidates splitting the remaining thirty percent. Dunne's candidacy proved a boon for Martin. He could safely keep his opposition to Roosevelt's proposals under wraps.

With Martin on the Democratic ticket and Dunne on the Republican side presenting the same ambiguous language on the public power issue, the advocates of public power development in both parties had no candidate for whom to vote. Into this void stepped State Senator Peter Zimmerman from Yamhill County, a progressive Republican from the George Joseph-Julius Meier faction of the party, to run as an independent candidate for governor on a public power platform. In addition to supporting public development of Bonneville power and the enactment of the initiative for state construction and ownership of power lines, Zimmerman sent shock waves through the ranks of mainline Republicans and Democrats alike when he called for old-age pensions similar to the Townsend Plan and an increase in inheritance and income taxes.

During the general election—one of the most tumultuous contests in state history that left national observers bewildered—no major Democrat publicly opposed Martin, although Mahoney, defeated by Martin in the primary, refused to actively work for the Democratic candidate. But the Republican factions took their battle to the public with charges and counter charges. Sam Brown, one of Dunne's opponents in the Republican primary, endorsed Zimmerman and made scathing attacks on Dunne. While the Republicans fought each other, Martin stepped up his campaign to identify himself with Franklin Roosevelt. He insisted throughout the campaign that he was one of the president's staunchest supporters in Congress. Late in the campaign, Martin planted a story countering the earlier press reports crediting Oswald West with convincing him to run. It now appeared that none other than the president himself persuaded Martin to run for governor. "General," Martin claimed Roosevelt said to him, "I don't like to spare you from Congress but I wish you'd go back to Oregon and be governor. When the Columbia River is harnessed I must have the cooperation of that state to save the resulting benefits from the light and power companies that are lying in wait for them." With the New Deal leader himself giving his blessing, who could deny the governorship to Martin?[39]

His feigned support for the New Deal and the authorization of the Bonneville project played well with the voters. Martin won the 1934 gubernatorial election with a plurality of 21,000 votes, thirty-nine percent of the total vote cast for governor. He later admitted his indebtedness to Republicans who tilted the election in his favor when he said "enough good Republicans came to my support to secure my election over a weak Republican candidate." Zimmerman finished second with thirty-two percent, followed closely by Dunne at twenty-nine percent. The grange initiative went down to defeat. Republicans captured Martin's Third Congressional District seat, voters reelected Walter Pierce in the Second District, and the Democrats captured control of the lower house of the state legislature for the first time since 1878.[40]

Now, at last, Charles Henry Martin had attained complete command. There were none who ranked higher than him. There were not 434 other members of Congress with whom he had to contend. Franklin Roosevelt sat in the White House, but Charles Henry Martin occupied the governor's chair in Salem. He could at last enforce order and discipline on a chaotic state.

NOTES

1. Oscar Theodore Barck Jr. and Nelson Manfred Blake, *Since 1900: A History of the United States in Our Times* (New York: Macmillan Publishing Co., Inc., 1974), 217.
2. Congress, House, Representative Thomas L. Blanton and Representative Charles Henry Martin, 72nd Cong., 1st session, *Congressional Record* (June 15, 1932): 13039–40.
3. Ibid., p. 13058–61.
4. Duane Hennessy, *Oregonian,* December 11, 1938; Undated fragment of a newspaper clipping; S.M. Mears to CHM, June 16, 1932; CHM to My dear Classmate, February 21, 1934; CHM to Mr. J.J. McGinn, January 4, 1934, CHMC, OHS.
5. Arthur M. Schlesinger Jr., *The Age of Roosevelt: The Crisis of the Old Order, 1919–1933* (Boston: Houghton Mifflin Company, 1964), 259, 261.
6. Ibid., 265; Merle Miller, *Ike: The Soldier as They Knew Him* (New York: G.P. Putnam's Sons, 1987), 261–68; Howard Zinn, *A People's History of the United States* (New York: Harper and Row, 1980), 381–82.
7. Barck Jr. and Blake, 329.
8. Schlesinger Jr., 289, 290; Typescripts of Martin's radio addresses, November 2, 5, and 6 1932, CHMC, OHS.
9. Robert S. McElvaine, *The Great Depression: America, 1929–1941* (New York: Times Books, 1984), 142–43; Martin's official voting cards, CHMC, OHS; 73d Congress, First session, p. 1680, 2128, 4368.
10. Most descriptions, such as Richard Lowitt, *The New Deal and the West* (Norman: University of Oklahoma Press, 1993), 160, and Steve Neal, *McNary of Oregon: A Political Biography* (Portland: Western Imprints and the Press of the Oregon Historical Society,

1985), among others, either completely neglect to mention or downplay Martin's roll in the approval of the Bonneville Dam project. Neal's biography of McNary is especially lacking in this regard. Neal mentions Martin only in passing, as if Martin's contribution to the discussions with FDR really did not matter because McNary carried the ball once Roosevelt got behind "McNary's project." Interestingly, Neal has a fascinating quotation attributed to FDR (page 145): "When Roosevelt signed the Bonneville legislation, he explained to McNary's colleagues, 'I've got to give Charlie his dam.'" Neal cites no sources for this quotation however. Which "Charlie" was FDR referring to—could he have meant Martin who personally lobbied FDR much harder than McNary?; CHM to FDR, June 21, 1933, CHMC, OHS.

11. Typescript of a memorandum titled "The Beginning of Bonneville" by General Charles H. Martin, undated, CHMC, OHS, subsequently referred to as Memo 1.

12. Army Corps of Engineers report as quoted in the *Oregon Journal,* November 22, 1931.

13. Memo 1 and typescript of a memorandum titled "Negotiations Held in the Spring of 1933 Which Lead Up to the Authorization for the Construction of the Bonneville Dam on the Columbia River," undated, CHMC, OHS, subsequently referred to as Memo 2. Both memos relate the same events with some minor differences. For an extended discussion of the Congressional debates and maneuvering over Bonneville and other public power projects see, Philip J. Funigiello, *Toward a National Power Policy: The New Deal and the Electric Utility Industry, 1933–1941* (Pittsburgh: University of Pittsburgh Press, 1973), Richard Lowitt, *The New Deal and the West,* Arthur M. Schlesinger Jr., *The Age of Roosevelt: The Politics of Upheaval,* Richard White, *The Organic Machine* (New York: Hill and Wang, 1995), and William Dietrich, *Northwest Passage* (New York: Simon and Schuster, 1995).

14. Ibid.

15. Memo 2.

16. Memo 1, Memo 2, and typescript of a document titled "The Story of Bonneville Dam as told by Governor Martin, July 20, 1936," author unknown, CHMC, OHS, subsequently referred to here as The Story. Whoever produced "The Story" document did so at a time of open hostility between Martin and the Roosevelt administration. It employs considerable denigration of FDR and Harold Ickes not present in the other two accounts, which seem to have been written contemporaneous to events when Martin was still cooperating with FDR. The document is related in the first person, so it is assumed that Martin either wrote or dictated it.

17. Ibid.

18. The Story, 2.

19. Ibid.

20. Ibid.

21. Memo 1, Memo 2, and The Story, 3.

22. Memo 2 and The Story.

23. Ibid.

24. Ibid. For a chronology of these events as they appeared to the public see the *Oregonian* for April 26, 1934, and September 2, 6, 8, 10, 17, 20, 23, 24, 26, and 27, 1933.

25. *Salem Capital Journal,* May 10, 1934; Pierce, quoted in Arthur H. Bone, *Oregon Cattleman/Governor Congressman: Memoirs and Times of Walter M. Pierce* (Portland: Oregon Historical Society, 1981), 387.

26. Rosemary Schenck to CHM, October 24, 1933, CHMC, OHS.

27. Walter W.R. May as quoted in, Robert E. Burton, "The New Deal in Oregon," in, John Braeman, Robert H. Bremner, and David Brody, eds., *The New Deal: The State and Local Levels* (Columbus: Ohio State University Press, 1975), 76.

28. *Oregon Journal,* October 15, 1933.

29. The *Spectator,* undated editorial found in one of five scrapbooks, CHMC; *Oregon Democrat,* March 21 and April 6, 1933; Carl Donaugh to Ralph Watson, January 3, 1934, on Martin's official congressional stationary; Ralph Watson to Carl Donaugh, January 6, 1934; Donald J. Sterling to CHM, January 8, 1934; CHM to Donald J. Sterling, January 15, 1934, CHMC, OHS.

30. Richard L. Neuberger, *Our Promised Land* (New York: The Macmillan Company, 1938), 318; for West's role see the *Oregonian,* January 14, 1934, and *Salem Capital Press,* February 9, 1934; Donald J. Sterling to CHM, January 24, 1934, CHMC, OHS.

31. Ibid., March 2, 1934, CHMC, OHS.

32. Cornelia Pierce as quoted in Bone, 387–88.

33. CHM to Colonel R.W. Hagood, March 27, 1934; *Salem Oregon Statesman,* February 9, 1934; *Salem Capital Press,* February 9, 1934; CHM to Colonel R.W. Hagood, March 27, 1934, CHMC, OHS.

34. Bert Haney to CHM, May 19, 1934; Dorothy Lawson McCall, mother of Oregon's future governor Tom McCall, to Mrs. Josephine French, May 3, 1934, CHMC, OHS.

35. Robert E. Burton, "The New Deal in Oregon," in John Braeman, Robert H. Bremner, and David Brody, Eds., *The New Deal: The State and Local Levels* (Columbus: Ohio State University Press, 1975), 357.

36. O.O. Hood to CHM, August 4, 1934; Bert Haney to CHM, May 19, 1934; Donald J. Sterling to CHM, June 5, 1934, CHMC, OHS.

37. Charles Martin for Governor campaign poster, CHMC, OHS; Alan Brinkley, *Voices of Protest: Huey Long, Father Coughlin, and the Great Depression* (New York: Vintage Books, 1983), 223.

38. E.R. Lafferty to CHM, September 19, 1934; CHM to E.R. Lafferty, September 24, 1934; E.R. Lafferty to CHM, September 28, 1934, CHMC, OHS.

39. *Oregon Democrat,* October 6, 1934.

40. CHM to Charles G. Dawes, June 21, 1935, CHMC, OHS.

Chapter Ten

GOVERNOR MARTIN

Our system of selecting officers in all branches of our combatant service is to pick them from the people. They are the sons of mail carriers, bank presidents, street car conductors, clergymen—in fact they are from all walks of life, without any class distinction. American officers never lose their touch with the people they serve.
—Charles Henry Martin

AT THE INAUGURAL RECEPTION on the night of January 14, 1935, Charles Henry Martin shook the hands of thousands of constituents who lined up to pay their respects to the new governor and his wife. "With true Jeffersonian simplicity," gushed the *Salem Capital Journal*, "it was open to everyone." Standing next to Martin and his wife in the receiving line were Henry L. Corbett, president of the state senate and scion of the wealthy Portland family; speaker of the state house John E. Cooter; and Howard Hulsey, president of the Salem Chamber of Commerce.

Notable by their absence, neither representatives of the Oregon Grange and organized labor nor Walter Pierce and proponents of public power stood beside the new governor shaking hands. Missing also, said the *Capital Journal*, was the uniformed and armed chauffeur-guard who had stood at attention beside Julius Meier four years previously. Martin's good sense, "his democratic qualities and his kindly feelings towards the people of his state, prompts the ending of heroics and the maintenance of the open door," trumpeted the *Journal*.

Later in Martin's term, a swinging door at the dedication of the new state capitol, erected where the old building had burned down, proved more difficult to open. The governor, dressed in "tall silk hat" and "cutaway suit," finished a dedicatory speech, cut the ribbon, and invited the citizens to enter their new capital building. When the crowd surged forward and crushed people trying to get through the swinging doors, Martin jumped forward shouting "Get back, you bastards, get back!" "It was just like a blowtorch," former Oregon Senator Mark Hatfield recalled, "the people fell back because that was his military background."[1]

Martin's election held a great, inchoate promise for the Democratic Party. He had campaigned as a New Deal champion, and voters in the state stood behind Martin because of this. After more than a decade of internecine party warfare, Martin conceivably could have healed the breach among Democrats. He held an unparalleled opportunity to reshape Oregon politics and wrest control of state government away from the dominant Republicans. Instead, Martin's actions eventually solidified the Republicans' position at the state level. Also, he launched a political tyranny that caused progressive Democrats to view Martin's iron-fisted party control as reactionary. Martin's actions as governor proved to be a disaster for Democratic Party unity. His authoritarian inclinations and lack of political acumen appeared almost immediately after his election and kept the state in turmoil throughout his administration.

Martin turned first to settling personal scores by instigating a petty action against Walter Pierce that one newspaper called "a vicious one inspired by personal spite." Martin had bills introduced in both legislative houses "that would prohibit persons holding party office—precinct to national committeeman—from holding any remunerative public office." The bills directly attacked Pierce, who held the office of Democratic national committeeman and represented Oregon in the Second Congressional District. When the House defeated the bill, "Governor Martin started calling the boys into his office. Apparently he talked turkey because in the afternoon, the bill was reconsidered and passed smoothly." Possessing somewhat less power in the Senate, however, the governor proved unable to convince senators to bring the bill to the floor for a vote.[2]

Prior to the attempted legislative assault on Walter Pierce's political life, Martin had gone after his wife, Cornelia Pierce. "Three days after his inauguration Martin asked for her resignation from the State Board of Higher Education, to which she had been appointed by Governor Julius Meier." Martin claimed the best motives in his action, but the *Oregonian* reported that her removal "was in retaliation for the refusal of Walter M. Pierce to resign as Democratic National Committeeman from Oregon." Mrs. Pierce refused to resign, so Martin fired her. She struck back in a 6,000-word letter "that appeared on the front pages of newspapers throughout the state." She lamented Martin's ability to control the state board through his appointees because his inaugural address "made it quite clear that he knew little of Oregon, its people, its traditions or its ideals." Dredging up old wounds from their days together in Washington, D.C., where "neither the general nor his wife ever thought it worthwhile to speak a civil word to her or to her husband," Cornelia Pierce blasted Martin for bullying "the aged" and alluding to a farmer neighbor as "an old bum." Martin was consumed by contempt she claimed, "contempt for the electorate, contempt for popular government" and he desired only "dictatorial powers." Fully conscious "of this contempt," Pierce concluded, "I know how offensive it must be to you to have in your official family a person like myself who belongs to the farming class."[3]

Turning his attention to the national scene, Martin opposed New Deal programs for public power, relief, welfare, and most especially, federal labor legislation, which he believed, as administered by Secretary of Labor Frances Perkins, coddled communists and various other "crack pots." After that remark in 1935, 41,000 disgruntled workers joined what they called the Cracked Pot Club. They wore buttons displaying a cracked pot, emblematic of the governor's attack on workers. Martin did not oppose the entire New Deal agenda, however. Between 1935 and 1939, he selectively supported some initiatives, allowing federal programs that benefited thousands of Oregonians to function effectively.

Martin, for example, supported New Deal programs for reclamation and conservation. Under the auspices of the Bureau of Reclamation, 696 miles of canals and drains were completed in eastern Oregon. The Land Utilization Division of the Department of Agriculture spent millions in Oregon on programs to reseed forests that had been cut over and burned. In one project, federal funds financed the restoration of more than 15,000 acres of burned land resulting from the disastrous 1936 Bandon fire. The Land Utilization Division also provided funding to control range land use in eastern Oregon. More than 183,000 acres eventually came under the management of New Deal projects. Martin continuously wrote Roosevelt, attempting to convince the president to invest more federal money in Oregon. Roosevelt obliged. Several times the federal government purchased forest land from private companies, in one case acquiring 6,595 acres from the First National Bank, the Northwest Timber Company, and the Spaulding Logging Company to secure a watershed for Corvallis and Philomath. FDR prodded Martin to introduce legislation for soil conservation; Martin eventually submitted the Standard State Soil Conservation Districts Law to the Oregon Legislature. In addition, FDR channeled money from the

Agricultural Adjustment Administration into the Oregon hop industry and secured significant funding through the Works Progress Administration (WPA) for constructing an airport in Portland.[4]

Though he disapproved of and criticized the WPA, Martin allowed the agency to function in Oregon. The WPA and the Civilian Conservation Corps (CCC) built trails through national forests, established wildlife refuges and ranges, and supplied money and manpower for erecting five major bridges on the Oregon coast highway. The fifty-three-room Timberline Lodge, located at the 6,000-foot level on Mount Hood and constructed with CCC and WPA labor, ranks as one of the state's most popular attractions. WPA artists painted murals in public buildings, including the magnificent C.S. Price artwork in the Portland public schools, which even today reminds one of the New Deal's pervasive nature despite the governor's opposition. The WPA eventually spent more than $40 million in Oregon, ranking the state eleventh per capita in total funds expended by the New Deal.

In addition to Bonneville Dam, the Corps of Engineers completed nineteen other major projects in Oregon. By August 1936, more than 6,000 men worked on highway construction as the Bureau of Public Roads built more than 1,200 miles of roads at an expense in excess of $20 million. While these programs and projects prospered, however, Martin earned the enmity of New Deal supporters by his reactionary stance in opposition to public power, relief, and welfare, and his militarist response to organized labor.[5]

The issues surrounding public power continued to divide factions within both major political parties after the 1934 election. The Army Corps of Engineers began construction of Bonneville Dam in 1933, completing the massive project four years later. Throughout that period, Governor Martin, the Corps of Engineers, the Bureau of Reclamation, and private power interests waged a continual war of words with FDR's administration and public power supporters. Central to the dispute were questions concerning who would control the power generated by Bonneville Dam, how the power would be distributed, and who would benefit by the power generated—private utilities or PUDs. Congress took up the issue of Northwest electric power marketing in 1935 when Idaho Democratic Senator James P. Pope and Washington Congressman Knute Hill, both public power advocates, introduced legislation that would have created a Columbia Valley Authority (CVA) modeled on the Tennessee Valley Authority (TVA), a government-owned facility that pioneered radically low-rate structures for public power. Over the next two years, the proposal failed in Congress five times. Meanwhile, private industry in Oregon, aided by the governor, put up fierce resistance to what they considered a socialist threat to destroy private profit in the power industry.[6]

Support for a CVA came quite naturally from the grange, representing Oregon's farmers. Prior to the 1930s, private utilities, wedded to quick and certain profits, which in their analysis would not come from extending power lines across Oregon's vast open spaces, kept Oregon farmers out of the electric age and literally in the dark. The State Federation of Labor joined the Oregon Grange in supporting public power. Labor interests believed it would spur growth in the state's largest metropolitan areas providing work for their members. Both groups believed that federal allocation of Bonneville power should principally benefit individuals and strip the private utilities of their stranglehold. To ensure low rates, proponents of public power supported either state or federal construction of transmission lines from Bonneville Dam. They stressed the need for electricity costs to be uniform throughout the state so that a farmer in eastern Oregon would pay the same rate as a manufacturing plant in Portland.

FDR made his position on Northwest power development crystal clear at the Bonneville Dam site dedication in August 1934. With gubernatorial candidate Martin present, the president emphasized the need for rural development. He claimed Portland would benefit from Bonneville regardless, or perhaps even to its detriment because cheap Bonneville power might induce the city to grow too fast. This growth would come, Roosevelt said, at "the expense of smaller communities." The president favored developing Portland as a decentralized hub for regional growth as opposed to having the city become "a huge manufacturing center close to the source of power, a vast city of whirling machinery," as had happened so often in the east.[7]

To bring his vision to fruition, FDR created two New Deal agencies— the National Power Policy Committee and the National Resources Committee. By the time Roosevelt spoke at the Bonneville site in August 1934, the agencies had formulated broad criteria for government power distribution. The plan called for the federal government to set up a central grid system, "a power network co-coordinating both existing and new generating and transmission facilities into a single unit, making available large blocs of power at low rates uniform throughout the area." This would "connect Bonneville and Grand Coulee and would insure that nonprofit-making agencies could receive preference in the distribution of public power." When Congress later took up Roosevelt's suggestion to divide the nation into seven mega-utility districts, Martin wrote "confidentially" to an old colleague still on the Rivers and Harbors Committee in the House. Martin did not want to be quoted in public opposing the president, but he advised the congressman "to throw all this crap into the ash can. What nonsense to talk about further harassing business!"[8]

Portland Central Labor Council president and state
senator Phil Brady, one of Martin's nemeses. *Oregon
Historical Society, 000005*

Walter Pierce, as usual, led the state Democratic Party public power
faction supporting FDR's vision for a CVA. With Nan Wood Honeyman,
Phil Brady of the Central Labor Council in Portland, Willis Mahoney, and
other Democrats, most of whom did not occupy high positions in party
hierarchy, Pierce challenged private utilities, Oswald West, and especially
Governor Martin. He took delight in castigating Martin, "one of the few
political figures whom Pierce could not find some reason to praise." Writing to a colleague, Pierce said he thought "the old fellow should be repri-
manded by the people of Oregon." Honeyman, Brady, and others won
election to the state legislature in 1934 and 1936, where they continued their
unrelenting opposition to Martin. The feuding erupted into internecine warfare between the Democratic majority in the lower house and the governor.

Martin, frustrated, vindictive, and ever the warrior, lashed out at his Democratic Party rivals. He saw his opponents as a danger to society. "Oregon is stirred from stem to stern," he wrote Paul R. Kelty, editor of the *Oregonian*, "and every subversive element is active in its efforts, desires and hopes of overthrowing organized society and the governor, not of their ilk, would naturally be the one official that they would strike at." All the legislative leaders sought only self aggrandizement, Martin lamented, "[they] have thumbed their way into the party car only to get out their knives to try to kill the chauffeur. For Instance—my most virile enemies in the legislature are Democrats and most ardent supporters are Republicans." "I have been bedeviled from morning to night by a lot of small, mean, contemptible people," whom he then went on to list. In another letter that Roosevelt himself could have written about Martin, the governor rebuked the Democrats in the Senate, claiming that "from the beginning to the end of the session they opposed me in every way possible, while expressing deepest loyalty." The spectacle of warring Oregon Democrats and Martin's intransigence coupled with the long intractable battle over Bonneville power eventually led "Brother Ickes" to repudiate the governor, claiming, "Martin is at heart no New Dealer."[9]

While the Pierce faction continued its denunciations of the governor, Martin held the reins of power in the party. Even before Roosevelt's Bonneville dedication speech, Martin and the president had clashed over electric power policy. Martin's faction, including Oswald West, Portland Mayor Joseph K. Carson Jr., and others, supported by private utilities, industrial interests, and the Portland Chamber of Commerce, continued to press for industrial development and private supply. Private power supporters, while favoring federal financing of Bonneville Dam, maintained that a system of low charges to manufacturing interests located near the dam and controlled by private utilities, known as the "bus-bar rate," should be established. Under the bus-bar system, each mile from the dam would mean a higher rate. Clearly the bus-bar system favored industrial development at or near the dam and in Portland over residential users in the state's further reaches. Even though Martin and his supporters argued that the power produced at Bonneville should benefit private and public use, inexpensive power for industrial purposes under the control of private utilities remained their prime concern.[10]

The legislature, in an attempt to thwart Martin and urged on by Secretary Ickes, FDR, and the grange, passed a bill to have the state build power lines from Bonneville Dam and deliver electricity to consumers at cost while establishing a State Power Commission. Martin claimed the grange "didn't know a damn thing about building power lines" and he called the proposal a "tin-horn bill." He promptly vetoed the measure. "I secured Bonneville," Martin wrote, "and think I understand the best policy for the distribution of power for the benefit of all the people." Opposition Democrats could not muster the votes to override the governor's veto.

Opponents lashed out at the governor. Representative J.F. Hosch later charged that Martin had "used every effort to keep power out of the hands of the people; by his veto of . . . power bills . . . the governor has indicated his stand—a stand which no amount of saber rattling denunciation or lung splitting profanity can alter." Cornelia Pierce directed comments directly at Martin, saying the veto illustrated "your apparent surrender to powerful groups who appeal to you more strongly than do the farmer-taxpayers of Oregon." To Cornelia Pierce at least, Martin had exposed the fraudulent face of his governorship. "You made your campaign on the support of the Administration and as the 'friend of the President,'" she screamed at Martin from the front pages of newspapers throughout the state, "and then you vetoed the power bill which would have given the people of Oregon the undoubted right to the beneficial use of the great water power of the Columbia River.[11]

Public power advocates became increasingly frustrated as conservatives in control of both major political parties denied them a voice in party debate. They eventually turned their disgust to political activism in 1937 by assisting in the formation of the Oregon Commonwealth Federation (OCF). "We . . . declare our purpose," the preamble to the OCF constitution stated, "to unite the progressive forces of our state, irrespective of race, religion, or political affiliation. . . . Our task shall be done only when our people live in the society of peace, security, and abundance which is our rightful American heritage from the work which our fathers have done."

Unlike their counterparts in Washington, where communists maintained significant control over the Washington Commonwealth Federation, the OCF "shut out" communists. Although Charles Martin considered his fellow governor and namesake Clarence Martin of Washington "conscientious [and] fair-minded," he exhibited disgust with Washington politics. "That state is too much influenced by Seattle, which sad to relate early became a dumping point for the refuse of Alaska and the Orient," Martin wrote to General J.A. Ryan. "Seattle is today Russian territory," Martin concluded, "and I hope before long it will again become part of the United States."

Meanwhile, the membership of the OCF included "the unemployed, loggers, farmers," Democrats, Republicans, and Socialists, with radicals clearly in control of the agenda. At its Portland organizing convention in late August 1937, the OCF adopted resolutions supporting "New Deal programs; a

Senate La Follette Committee to investigate government spying on organized labor; anti-lynching legislation then in the Congress; nationalization of war industries; and public ownership of all natural resources, utilities, banks, and monopolies." Though opposition to Martin provided an impetus to organizing, the issues surrounding Bonneville power served as the catalyst to OCF formation. The OCF reserved a special place for public power in its founding document, urging "that all people be given equal preference to the power made available by the completion of Bonneville Dam[,] . . . Federal or state construction[,] and operation of trunk transmission lines[, and] . . . a blanket rate to be established at the terminal of the trunk lines . . . creating . . . People's Utility Districts, farmers cooperatives and municipal district agencies to make available at the lowest cost electric power to farm and city users." The OCF singled out Governor Martin and Portland Mayor Joseph Carson for special condemnation, claiming that their actions subverted the "real purpose of the Bonneville Dam, namely, to promote the general welfare of all people . . . by insisting that the power be used to the advantage of industry."[12]

Indeed, the dominant thrust of the OCF until its demise in 1942 centered around the battle for public power. The OCF would later join with progressive Democrats, many of whom became members of the OCF, in plans to defeat Martin in the 1938 Democratic gubernatorial primary. Meanwhile, at the organization's convention in 1937, after passing a convention resolution denouncing the "tyranny of the Martin regime," the delegates satirized Martin in song. To the tune of "Fare Thee Well," the convention sang:

> There is a general in the town, in the town
> Oh how he's let the people down, let us down
> And we'll vote, vote, vote until we've won the day
> And brought the New Deal here to stay![13]

The OCF's founding came as no surprise to the governor. "I had two state policemen in plain clothes present at the organization," Martin wrote. On April 13, 1937, Oregon State Police Major Lawrence A. Milner, on assignment as a special undercover agent, reported on an OCF Executive Committee planning meeting for calling a convention. Milner reported, erroneously, but in keeping with the anticommunist paranoia that developed during Martin's tenure, that the OCF "is a subsidiary to the Communist Party of the Soviet Union."

Two days later, Sergeant Carl A. Glen delivered a report to the governor that contained brief biographies of each participant, including among
others David G. Epps, son of a Portland police captain; Harry Gross, an
activist leftist attorney and member of the American Civil Liberties Union,
who "always [follows] the [Communist] Party Line in placing control of the
unions under the Communist Party [and] has a personal friendship with
Harry Bridges . . . and other radicals . . . [and] is not a member of the Communist Party for the reason he fears if he joins the Party he will be disbarred";
S. Stevenson Smith, a University of Oregon professor; and Peter Zimmerman,
Martin's former gubernatorial opponent. Milner, always eager to ingratiate
himself with Martin, reported that "the Communist party issued instructions that the Governor of Oregon would be made the butt of all attacks
by the various speakers during the Convention."

Martin also received reports on the OCF convention from young attorney Harley Osburn, who was assigned to attend the convention by his
employer, John J. Beckman, at the governor's request. Beckman, in his cover
letter to Osburn's report, confided to Martin on April 26, "I had several
observers at the convention, but the man who made the report that I en-
close is skilled in this type of work . . . he knew the real label of a good many
of these agitators and can relate a great deal of what went on behind the
scenes and who was who and why. I can, no doubt, make him available at
any time." By August Martin wanted more information on what he termed
"[those] gang . . . of young Jew[s] . . . communists, C.I.O.'s and crackpots!"
He directed the Oregon State Police to keep a close eye on the OCF.
In a memo to the chief of the state police, Martin ordered weekly reports on
OCF activities.[14]

Martin maintained his militant opposition to a Columbia Valley Authority right up to the completion of Bonneville Dam in 1937. Supporting a Corps of Engineer's analysis, he insisted at 1937 committee hearings
in Washington, D.C., that "there was no power market among domestic
consumers in the region." He warned the House committee that the
Bonneville investment could be repaid only by encouraging new industries
making heavy use of electricity to come into the area, and that this could
be accomplished only through a system of preferred rates.

In August 1937, after numerous proposals, modifications, and counter
proposals, Congress passed the Bonneville Power Act, a reconciliation of
Senate and House versions of the bill. The act, "a compromise to all interests," created "a balanced and segmented sharing of authority and preference over the power and rates of Bonneville's energy." Bonneville would have
a civilian administrator falling under the jurisdiction of Secretary of Interior

Ickes with the Corps of Engineers actually operating the dam. "The administrator would market the electricity and set the rates." The act directed the Bonneville Power Administration (BPA) to give preference and priority to public utility districts and cooperatives in the distribution of electric power generated by Bonneville Dam. With few PUDs operating in Oregon, however, private power interests were able to maintain their hold on most residential customers and defeated most initiatives to establish new PUDS.

Martin and his supporters immediately turned their attention to the appointment of the Bonneville administrator. They attempted to thwart Ickes' appointment of J.D. Ross, head of the Seattle City Light Department, whom his detractors called a municipal socialist. Eventually, during October 1937, over Governor Martin's vociferous objections, FDR chose Ross who shared FDR's belief "that cheap electric power would unlock the door to a higher living standard for all Americans," thereby fully supporting the yardstick principle.[15]

Though Martin sometimes at the insistence of his staff softened his public rhetoric regarding power issues, he conducted an unrelenting attack on New Deal relief and welfare programs to aid the poor and support the needy. He never understood the hopes and aspirations of desperate people attempting to hold on in hard times—unless they were related to him, for now and then, he did provide a modicum of empathy accompanied by ten or twenty dollars to destitute relatives. He viewed war as the normal state of mankind, so for him each day presented just another in a series of battles where only the fittest deserved to survive. As governor, with thousands of citizens prostrated by the Depression, Martin viewed his task as providing order and discipline in his corner of a chaotic world. "I am attempting to teach our people to show the courage and fortitude of good soldiers," he wrote not long after taking office. "Democratic nations," he asserted, "have lost their moral force through pampering their people."[16]

Like Herbert Hoover—and after all Martin described himself as a "Hoover Democrat"—Martin steadfastly maintained that counties and cities, not state or national governments, held the responsibility for public welfare and relief. He badgered the Oregon State Relief Committee to tighten control over those to whom it dispensed relief. When Multnomah County ran out of funds in June 1935, a crisis for which responsibility lay, the governor claimed, in "labor troubles . . . with their abundant lawlessness which has prevented men from working who want to work," the governor cautioned Judd Greenman, chairman of the state relief committee, against sending more aid. "It must be distinctly understood," Martin wrote to Greenman, "that there are other unfortunate people in this state to be considered than those in Multnomah County who seem so helpless to care for their own affairs." Greenman, however, told the governor that he would "not permit a single Oregon citizen who is entitled to any of the funds provided by the Legislature for . . . relief . . . to suffer."

Entitlement became a component of Martin's mantra against those he perceived to be receiving relief unjustly. He did not mind taking care of "old folks," he said, "but I'll be damned if I'll feed the young ones. Are we going to feed them for the rest of our lives? Hell!" he said, "Let them work!" When destitute refugees from the Dust Bowl and others from the northern Great Plains arrived in Oregon, Martin called them "alien paupers" and suggested that if they wanted to eat, selling their "rattletrap automobiles" should provide the necessary funds. These depression migrants sought economic opportunity in Oregon mainly in the agricultural sector. Martin and his like-minded associates labeled the newcomers as a threat, viewing them as "competitors for scarce jobs, as sources of increased taxation for relief, and as socially dangerous malcontents." Attempting to discourage "Okies" from taking up residence in the state, Martin ordered Greenman to close down the so-called Roosevelt Transient Camp in Roseburg. In reality, the governor said, the camps "were Tramp Camps," and the transients "should be kept moving out of our state the same as criminals." Martin reviled able-bodied unemployed men, claiming that Oregon would provide no assistance to them because "the need for the necessities of life will force these people to get some kind of work and care for themselves."[17]

Martin prided himself on his egalitarianism, or what he called his "Jacksonian" qualities—his ability never to allow any man to interfere with the great truths that he advocated and his facility to see and treat all citizens equally. "One of the finest things in our form of government," he told a crowd of young Democrats, "is that we have evolved a truly classless society. We recognize our fellow citizens and grant them preferment only on the basis of their ability to serve the common good." In this "truly classless society," with millions in America unemployed, where his accumulated wealth stood near $500,000, where his salary as governor coupled with his army retirement pension netted him an income of more than $1,100 per month, Martin declared that the physically and mentally disabled could adequately care for themselves on $10 per month. What of citizens who lacked the ability to serve the common good? Martin supported a plan to chloroform the "aged and feeble-minded wards of the state." To fulfill his promise to balance the budget, Martin suggested that the state could save $300,000 in the next biennium by putting 900 of the 969 inmates at the Fairview Home in Salem "out of their misery."[18]

In 1936 the governor peremptorily announced the end of the Depression in Oregon and told Harry Hopkins, head of FDR's relief program, to keep his money out of the state. Martin had barely held his dislike for Hopkins and relief programs under wraps while he sat in Congress, but not long after his inauguration in 1935, when Congress passed the Social Security Act and the Emergency Relief Appropriations Act, he threw off the cloak of caution, fiercely attacking the relief measures. He despised both measures, calling Social Security a "program . . . driving this country into national socialism." His distaste grew so overpowering that he attempted to block Social Security's implementation in Oregon. He delayed providing matching funds for old-age assistance, aid to the blind and disabled, and care for dependent mothers and children. Citing his 1934 campaign promise to balance the state budget and lower taxes, the governor dragged his feet in allocating state revenues for federal programs. He readily acceded to increased budgets for the National Guard and the state police but balked at "Socialist" public welfare programs. After the people twice refused to adopt a sales tax, referred to them by the legislature to provide the necessary state matching funds for Social Security, the governor finally acquiesced to having the legislature set aside several million dollars from state liquor revenues to provide relief and welfare services.[19]

In the years after Martin left Congress, destitute veterans had continued unsuccessfully in their attempts to have Congress pass a bonus bill. In Oregon many veterans supported Martin for governor, forgiving him for his vote in Congress against the 1932 Bonus Bill, hoping he would be sympathetic to their plight. When some veterans began to default on state loans in 1936, Martin called them "skunks" at a Portland Press Club luncheon. The remark set off a firestorm. "The Veterans of Oregon have forgiven you much, but this latest outrage of yours . . . cannot be overlooked," one correspondent wrote. "Has it occurred to you that there are thousands of these so-call 'skunks' in the state . . . all of whom bitterly resent your . . . remarks?"

The mother of a soldier killed in action wrote from The Dalles, "I am a 100% mother. My people arrived in America on The Mayflower's first voyage. . . . I do not feel [they] merit being called a skunk." Martin excoriated the press for quoting him. He claimed that his comments had been made "off the record" to a group of reporters "with the understanding that my remarks were confidential and not for publication." When Major Leo J.A. Fironi, president of the Commanders' Council of Veterans' Organizations in Multnomah County, demanded an apology from the governor, Martin's executive assistant Wallace Wharton fired off an angry rebuke. "Your peremptory demand that the Governor of the state of Oregon 'retract' or 'apologize' is insulting," Wharton fumed, "and displays an utter lack of courtesy."[20]

At the State Relief Committee, Greenman barely maintained his loyalty to Martin but the governor at one time or another antagonized most other members of the commission by constantly obstructing the committee's work. When the state started using liquor revenues for relief and welfare, on Martin's instructions it required the counties to match the state dollar for dollar, which proved to be a totally unrealistic expectation. Finally, even Greenman crossed swords with the governor. When Martin refused to disburse funds already allocated for relief, Greenman testily wired the governor at the El Cortez Hotel in Reno where Martin vacationed: "I feel that compliance with your instructions . . . [is a] violation of the statutes." Greenman ordered relief officials to disregard the governor's instructions.

Martin just hardened his stance. He told the newspapers that the state committee overspent its budget supporting "loafers" and "chiselers." With plenty of jobs, "there is no need why anyone willing to work cannot find it in this state with crops to be harvested" and the Depression over. Martin warned that relief and welfare sapped the moral force of the country. "It is desirable," the governor said, "that the government should get out of running everything and give some chance to private initiative. . . . For those who are in need and who are unable to work the relief committee will make provision, but for the slackers there will be lean pickings." Disgusted at Martin's unwarranted assault on relief recipients, Greenman showed solidarity with other members of the committee by joining them in resigning.[21]

While many Republicans supported Martin throughout his battles with relief organizations and proponents of a CVA, most Democrats, even those who had voted for him, developed a strong distaste for the governor. "Whenever I recall that I voted for him," one Democrat wrote Walter Pierce, "I am so humiliated that I feel like migrating to South America to live among the Indians of the upper Amazon for the balance of my natural life."[22]

Some politicians and voters, including among their number Democrats, Republicans, Socialists, and members of the grange, formed an alliance in early 1935 to recall the governor. Martin's undercover agent, Lawrence Milner, who was surreptitiously positioned within the radical movements in Portland, began delivering reports to his superiors at the outset of the recall agitation. His reports detail the clandestine maneuvers of several Democratic members of the state legislature, including Senators Zimmerman, Carney, Stringer, Strayer, and Hess, to steer the movement while remaining on the sidelines. State Senator W.E. Burke, however, moved quite openly in Portland, attempting, unsuccessfully, to raise funds necessary to support the effort.

Milner related Burke's frustration in one report, claiming Burke "could not understand what was the matter with Portland people as they were willing to discuss the subject but when it came time for action and putting up the cash it was a different matter."

Not knowing Milner was a spy, Burke expressed exasperation to Milner about Richard Neuberger, a young reporter at the *Oregonian* who claimed that his job at the paper precluded his open support for the recall. Learning about Neuberger's surreptitious support of the recall, Martin interceded to have Neuberger fired from his position at the paper, but his friend Paul R. Kelty, the *Oregonian* editor, refused. "The statement that young Neuberger is active in the movement is an error, to my certain belief," Kelty wrote Martin. "Neuberger was asked if he would participate and refused, further than to say that he would vote for your recall if it were placed before the voters. I am positive he meant what he said. I have known him since he was a little boy and he does not lie." Without being able to reveal the source of his information, Martin let the matter drop. The governor also took seriously the secret information that the son of Portland Police Captain William Epps sat on the organizing committee. Writing to his ally Mayor Joseph Carson early in May 1935, Martin requested that the mayor look into the situation.[23]

Throughout the summer, as the recall movement gained strength, editorial opinion from around the state consolidated in support of the governor and against a precipitous recall movement. Martin kept Milner on the job while publicly dismissing the recall backers. Privately he vented his rage. "They have their secret meetings, their newspaper releases . . . any means that their deviltry can think up to break me down," he wrote to Paul Kelty in November. Undaunted, Martin claimed his opponents gave him strength. "These assaults will encourage and nerve me to adhere more strictly to the path of honor and of duty. I would be glad to sign one of their recall petitions and would urge my friends to do likewise that once and for all time it might be determined to what extent Oregon has been undermined by such scoundrels." The recall movement collapsed almost as suddenly as it arose. Organizers never managed to raise sufficient funds to finance their efforts and the major charge against the governor—that he could not serve as governor while collecting a pension from the federal government—never resonated with voters.[24]

Martin's position on public versus private power further exacerbated the factional splits in both the Republican and Democratic parties and his contempt for citizens suffering the ravages of the Depression alienated a significant portion of the electorate. But his militarist, uncompromising actions directed against union activities, commencing almost immediately with his assumption of office, attracted organized labor's everlasting enmity. Deep conflicts between labor and capital in Oregon had preceded Martin into office and would bedevil him throughout his term.

One piece of New Deal legislation, passed right after Martin surfaced from his unexplained absence in Congress during the "hundred days," recognized workers' rights to organize and bargain collectively. For the first time in the history of the United States, federal law recognized workers' organizations. The legal right for workers to withhold their labor and to strike joined, briefly, the pantheon of basic freedoms. Section 7-(a) of the National Industrial Recovery Act (NIRA) invigorated organized labor. Oregon's workers, like their counterparts throughout the country, demanded their right under section 7-(a) to bargain collectively through unions of their own choosing. They expected government to make good on a promise imbedded in the act that "prohibited employers from any interference, restraint or coercion" in the process. New York Senator Robert F. Wagner chaired the National Labor Board established by the act to oversee employee elections to determine their bargaining representatives.[25]

Workers on the West Coast immediately began agitating for their rights, led by the most militant unionists in the dock workers and longshoremen's unions. Ship owners, horrified at what they viewed as economic revolution and an organized communist plot, were determined to resist and fight back. They stood their ground on traditional private property and ownership rights. These two polarized positions set the stage for a monumental struggle that would erupt in 1934 and continue through Martin's term as governor.

Notes

1. *Salem Capital Journal*, January 15 and February 9, 1935; Mark Hatfield, "History Can Give You Connections: An Interview with U.S. Senator Mark O. Hatfield," *Oregon History Magazine*, V. 37, Summer 1993, 2.
2. Arthur H. Bone, *Oregon Cattleman/Governor Congressman: Memoirs and Times of Walter M. Pierce* (Portland: Oregon Historical Society, 1981), 389.
3. Bone, 389–91.
4. FDR to CHM, October 16, 1936; February 23, December 15, and November 6, 1937, CHMC, OHS.
5. Richard D. Burton, "The New Deal in Oregon," in John Braeman, Robert H. Bremner, and David Brody, Eds., *The New Deal: The State and Local Levels* (Columbus: Ohio State University Press, 1975), 367–68.
6. Philip J. Funigiello, *Toward a National Power Policy: The New Deal and the Electric Utility Industry, 1933–1941* (Pittsburgh: University of Pittsburgh Press, 1973), 174–75.

7. E. Kimbark MaCColl, *The Growth of a City: Power and Politics in Portland, Oregon, 1915 to 1950* (Portland: The Georgian Press, 1979), 446.

8. Arthur M. Schlesinger Jr., *The Age of Roosevelt: The Politics of Upheaval* (Boston: Houghton Mifflin Company, 1960), 378; CHM to Eugene Lorton, November 22, 1937, CHMC, OHS.

9. Bone, 386; Walter Pierce to Tom Quigley, May 26, 1937, as quoted in Burton; CHM to Paul R. Kelty, November 21, 1935, and CHM to A.E. Reames, November 21, 1935, CHMC, OHS; Harold Ickes to Henry Hess, May 14, 1938, as quoted in Burton, 364.

10. *Oregon Journal*, October 15, 1933.

11. CHM to Colonel C.A. Robertson, August 20, 1935; typescript memorandum, "Record of Legislature Dispels Dispute over Public Power Issue," by Ralph Watson, October 1937, CHMC, OHS; Cornelia Pierce as quoted in Bone, 390–91.

12. Redacted rendition of the Oregon Commonwealth Federation Constitution, prepared by Major Lawrence A. Milner of the Oregon State Police; CHM to General J.A. Ryan, September 2, 1936, CHMC, OHS; Monroe Sweetland in an interview with the author, May 24, 1998.

13. Robert E. Burton, *Democrats of Oregon: The Pattern of Minority Politics, 1900–1956* (Eugene: University of Oregon, 1970), 84.

14. Typescript copy of Milner's report, April 13, 1937, CHMC, OHS; Typescript copy of report, April 15, 1937, Sergeant Carl A. Glen, Governor Martin Papers, State of Oregon Archives [referred to hereafter as Martin Papers]; CHM to Roy W. Ritner, April 30, 1940, CHMC, OHS; Report of Lawrence A. Milner on the Oregon Commonwealth Federation convention, undated; John J. Beckman to W.L. Gosslin, Secretary to the Governor, April 26, 1937, Martin Papers; CHM to Charles Pray, August 10, 1937, CHMC, OHS.

15. Funigiello, 188-89, 194-96; Craig Wollner, *Electrifying Eden: Portland General Electric, 1889–1965* (Portland: Oregon Historical Society Press, 1990), 156–72.

16. Martin as quoted in the *Oregonian*, December 25, 1938; CHM to Jesse E. Moseley, October 5, 1935, CHMC, OHS.

17. CHM to Erwin A. Taft, June 13, 1935; CHM to Judd Greenman, June 13, 1935, CHMC, OHS; Gordon B. Dodds, *Oregon: A History* (New York: W.W. Norton and Company, 1977), 186; Judd Greenman to CHM, June 9, 1935, Martin Papers; Richard L. Neuberger, *Our Promised Land* (New York: The Macmillan Company, 1938), 314; *Oregonian*, January 15, 1936; *Salem Capital Journal*, July 14, 1936.

18. Typescript of a speech to Young Democrats in Marion County, April 7, 1938, CHMC, OHS; *Salem Capital Journal*, March 12–15, 1936; *Oregonian*, March 14–19, 1936.

19. *Salem Capital Journal*, October 14, 1938.

20. Dwight E. Alderman to CHM, February 26, 1936; "Mother" Viluria L Lent to CHM, February 26, 1936; CHM to Viluria L. Lent, February 29, 1936, CHMC, OHS; Wallace S. Wharton to Major Leo J.S. Fironi, March 3, 1936, Martin Papers.

21. Judd Greenman to CHM, June 15 and 29, 1936, Martin Papers; CHM to Prescott Cookingham, August 14, 1935; typescript of press statement, August 11, 1937, CHMC, OHS.

22. Wilbur F. Brock to Walter Pierce, June 3, 1937, as quoted in Burton, 82.

23. Report of Lawrence Milner, December 7, 1935; Paul R. Kelty to CHM, November 25, 1935; CHM to Joseph Carson Jr., May 11, 1935.

24. CHM to Paul R. Kelty, November 21, 1935, CHMC, OHS.
25. Section 24 7-(a) had read as follows: "Employees shall have the right to organize and bargain collectively through representatives of their own choosing, and shall be free from the interference, restraint, or coercion of employers of labor, or their agents, in the designation of such representatives . . . no employee and no one seeking employment shall be required as a condition of employment to join any company union or to refrain from joining, organizing, or assisting a labor organization of his own choosing." Arthur M. Schlesinger Jr., *The Age of Roosevelt: The Coming of the New Deal* (Boston: Houghton Mifflin Company, 1959), 137.

Chapter Eleven

HUNTING REDS

War is the normal state of man in spite of all the wistful thinking of pacifists.
—Charles Henry Martin

THE WEST COAST WATERFRONT had long been an arena for conflict between management and labor. Although worker-employer conflicts dated back to the 1860s in parts of California, violence had escalated in 1916 when longshoremen and seamen aggressively pressed their demands to organize for their mutual benefit. By using strikebreakers and armed guards, waterfront employers met a series of 1916 longshoremen strikes for higher wages. Working men on both sides suffered maulings and beatings. A number were killed. In response to the strikes, California shipowners, industrialists, and other employers formed the Law and Order Committee. The committee amassed pledges of a million dollars from its members, "to bust the unions." Eventually, the Law and Order Committee helped pass an antipicketing ordinance in Los Angeles. They claimed there was "no such thing as peaceful picketing. . . . picketing is an instrument of violence. It is un-American," a stance later adopted by Governor Martin.[1]

In 1919 workers acted again. As with the 1916 strike, a combination of an unfriendly press, police, courts, state and city officials, strikebreakers, and armed guards allowed the owners to defeat port labor. One result of the strike was the founding of the Blue Book, the waterfront-employer controlled and dominated union, "an infamous organization to which men were compelled to pay tribute in order to work on the docks."[2]

The waterfront remained relatively quiet between 1919 and 1934, with one brief shut-down in 1922 by the International Longshoremen's Association (ILA), which affected all major West Coast ports. Shipowners deployed an army of 1,500 mobile strikebreakers from harbor to harbor, successfully breaking the strike. Following the unsuccessful 1919 and 1922 strikes, union membership plummeted. The International Seamen's Union (ISU), an amalgamation of a number of separate craft unions of which the Pacific Coast Marine Firemen, Oilers, Watertenders, and Wipers Association (MFOW) were a part, declined from a high of 106,000 in 1920 to 14,000 in 1929. The Blue Book controlled access to jobs. Wages remained low, hours were long (eighty-four hours per week), employers eliminated overtime pay, and feudal conditions existed on the ships. In fact, no standards existed for working conditions. "Seamen stood two watches a day, lived in small, over-crowded quarters with unsanitary latrines, slept on 'donkey's breakfast' mattresses, and did all their bathing and laundering from a single bucket, using sea water and salt water soap."[3]

When section 7-(a) became law, Longshoremen reorganized through-out the West Coast as one union. Early in 1934, as they pressed for union recognition and improved working conditions, they met an adamant, united rejection from employers. President Roosevelt averted a strike planned for March by personally intervening in the dispute. Through arbitration con-ducted by a regional mediation board set up by Senator Wagner, elections in Los Angeles and Seattle gave the ILA an overwhelming mandate among workers. The ILA scheduled elections for May 11 in Portland, but by then the waterfront owners had had enough. They repudiated the first two elections, announcing their intention to carry a suit to the U.S. Supreme Court. Knowing that a suit would drag on for over two years, the ILA decided to strike. On May 9, 1934, all ILA members on the West Coast walked off the job.

In Portland, shipowners actually welcomed a strike, believing "that they could break the union as they had done back in 1922. The Waterfront Employers' Association and the Chamber of Commerce clearly expected to defeat the union if they received sufficient support from governmental au-thorities."[4]

The strike paralyzed shipping, and maritime commerce ceased. Most of the grain intended for export from the state began to rot. Sawmills halted the production of lumber for export. The 3,000 waterfront workers idled by the strike were joined by 15,000 other workers in Portland and 50,000 workers statewide who also sat idle. As violence escalated, employers and the Chamber of Commerce first labeled the strikers "rioters" and then, hoping to hit a more responsive chord with paranoid politicians, began labeling the irate workers "Reds" and "Bolsheviks." Even though the police, many of whom felt sympathy for the workers, clubbed and arrested picketers, and police courts convicted them without evidence, the chamber complained of lax law enforcement. Mayor Carson appealed to Governor Julius Meier to call out the National Guard but Meier refused.

In San Francisco on July 5, 1934, "Bloody Thursday," police killed two strikers, shooting them in the back. Generally sympathetic toward working people after four years of the Depression, the people of San Francisco supported a general strike, lasting from July 16 to 19, 1934. Phil Brady at the Portland Central Labor Council threatened similar action if Governor Meier called out the National Guard. Meanwhile, laboring men turned out in force at a Portland memorial for the San Francisco dead.

President Roosevelt, due to arrive in August for a dedication ceremony at the Bonneville Dam site, dispatched Senator Wagner to Portland, hoping he could negotiate a settlement. On July 20, the Waterfront Employers' Association reluctantly agreed to submit all of the strike issues to arbitration. When workers returned to their jobs on July 31, they ended "the most devastating work stoppage in Oregon's history"—an action that wreaked havoc on Oregon's economy. By prevailing, unions proved that section 7-(a) actually had teeth and FDR proved that he would support the law. Thus encouraged, the waterfront unions formed the Maritime Federation of the Pacific, an action that would eventually affect Martin's governorship in 1937.

When timber workers began a strike in early May 1935 against recalcitrant wood products employers, Martin reflected on the failure of Governor Meier to act decisively and steeled his own resolve to be the "law and order" governor. Martin immediately revealed his solidarity with employers, complaining that organized labor was out to get him. "These pestiferous peewees would go to any lengths to embarrass me and my administration," he complained. He responded militaristically, reflecting his life's training.

When Sheriff Oscar Weed of Columbia County wrote to the governor for advice, claiming he might not be able to control strikers in his county, Martin replied with a stinging rebuke, which he made public in the *Oregonian*. "It should not be necessary," Martin wrote, "for me to remind you of your duty as sheriff, but your letter makes it necessary. . . . As governor of the state I expect you, and the sheriff of every other county to do his full duty in all respects . . . and if [you] fully perform [your] duties, no necessity will arise whereby you or any of the sheriffs will have to call upon the governor for assistance." Not content to leave the rebuke at that, Martin warned Weed that if he or any other sheriff did not do his duty, Martin would remove him and "appoint officers . . . who will enforce all the laws of the state, and maintain peace and order."

Multnomah County Sheriff Martin T. Pratt congratulated Martin for rebuking Sheriff Weed, claiming Weed got just what he asked for. "Bully for you!" Martin responded to Pratt. "I wish we had a sheriff like you in every county in Oregon. I did not mind when that weak-kneed sheriff of Columbia County gave me a chance to tell him where to get off!" Martin advised sheriffs to "beat hell out of 'em!" and "crack their damn heads! Those fellows are there for nothing but trouble—give it to them!"[5]

As picketing workers appeared at various locations around the state to press union demands, Martin appointed State Police Superintendent Charles P. Pray to head a state response team armed with tear gas and machine guns. At the Stimson Mill strike in Washington County, an action fairly representative of others around the state, striking workers adopted various strategies to force the mill owners to accede to union demands for recognition. When the Stimson owners refused to recognize the union, workers walked out and the owners hired strikebreakers. Union pickets made life for the "scabs" as difficult as possible and virtually shut down mill operations. For several days workers picketed the mill under the local sheriff's constant surveillance. Pray's representatives at the scene also watched and reported to their boss in Salem. As Martin received constant reports from Superintendent Pray, he met several times with Harold Miller, Stimson Lumber Company's manager.

On May 22, twenty-five cars loaded with picketers left the Labor Temple in Portland to join striking workers at Gaston. Early the next morning, with several hundred picketers gathered at Gaston, Martin ordered out the state police and the National Guard to protect strikebreakers, just as he would do on numerous other occasions across the state. Armed with gas grenades, riot gear, and machine guns, the military and police forces delivered an ultimatum to the pickets—leave or be shot. For several tense minutes, with machine gunners and two combat squads in place, the workers conversed with Labor Commissioner Charles Gram and Otto Hartwig of the Industrial Accident Commission. Then, as the state military forces readied their attack, the workers dispersed. By the barest margin, the workers' tactical retreat averted a slaughter. Though Martin would not use National Guard troops again against striking workers until the waterfront disturbances in 1937, state police forces, following the governor's orders, continued to mass at various strike situations around the state to threaten, harass, and arrest picketers.[6]

When the governor's tactics failed to extinguish workers' demands in the state's main urban area, Martin drew up plans to lead the charge himself at the head of the state police and National Guard. His staff prepared a "PROCLAMATION" that declared a "state of insurrection" to exist in Portland and Multnomah County where "the civil officers and authorities . . . are wholly unable to establish and maintain law and order." As "Commander-in-Chief of the Oregon National Guard," Martin decreed, "I do hereby proclaim that martial law exists . . . [I] assume military command and control of and over the City of Portland and County of Multnomah." As arrests mounted but no situation presented itself where drastic measures could be invoked, Martin instead appointed Assistant Attorney-General Ralph Moody as special prosecutor for the "goon" cases. When Martin later reflected on his term as governor, he recalled with pride his confrontation with the "un-American . . . viscous campaign of brutal intimidation by a group of bullies and racketeers purporting themselves to be labor leaders," pointing out that of more than 120 arrests, Moody had convicted 75 individuals, including Al Rosser, the head of the Teamsters, and five other Teamsters for burning down a box factory in Salem.[7]

Union membership burgeoned during the 1930s, reflecting the new government protection afforded first by the National Industrial Recovery Act, and then, by the Wagner Act passed in 1935. But this constituted only part of labor's story. Capitalism's collapse during the Depression disillusioned millions of workers. They lost faith in capitalist leadership and became unwilling to simply trust their destiny to the whims of employers. They wanted union contracts that clearly defined the terms and conditions of employment. As union ranks swelled, two factions emerged within the nationwide American Federation of Labor (AFL)—one advocating broad industrial unions and the other supporting the more traditional AFL focus on craft unionism. They joined in a national battle that remade unionism in Oregon and plunged the state into a deepening crisis.

After a tumultuous struggle at the annual AFL national convention in November 1935, defeated proponents of industrial unionism formed the Committee for Industrial Organization, which later became known as the Congress of Industrial Organizations (CIO). Throughout 1936 and 1937, the rivalry that emerged between the AFL and the CIO led to hundreds of strikes across the country. In Oregon, these struggles mainly involved the timber and port unions. Citizens not directly involved became exasperated by disputes that led to work stoppages having nothing to do with basic labor-management relations but centered instead on union jurisdictional disagreements. This exasperation eventually led Oregon in 1938 to adopt draconian antilabor legislation in the form of a ballot initiative financed by several employer organizations. The political battle fueled Martin's war of words with Labor Secretary Frances Perkins and pitted the governor against unions in general, although he reserved a particular dislike for the CIO.

The FDR-sponsored National Industrial Recovery Act (NIRA), which established the National Labor Board (NLB), was in effect for only a brief period. Critics on the right claimed the NLB favored unions; meanwhile union leaders claimed it favored management. By the end of 1935, with the NLB at the end of its tether and finding it harder and harder to secure compliance, a federal district court delivered the coup de grace by declaring section 7-(a) of the NIRA unconstitutional. The U.S. Supreme Court followed suit soon after, declaring the act unconstitutional. Working with FDR, Senator Robert F. Wagner supplied the remedy in the 1935 Wagner Act, which incorporated much of the same protections guaranteed in the NIRA, including the 7-(a) protections allowing unions to organize.

By 1939, Martin would view the Wagner Act as a malevolent piece of work. He condemned it as causing "four years of tumultuous and destructive labor strife, violence, and controversy." All of his problems, the governor declared, had their "inception in the Wagner act" and the "maladministration" of the act by Secretary Perkins or "the Madame Secretary" as Martin sarcastically referred to her.

Martin commiserated with a group of Washington businessmen in their travails with the act when addressing the Tacoma Chamber of Commerce in 1939: "I can fully appreciate the dilemma in which many of you gentlemen in other states find yourselves, in attempting to operate profitably and in harmony with your employees under the inadequate one-sided machinery for handling labor disputes provided by the Federal statutes" and supported by "labor union officials, sympathizers, and parlor-pink magazine writers and newspaper columnists."[8]

The struggle between the AFL and the CIO played itself out in Oregon in the timber industry and on the waterfront in a series of on-going strikes from 1935 to 1938. Martin believed the union conflict was a sinister plot. "The purpose of both is the same," he wrote to a fellow army general, "to seize control of the government." Martin labeled labor organizers gangsters and racketeers. Martin continually stressed his belief that unions leaders such as Dave Beck of the AFL and Harry Bridges of the Longshoremen's union exploited "the ranks of labor" while "disrupting the peace and order of the community in their efforts to force jurisdictional control for their own aggrandizement." Martin desperately searched for instances of fraud among labor leaders and their supporters, having the state police investigate the tax returns of union officials and legislators who supported the union movement. He had other investigations in mind for resident aliens involved with labor struggles. "Several of these self-appointed leaders [referring to Harry Bridges] are not even American citizens and their un-American affiliations will bear looking into." But then Martin had already been "looking into" Bridges for some time.[9]

Increasingly, both publicly and privately, and particularly to military colleagues, Martin directed his disgust over labor conflicts toward what he viewed as its source—Franklin Roosevelt's policies and the actions of Secretary of Labor Frances Perkins. Seeing rank and file unionists under the spell of labor leaders, Martin viewed the electorate as being under the spell of another wizard. "Whether the idolatrous following which the President has had in this state will see the handwriting on the wall remains to be seen," he wrote to General C.R. Howland in Washington, D.C. "I think personally that things are going to get much worse before they turn and further that the turn can only come by an about-face in Washington." By this time, Martin had claimed the Depression at an end in Oregon and asserted that "things were going fine with us out here until this maritime strike," which turned bliss to chaos. "The laboring men are in an ugly mood," he told Colonel Clarence Hotchkiss, "thinking they put the President in the White House . . . [they] feel it is now up to them to run the country."[10]

Though not openly criticizing FDR in public, Martin lashed out at the National Labor Relations Board (NLRB) and Secretary Frances Perkins. The NLRB "has shown complete ineptitude in bringing about [any] settlement," Martin told a radio audience. Worse, "this autocratic federal body has heretofore assumed powers in rendering decisions . . . strangely paralleling procedure in Russian courts of so-called justice." "I do not intend," Martin thundered, "that the Bolshevik-Soviet system shall be introduced into this state."

Martin laid the ineffectiveness of the NLRB at the feet of the head "Red" in the Roosevelt administration, "that miserable Secretary of Labor." "That Madam Secretary is responsible for most of our troubles," he wrote to General Nathaniel F. McClure, concerning Perkins. "I think at heart she is a red. If the President would give her the gate like he has some of those other Reds around him, it would be a mighty fine thing for the country." Martin viewed Frances Perkins as being in league with the devil—"I think these very conditions are what brother Bridges and his Reds want to bring forth," he said of the waterfront strikes in 1936, "while the Madam Secretary smiles and will do nothing that will hurt 'her boys.'"[11]

With democratic government under attack by "Jew Communists" or "shanty Irishmen" as Martin claimed, he wanted swift, decisive, militaristic counteraction. Forget the niceties afforded by democratic government: the threat to democracy would have to be handled undemocratically. Martin perceived Western civilization as a whole being threatened by a "madness abroad in the world today, which threatens our American institutions and government with inundation by waves of unreasoning emotionality," by "these dear soft people who want to alleviate all suffering," but surely "will in the end find themselves the greatest sufferers." "This continued prating about human rights being placed above property rights is certainly bearing bitter fruit. I believe eventually . . . people . . . will crush it," he warned.

An aroused citizenry must take action, Martin claimed, before the Reds succeeded in their aims—the "destruction of our liberties." "These forces want to do away with the capitalist system. They are playing the same game as they played in Italy and Germany—strikes, confusion, and turmoil." If Reds wanted to destroy the American system, Martin had the answer. "If things come to a crisis, there are enough strong men left in the country to handle it properly. . . . The Italians wouldn't submit; they organized their blackshirts. The Germans wouldn't submit; so they had their brownshirts and Hitler. I don't believe Americans will submit," he claimed, leaving the conclusion dangling. At any rate, "certainly the politicians will have to be thrown overboard."[12]

Following Martin's inauguration as governor, the *Salem Capital Journal* stated that Oregonians would miss watching the antics of amateur detectives, employed by Martin's predecessor Julius Meier to "snoop around the several departments." Martin inherited an infant state police force designed for Meier by retired Marine Corps General Smedley Darlington Butler, a two-time Medal of Honor winner. A charismatic speaker and brilliant organizer, General Butler later claimed that the reactionary American Liberty League offered to make him dictator of the United States if he would lead a coup d'etat against FDR. Martin quickly reorganized the state police, expanding its undercover capabilities. The governor's special agents would operate amateurishly at times and most certainly out of the public eye, but Martin built one of the most nefarious spy networks then existing in any state in the country with the possible exception of California. "Red Squad" agents hunted down radicals all along the West Coast, from Los Angeles to Seattle. The operatives' loyalty and obedience to the governor matched that of any military unit.[13]

In this period and later, people of Martin's ilk considered communists to be of foreign origin, the ultimate strangers, and certainly "Un-American."[14] Consciously or not, Martin had spent his whole adult life rehearsing and preparing for his role as an anticommunist crusader bent on stamping out the Red menace—and saving American civilization. His early adult socialization had occurred at West Point, where education and training emphasized Duty, Honor, Country, while also generally inculcating chauvinistic and ethnocentric views supporting the status quo in American society, economics, and politics at the time. Except for patrolling Northwest Indian reservations as a junior officer from Vancouver Barracks, Martin missed participating in the last conquests of Native American tribes, although he did claim falsely while making his first congressional bid to have taken part in "the last of the big Indian campaigns, that against the Sioux in 1890."[15]

That natives and other races aspired to a higher station in life grated on Martin's nerves. He considered them naturally inferior. "We find it impossible to get a clean intelligent servant in Peking," he wrote to Louise from China in September 1900. "All from high to low are base, filthy, ignorant beasts. . . . I should say that the world would be better off rid of the whole brood."[16] Eighteen years later, when commanding black American soldiers, Martin found himself charged with subduing "marauding bands seeking night life"—a people who lacked "intelligence, education, common sense, initiative, determination and pride."[17] In the early 1930s when FDR threw his support to labor, the first U.S. president to do so, and tenuously held out the hand of reconciliation to African-Americans, Martin and other similar political leaders perceived the collapse of America. As he assumed the reins of power, Martin intended to use the means available to him as governor to forestall that downfall.

Martin's Red Squad coordinated the efforts of the Portland police, state police, the National Guard's intelligence unit, and his own special agents. In Portland, Walter B. Odale, M.R. Bacon (whose usefulness proved short lived as the Communist Party expelled him after exposing him as a spy), Bill Brown, and J.J. Keegan formed the Portland Police Department's Red Squad. They sent hopelessly mundane, convoluted, "Weekly Reports of Communist Activities" to the governor's office for years, running to hundreds of pages. Red Squad agents attended every gathering even remotely connected to radical politics. They reported on labor unions, the Oregon Commonwealth Federation, the Communist Party, the Oregon League Against War and Fascism, the American Civil Liberties Union, and on individuals—from policemen and college professors to newspaper reporters and state legislators.

J.J. Keegan, the captain of Portland's Red Squad, traveled as far as Los Angeles to obtain evidence for Martin in the latter's ongoing vendetta against radical labor leader Harry Bridges. When questioned at a U.S. Department of Labor hearing looking into Bridges' Communist affiliations, Keegan admitted that he worked closely with Martin's special agent Stanley Doyle and other associates. When asked where the money came from to finance the far-flung investigation, Keegan at first claimed that the Portland Chief of Police lavished funds on the undercover unit and never asked questions. When pressed on this answer and presented with signed receipts, Keegan admitted that substantial contributions "came from the Portland Teamsters

Union, with the blessings of Dave Beck. As staunch AFLers, the Teamsters were anxious to see the CIO, and its west coast organizer, Bridges, routed."[18]

The undercover work of Major Lawrence A. Milner, Martin's agent at the state police, actually had begun earlier at the request of the National Guard in 1933. From 1933 to 1937, Milner investigated subversives by ingratiating himself to various organizations including the Communist Party. Milner served a purpose for these organizations; he owned a large seven-passenger car and often volunteered as a chauffeur for group members needing to travel. Milner filed extensive reports detailing the conversations he overheard while driving, sometimes as far afield as San Francisco or Seattle. Milner's reports encompassed more than 1,400 pages during his undercover years. Always eager to please and ever the sycophant, the focus of Milner's reports range from the dreary to the disgusting. He lied, he flattered, he acted as an agent provocateur for mob violence, and he gained the confidence of committed radicals and progressives so he could report on their every word and action.

Milner stated it was "my duty as a military intelligence officer to do anything to gain my purpose without being disclosed." James M. Landis, dean of Harvard Law School, summed Milner up best: "an undercover operator anxious to flood his superiors with information regardless of its relevancy or accuracy . . . . Milner can best be dismissed as a self-confessed liar, a man who has admittedly tried twice—once successfully—to make falsehood parade as truth."[19]

Special Agent Stanley M. (Larry) Doyle, operating directly under the governor, became Martin's most disreputable agent in the anticommunist struggle. Doyle, a former American Legion national official, first came to the attention of government antilabor circles as the prosecutor in the Dirk DeJonge case. A dedicated socialist who joined the Communist Party after the 1934 waterfront strike, DeJonge landed in jail for violating the Oregon syndicalism law when he spoke at a rally in downtown Portland criticizing the Portland police force's "brutal practices."

At DeJonge's trial, Doyle claimed "it was only necessary to show that DeJonge was a Communist and had been present at the public meeting to prove his guilt under Oregon's syndicalism law." The law, a desperate attempt to curtail free speech, defined criminal syndicalism as "the doctrine which advocates crime, physical violence, sabotage, or any unlawful acts or methods as a means of accomplishing or effecting industrial or political change or revolution." To prove that DeJonge indeed belonged to the Communist Party, Doyle solicited testimony from Portland Red Squad undercover agent M.R. Bacon, a former bootlegger.

Doyle also called to the stand DeJonge's supposed Communist Party comrade, undercover agent Lawrence Milner. Milner, however, testified that he "didn't know DeJonge was a communist." During a recess in the trial, Doyle requested that Milner change his testimony. Milner refused, because he found Doyle personally offensive, yet when he resumed his testimony he denied under oath that Doyle had made any such request. In proceedings "tantamount to a Kangaroo court," presided over by Judge Jacob Kanzler, "an active member of both the American Legion and the Veterans of Foreign Wars, and a loyal Republican," DeJonge did not stand a chance.

However, two years later, the U.S. Supreme Court overturned DeJonge's conviction. Chief Justice Charles Evans Hughes's opinion, while not ruling the syndicalism law unconstitutional, did represent a victory for radicals. The court ruled that membership in the Communist Party in and of itself did not constitute a punishable offense, that DeJonge's "sole offense [was] that he had assisted in the conduct of a public meeting, . . [that] peaceable assembly for lawful discussion cannot be made a crime."[20]

As Martin's special agent, carrying badge number 280, Doyle ranged up and down the West Coast attempting to fulfill Martin's promise to rid waterfront employers of Harry Bridges. Bridges had risen to prominence because of his leadership in the 1934 maritime strike. As he consolidated his union's power, the federal government, the Immigration Service, Governor Martin, Governor Merriam of California, Governor Clarence Martin of Washington, and police Red Squads from Los Angeles to Seattle carried on an unremitting campaign to deport Bridges as an alien Communist.

As demands emanating from waterfront employers, the American Legion, and government officials bombarded the Immigration Service, undercover agents gathered affidavits and other evidence to try to prove Bridges' connection to the Communist Party. The chief agents assisting Harper Knowles, chairman of the Subversive Activities Committee of the California Department of the American Legion, were from Martin's Red Squad, especially Captain John Keegan and Stanley Doyle. Many of Doyle's escapades later came to light, in part, through the findings of a U.S. Labor Department hearing conducted by James M. Landis. The Landis report painted a sordid picture of Governor Martin and state power run amok.[21]

Following Martin's instructions and working closely with Captain Keegan, Doyle also cooperated with the San Francisco Industrial Association and the Waterfront Employers' Association in gathering evidence to implicate Bridges as a Communist. In the process, however, he hopelessly compromised himself by taking "so much money from so many people" that any effectiveness he might have had as a witness against Bridges vanished. Eventually "he was no longer of any use."[22]

Doyle several times attempted to bribe witnesses against Bridges. In 1935, Charles G. Bakcsy, working as an undercover agent for the Matson Navigation Company, set about uncovering connections between Harry Bridges and Russian Soviet agents in Carmel, California, a mecca for writers and artists and the home of the great "muckraking" journalist Lincoln Steffens. Bakcsy established himself in Steffens' circle of friends, hosting lavish parties at a rented beach house equipped with "hidden microphones and cameras, a fingerprint laboratory, to which guests' liquor glasses were rushed as soon as they were through with them, and an arsenal of guns." Despite his elaborate efforts to steer conversations toward revolution, Bakcsy gained no evidence against Harry Bridges after several months of work.

One fall night, Stanley Doyle appeared at the beach house demanding that Bakcsy sign an affidavit saying "he had seen Bridges at a communist meeting at Steffens's home." Bakcsy refused, but Doyle pressed the point, even producing an affidavit he carried in his pocket. Doyle threatened to have Bakcsy fired from his job with Matson if he did not cooperate. True to his word, when Bakcsy again refused to sign, Doyle carried out his threat. The Matson Navigation Company terminated Bakcsy's undercover work. Even though Bakcsy and Lawrence Milner, too, worked undercover for organizations bent on prosecuting radicals, Doyle proved unable to persuade the men to commit perjury.[23]

Doyle spent much of his time with Harper Knowles of the American Legion's Subversive Activities Committee, as well as Arthur Scott, another undercover agent for several employers' groups, plotting against Bridges and his comrades. After the murder of Chief Engineer George Alberts aboard the *Point Lobos* in Alameda harbor on March 22, 1936, the three undercover agents hatched a plan to frame Earl King, one of Bridges' union supporters, for the crime. King headed the Pacific Coast Marine Firemen, Oilers, Watertenders and Wipers Association (MFOW).

About two weeks later, Arthur Scott met with Colonel Henry R. Sanborn, "the publisher of the rabidly anticommunist newsletter, American Citizen." Sanborn agreed to pay Scott for information on Bridges and for helping construct the frame-up of Earl King. Two days later, Scott, accompanied by Doyle, called on Sanborn for the first payment. Scott continued to be paid for some time afterward, receiving money from both Sanborn and Doyle. In August, five months after the murder, Earl Warren, the Alameda County district attorney, announced that through "undercover work on the waterfront," he had the murderers in custody. "It was a paid killer's job," Warren said, "it was a paid assassination job and the basis of the plot was communistic." While the evidence is not conclusive, it seems that a full four months prior to the arrests of Earl King and his co-defendants, Ernest Ramsay and Frank Conner, Doyle successfully conspired to concoct the union leaders' frame-up. Warren convicted King, Ramsay, and Conner, knowing full well the case against them turned on perjury and manufactured evidence.[24]

In August 1937, Doyle contacted Ernest Ramsay's wife, Gwendolyn. Doyle asked Mrs. Ramsay if she wanted to see her husband released from jail. He also questioned her about Harry Bridges, asking if Bridges, her husband, or Earl King belonged to the Communist Party. She responded that she knew her husband had no connection to the party, she did not think Bridges belonged, and she did not know about King. More importantly, she wanted to know how Doyle could get her husband out of jail. Doyle informed her that all she needed to do "was sign a statement that Harry Bridges was a communist and that she had seen him at communist meetings." Doyle told Mrs. Ramsay, "You won't have to worry about the rest of it, because it will be made out for you. All you have to do is sign it, and then your husband will be released from San Quentin." Mrs. Ramsay wanted to know what authority Doyle had to make such a promise. He was "a secret service man working for the Government," he replied, flashing his gold badge. Wisely, Mrs. Ramsay refused to join in the conspiracy.[25]

A few days later, Doyle invited Mrs. Ramsay to accompany him to San Quentin where the three convicted union men languished behind bars. Mrs. Ramsay had been to the prison numerous times. Always before she had signed in, following prison regulations, but not this time. Doyle greeted the guards as if he knew them, checked his pistol, and led Gwendolyn Ramsay to the captain of the guard's office where Ernest Ramsay joined them. Doyle, introducing himself "as a secret service agent for the Immigration Service and the governors of California and Oregon," offered Ramsay the same deal he had earlier offered Mrs. Ramsay. If Ramsay would sign an affidavit swearing to Bridges' connection to the Communist party, Doyle could arrange his release from prison. The soft-spoken Ramsay instantly declined Doyle's offer. Doyle seemed resigned to defeat but told Ramsay, "if he changed his mind he could reach Doyle through Governor Merriam's office."[26]

On September 30, Doyle returned to San Quentin, this time to see Earl King. Doyle introduced himself, presenting the gold badge, which, King carefully noted, said "Special Agent—State of Oregon," badge number 280. Doyle made King the same offer he had presented to Ramsay:

I have spoken to a number of gentlemen and if you will testify against Bridges, state that you sat in top fraction meetings of the Communist Party at places that I can give you—I will give you the addresses and the dates—we will get you to come up to Oregon. We will have a hearing up there behind closed doors. If you will testify to that your testimony will be very convincing and it will be clinching and we can deport him.

Doyle threatened King with severe consequences if he failed to cooperate, pledging to frame King for another murder. King flatly refused. "Are you crazy?" Doyle asked. Doyle could not fathom a moral man, could not understand a man with conscience and conviction. King explained:

Well, I am about 45 years of age, I have been to a lot of places, and done pretty near everything I wanted to do, had a good time, had good friends. Nobody can make me perjure myself. . . . I am not going to lie against Harry Bridges just to get out of here. I don't care what happens to me now. I have only got my self respect left; I am going to keep that.

Doyle, however, had long before sacrificed his own self respect on the altar of anti-Communism. He left.[27]

Martin carried his vendetta against Bridges and labor all the way to FDR. In a conversation with Roosevelt on September 28, 1937, Martin told the president that "it would be necessary to resort to troops in the near future" to quell the waterfront strikes. Roosevelt finessed the governor, calling "the labor troubles . . . principally growing pains." Martin pressed the point. No, he assured FDR, "they were far more serious than that . . . [and] the principal offender and cause of the controversy [was] Harry Bridges, [an] alien and proven Communist." The president expressed surprise and again assuaged Martin by promising a federal probe.[28] (By 1939, with Martin repudiated in his reelection bid the previous year, the out-of-work spy Stanley Doyle achieved the obscurity he so richly deserved, practicing law in Minnesota. The efforts to deport Harry Bridges, meanwhile, would continue, unsuccessfully, until 1954.)

Doyle exemplified the unethical, illegal aspects of Martin's administration. It cannot be denied that an intent to subvert democracy existed. As dangerous as the threat was, it also had its comic aspects. By 1937, the governor's search for un-American activities had grown so vast, with the number of secret agents increasing exponentially, that his staff frantically attempted to trace and rescind some of the badges. In one case, a special agent's family pleaded with the governor to cancel an appointment. "My brother was appointed Special State Police Officer several months ago by you," wrote Portlander William Schmitz. "My brother has no right to have this power," he said, "as he is irresponsible, inclined to be rattle-headed and is just as apt to shoot somebody for no just reason. So please use your power to cancel this commission given him by you." Worrying about turning on his brother, Schmitz closed the letter by begging Martin to "keep this letter strictly confidential so as to avoid ill feeling on his part."

In another case, a thug named S.A. Mendenhall used his special agent's badge to line his own pocket. He hired out his services as a special agent to collect debts owed to gardeners at the Italian Market in Portland. Eventually police arrested Mendenhall for beating an elderly man with a loaded revolver, charging him with assault and intent to kill.[29]

As the 1938 primary election approached, the forces arrayed against the governor appeared formidable. Even though the AFL leadership plotted with Martin against their CIO counterparts, the rank and file in both unions firmly opposed sending Martin back to Salem for a second term. By joining with organized labor, the Oregon Commonwealth Federation, public power advocates, the grange, citizens seeking relief, veterans, pensioners, and the Pierce faction of the Democratic Party all sought to bring the governor down. Martin even found opposition at home. Louise grew weary of the controversy swirling around her husband. For more than a year, she had badgered Martin to relinquish the fight. She "has been violently opposed to the whole business so that I have had to carry the burdens all alone," Martin complained.

As he campaigned, and indeed throughout his term as governor, Martin aided his opponents by consistently using reckless, inappropriate language usually reserved for raw recruits in basic training. His opponents, and many supporters as well, claimed that he "dug his political grave with his own tongue." Some laid this propensity to the "petulance of old age," but the State Federation of Labor probably came closer to the mark, claiming Martin was "intolerant of the views of opponents, domineering and given to continuous explosions of profanity." Recordings of Martin's radio addresses do not survive, but if former Oregon Senator Mark Hatfield is correct, Martin rarely managed to conclude a broadcast. "They cut him off of any radio speech," Hatfield recalled, "he never finished a radio speech, because he would start swearing." Many voters simply rejected Martin because of his belligerent rhetoric, his repeated threats to resort to state-sponsored force, and because he counseled violence by private citizens.[30]

Martin found formidable opposition to a second term among all factions of the Democratic Party leadership—not only from the Pierce faction, but from those who supported his first election as well. "We are all presumably united behind President Franklin D. Roosevelt," one Democrat said, "and hence, should be united in removing a traitor from his path. . . . It is high time to repudiate Governor Martin who has repudiated Franklin Delano Roosevelt."

The governor had gained the ire of many Democrats by turning a deaf ear to repeated appeals for supplying party patronage. Party leaders demanded that the governor fill all patronage positions with Democrats. Martin, however, had either retained or appointed Republicans in positions Democrats felt should be theirs. The plum appointment—leading the State Highway Commission—Martin gave to a Republican. Among other blunders, he retained Republican Charles Pray as head of the Oregon State Police, staunchly refused to give up Republican Elmer Goudy as state relief administrator, and appointed his old Arlington Club crony D.A. Bulmore, former vice-president of the First National Bank, to the State Unemployment Compensation Commission.

Vernon Williams, prominent editor of the *Oregon Democrat*, blasted the governor in a lead editorial titled: "CHARLES H. MARTIN HAS PROVED TRAITOR TO THOSE BY WHOSE VOTES HE WAS ELECTED." "By word and deed," Williams asserted, "Charles H. Martin has demonstrated that at heart he is not a Democrat, that he never was a Democrat, and that his endorsement of Democratic principles was a pretense and sham."

At the local level, Martin ignored county central committees in making appointments. County Democratic officials labeled him "no ballplayer." In the person of his personal secretary, W.L. Gosslin, the governor set up an almost impenetrable wall between himself and Democratic officials. No one saw the governor without first passing Gosslin's scrutiny. Gosslin, a Democratic outsider, never became familiar with local officials and often summarily turned away important persons who attempted to see the governor. When Martin eventually turned to those officials for support in his reelection, he found them working for his opponent, Henry Hess.[31]

Martin opened the patronage wound almost at the outset of the campaign in January 1938, when Oregon's Republican U.S. Senator, Frederick Steiwer, resigned. Elton Watkins, longtime Democratic activist, former congressman, and solid Martin supporter in 1934, sought the nod as Steiwer's replacement. "I have never asked you for anything," Watkins cabled the governor, "but now I respectfully request to be named Steiwer's successor. . . . [the Pierce crowd was] always against you and are now. . . . My work for you in last election deserves your favorable consideration." Watkins followed up on the telegram with a letter the next day, pleading for the appointment. "You know as well as I that . . . Pierce [has] always been against you, and will do everything in this campaign to hurt you. None of these gentlemen has ever attempted to do anything for you. I did when you needed help."[32]

Watkins attempted to call Martin, then to see him, only to be turned away by Gosslin. He telephoned the governor's executive assistant, Wallace Wharton, evidently in high dudgeon, demanding that Wharton intercede on his behalf. Watkins ranted at Wharton, claiming that he would be "deeply hurt and disappointed" if the appointment went to a candidate Oswald West endorsed. Wharton delivered a redacted version of the phone conversation to Martin, appending his impression. "Message delivered as requested," he wrote, "with the comment that such was the mouthings of a cracked person." Letters and telegrams from local Democratic leaders poured into Martin's office supporting Watkins's nomination. One even suggested that the governor appoint himself to the seat and run for that position in the May primary.

In the end, with a reckless determination that further antagonized party leaders, Martin appointed his old friend Alfred E. Reames, whom he had unsuccessfully attempted to lure into several other appointive positions. Reames, a lawyer and lobbyist for private utility companies, accepted the position. Watkins turned his previous support for Martin to implacable opposition. Initially he announced as a candidate against Martin, but then after conferring with party leaders he threw his support to Martin's other Democratic opponent, Henry Hess, and actively campaigned for him throughout the state. To blunt Watkins' effectiveness, Martin leaked copies of Watkins' pleading letters and telegrams to the *Salem Capital Journal*. In a blistering editorial, the *Capital Journal* chastised Watkins. "Without a blush, Watkins . . . charged that the leader of his party from whom . . . he was begging favors, cannot be elected," the paper scolded.[33]

Martin entrusted the leadership of his reelection effort to Oswald West and campaign manager Edward W. Smith. West, still bedeviled by his past as a lobbyist for the utilities, and Smith, working with Martin's conservative Republican supporters, devised what they considered a fool-proof plan to win the Democratic nomination for the governor. West helped organize Republican "Martin-for-Governor" clubs, urging Republicans to register as Democrats to vote for Martin in the closed primary. The strategy paid off with many Republicans.

"I believe it behooves us Republicans to get behind a sound man," Charles Evans wrote, "as both parties are badly contaminated with the radical element now days." In the Republican camp, leaders praised Martin, giving him credit "for the good work he has done in cleaning house," while others urged fellow Republicans to "vote in the primaries for a conservative

Republican—feeling certain that in the general election—all [conservatives] will elect governor Martin." Campaign manager Smith outraged Democratic leaders by claiming publicly that Martin "would win the republican, as well as the democratic, nomination." Smith insisted on a Republican write-in campaign early in the process, which he later abandoned, but the damage persisted.[34]

In the primary campaign, Martin threw off the liberal New Deal cloak he employed in 1934 to emerge openly as a conservative Hoover Democrat. In dozens of speeches given throughout the state, he stressed law and order. He railed against labor "goons" and "racketeers" to such an extent that he became a caricature of himself, essentially a buffoon, ridiculed by criticism "that he clowned around the state on the issue." Martin donned his anticommunism like a suit of armor to preserve the American form of government—democracy would be redeemed through a vote for "Iron Pants" Martin.[35]

In one of his bolder moves while campaigning, Martin claimed, and rightly so, that during his first four years as governor he led the fight to rid the state of the hated property tax. "The people must be made to realize," Martin told an audience of real estate brokers, "that [government] services cost money. They must be made to realize that government money does not grow on bushes, but comes out of their own pockets." Thus Martin claimed to have upheld his "principal plank" in the 1934 campaign—the "reduction of the tax load on real property." "I have succeeded," he boasted, "in having all property tax for state purposes eliminated for 1938." He decidedly did not boast about the beneficial effects these actions had on his own personal fortune, a fortune based on real estate speculation.[36]

Inevitably, news of the battle in the Democratic primary reached environs far removed from the struggle in Oregon. Having early on in his governorship shed his New Deal disguise, Martin had attracted the enmity of many inside the Roosevelt administration, most prominently Tommy Corcoran, Harold Ickes, Frances Perkins, Harry Hopkins, and, it seems clear, FDR himself. Martin shared this New Dealer enmity with other prominent conservative Democrats targeted by the Roosevelt administration, including "governors, like Albert Ritchie of Maryland and Joseph B. Ely of Massachusetts, Eugene Talmadge of Georgia, and Democratic elder statesmen, like Newton D. Baker." The *New York Times* called Oregon's Martin-Hess battle "a New Deal test race." Postmaster General James Farley attempted to head off the opposition to Martin within FDR's immediate circle, counseling the president to stay out of the Oregon primary at the least, or support Martin if he did decide to intercede in the local election. But Farley, also chair of the Democratic National Committee, already had lost his standing with FDR's advisors and the president. Farley lost out to Ickes and Corcoran, aided by Elton Watkins' hasty trip from Oregon to Washington, D.C.

When word leaked on May 10 that administration officials intended to publicly humiliate Martin by endorsing Hess, Oswald West hastily cabled Postmaster General Farley. "Please," he begged, "is there any truth in this?" Four days later, newly appointed U.S. Senator Reames, too, appealed personally and confidentially to FDR. "I sincerely hope that between now and May 20 you may find it convenient and advisable to say something in the Governor's behalf. . . . All of our supporters are behind the Governor's candidacy. . . . For you to follow the advice of Watkins at this time would, I am sure, be a serious mistake." On May 15, the White House denied Martin's claim that FDR had said to him during the president's 1937 trip to dedicate Bonneville Dam, "You and I made a good pair."[37]

Three days later, on May 18, two days before the primary election, Senator George Norris and Secretary Harold Ickes sent widely publicized letters to Oregon endorsing Hess. Senator Norris, whom FDR once called "the major prophet of American life," lambasted Martin as a "reactionary,"

Martin poses with his friend and supporter Postmaster General James A. Farley at the dedication of a new post office in east Portland, October 16, 1937. *Oregon Historical Society, 018922*

and encouraged farmers to vote for Hess. Ickes wrote that "Martin is at heart no New Dealer." On the same day, Elton Watkins, in a telegram from Washington, D.C., sent after a meeting with Roosevelt arranged by Ickes, claimed that the president "denounced the flagrant attempt of Governor Martin to deceive the people into believing that the New Deal Administration was supporting him." "I went to the White House today," Watkins cabled, "and in the presence of Secretary Ickes shook hands with and talked to the president. It's not proper to quote the president," he added coyly, "but let me say to . . . the Democrats of Oregon that what I heard from the lips of that great Democrat and what I saw in his beaming countenance . . . I knew and now say to you [Hess is] the man the Roosevelt Democrats of Oregon should nominate."[38]

Even with the advance warning, Martin's campaign failed to mobilize. "I was astonished," Martin later claimed, "that in the closing days of the campaign for the primaries in May, and before I could organize my followers against it, to find that the administration, including the President himself, had repudiated me." When Martin did respond, in a hastily arranged radio broadcast, he lashed out at Ickes, Norris, Watkins, and Richard Neuberger as his enemies. Later in the year, in a September meeting with PWA administrator Harry Hopkins, Martin complained bitterly and rather piteously of his shabby treatment by FDR and the president's minions. Repeating his old refrain, Martin told Hopkins that "I had never sought public office . . . I was drafted for Congress in 1930 . . . I was again drafted this time for the governorship . . . [in 1934] it was pointed out to me that I was the only candidate who could carry this state." Almost like the petulant child, unwilling or unable to accept responsibility for his own actions, Martin pleaded his innocence:

> I told Hopkins, I pursued the same policy of loyal, unwavering support, leaving no opportunity escape to express my admiration for the President and his progressive policies. I could not understand how the President could permit a man, . . . that son-of-a-bitch Elton Watkins . . . to be brought into his presence, chaperoned by a member of his cabinet, because it seemed to me that the President should have inquired as to who Watkins was before permitting him to tell lies about a loyal supporter. Had the President so inquired he would have found that Watkins was elected to Congress as a Klu Kluxer in 1922 . . . and that his whole policy is to disrupt and disorganize and that he is the worst type of a Southern hillbilly . . . [who] has so successfully . . . arrayed the administration against me.[39]

Martin claimed to be beset by enemies—a vicious communist conspiracy bent on seizing control of state government:

Hess . . . Elton Watkins . . . [and] Dave Beck of the International Teamsters . . . hatched their conspiracy . . . to buy off the candidates then
running against me so as to concentrate the labor vote, both CIO and
AF of L, and the subversive elements in the state headed by the so-called
Commonwealth Federation, against me, and with liberal finances run
all of these elements into the Democratic party. . . . Hess is now in the
position of being lined up with these destructive subversive elements . . .
which have now seized control of the Democratic party.[40]

The governor's repudiation by the Roosevelt administration proved
decisive as Hess emerged the winner in the primary with a 7,000 vote plurality, beating Martin 59,620 to 52,640, while the Independent O. Henry

Governor and Mrs. Martin cast ballots on election day, 1938. *Oregon Historical
Society, 013165*

Oleen garnered 8,220 votes. In a series of front-page articles devoted to the
results of the Oregon primary—rare treatment for an Oregon race—the *New
York Times* endorsed the analysis of Martin's nemesis Richard L. Neuberger
that Martin's defeat resulted from a "temporary truce between the AFL and
CIO to jointly back Hess . . . [as] decisive in the Portland area."

The intra-party schism left the Democratic party so weakened that Hess
proved to be the "cooked Goose" Martin predicted. The governor exacted
his revenge on his enemies by stoking the fire that cooked Hess. He openly

campaigned for the Republican candidate Charles Sprague against Hess. While denying that he had bolted the party or publicly supported Republicans, Martin told Harry Hopkins, "I was with the sound Democrats . . . but if it was expected of me that I could control the feeling and actions of the intelligent and sound Democrats . . . into supporting Hess they were giving me a power which I did not have and would not exercise even if I did have." The primary had split the Democratic Party, and many of Martin's supporters said that they would vote for the Republican Charles Sprague.[41]

He must have swallowed hard to throw his support to Hess' liberal Republican opponent, Charles Sprague, editor of Salem's *Oregon Statesman*. Sprague "endorsed the administration's public power program and proved far more friendly to Roosevelt than had Martin." Sprague led Republicans back into control of Oregon politics, a position they would hold for more than two decades.[42]

Martin, off balance, searched in vain for vindication from members of the Roosevelt administration. Finally, on Friday, July 15, 1938, Postmaster General James A. Farley telephoned his condolences. "General, how are you?" Farley inquired.

"I'm fine," the governor responded. "I can't tell you how sorry I am . . . I love you devotedly."

Farley interrupted. "I understand the situation entirely," Farley said. "I know how you feel and I want you to know it is reciprocated. I hope to see you soon. I'm glad you are all right. . . . When I have a chance to chat with you I will explain the situation to you."

Martin blurted out, pathetically, "I want you to understand I am a Democrat. You're just fine, Jim. God bless you."

"Goodbye, General," Farley said as he rang off.[43]

Notes

1. Frederick J. Koster, president of the Los Angeles Chamber of Commerce, quoted in David F. Selvin, *Sky Full of Storm* (San Francisco: California Historical Society, 1975), 39.
2. Herbert Resner and Aubrey Grossman, Application for Pardon [1938?], box 1, file "King Ramsay, Conner," Leo Huberman Papers, Special Collections, University of Oregon Library, Eugene, Oregon [UOL].
3. Miriam Feingold, "The King-Ramsay-Conner Case: Labor, Radicalism, and the Law in California, 1936–1941" (Ph.D. diss., University of Wisconsin, 1976), 2, 3.
4. E. Kimbark MacColl, *The Growth of a City: Power and Politics in Portland, Oregon, 1915 to 1950* (Portland: The Georgian Press, 1979), 469.
5. CHM to Walter E. Pearson, May 16, 1935, CHM to Oscar C. Weed, May 21, 1935, Martin T. Pratt to CHM, May 23, 1935, CHM to Martin T. Pratt, May 24, 1935,

CHMC, OHS; Richard L. Neuberger, *Our Promised Land* (New York: The Macmillan Company, 1938), 315.

6. Typescript "Chronology" prepared by the state police, May 28, 1935, CHMC, OHS.
7. Typescript "PROCLAMATION" and typescript record of convictions, CHMC, OHS; Typescript of a statement issued by the governor, November 28, 1936, Governor Martin Papers, State of Oregon Archives [referred to hereafter as Martin Papers]; "Martin Regards Goon Rout Best," *Oregon Journal*, January 1, 1939; Floyd J. McKay, *An Editor for Oregon: Charles A. Sprague and the Politics of Change* (Corvallis: Oregon State University Press, 1998), 73.
8. Typescript of a speech delivered September 11, 1939, Martin Papers.
9. CHM to General Eli A. Helmick, December 18, 1937, Typescript of a radio speech, undated, CHMC, OHS; State police report of investigation of income tax liabilities, October 17, 1938, Martin Papers; radio speech, undated, CHMC, OHS.
10. CHM to General C.R. Howland, November 23, 1937, CHM to Colonel Clarence R. Hotchkiss, December 3, 1936, CHMC, OHS.
11. Transcript of a radio speech, undated [probably November 1937], CHMC, OHS; Statement by Governor Martin at Salem, November 28, 1936, Martin Papers; *Oregonian*, December 7, 1937; CHM to General Nathaniel F. McClure, December 3, 1936, CHM to Colonel Clarence R. Hotchkiss, December 3, 1936, CHMC, OHS.
12. Typescript of a speech by Governor Martin at a Sigma Delta Chi luncheon, January 22, 1938, CHM to General C.R. Howland, March 17, 1937, CHM to General Avery Andrews, December 18, 1937, CHMC, OHS; *Oregonian*, December 18, 1937; CHM to General Avery D. Andrews, November 2, 1936, Martin Papers.
13. *Salem Capital Journal*, February 9, 1935.
14. Norman Ornstein, Andrew Kohut, and Larry McCarthy, *The People, the Press and Politics* (Reading, Massachusetts: Addison-Wesley, 1988), 113.
15. *Oregonian*, August 12, 1930.
16. CHM to LM, September 6, 1900, CHMC, OHS.
17. CHM, "Negro Manpower, Employment in Combatant Units," December 3, 1924, Archives Branch, U.S. Army Military History Institute, Carlisle Barracks, Carlisle, Pennsylvania.
18. See the collections of reports in the Martin Papers at the Oregon Historical Society, and there also is an extensive collection in the City of Portland Archives; Feingold, 633.
19. Several hundred pages of Milner's reports exist in the Martin Papers at the Oregon Historical Society, and hundreds more can be found in the Governor Martin Papers and the Military Department files at the State of Oregon Archives, although several linear feet of records are missing from the Military Department collection. I have been unable to access records from the Oregon State Police and have met significant obfuscation and stone-walling at that agency. No papers from the Oregon State Police are housed at the state archives; James M. Landis, as quoted in Feingold, 615–16.
20. MacColl, 483; Feingold, 614–15; Gerald Gunther, *Constitutional Law* (Mineola, New York: The Foundation Press, Inc., 1985), 1012–13.
21. For a full account of the hearings see, Charles Larrowe, Harry Bridges, and Estolv Ward accounts of the hearing.
22. Feingold, 635–37.
23. Ibid.
24. Ibid., 620, 631; Gary Murrell, "Murder on the *Point Lobos:* A Parallax Conspiracy" (Master's Thesis, University of Oregon, 1990), 9–10.
25. Feingold, 641.
26. Ibid., 643, 642.

27. Ibid., 646, 647–48.
28. Typescript of a conversation between President Roosevelt and Governor Martin, September 28, 1937, Martin Papers.
29. William Schmitz to CHM, February 9, 1937, E.M. Duffy to CHM April 9, 1936, Martin Papers.
30. CHM to General Eli A. Helmick, January 4, 1937, *Oregon Democrat*, January 1953, "Review of the Political Situation in Oregon," compiled by the Executive Board of the Oregon State Federation of Labor, 1938, Martin Papers; Hatfield in *Oregon History Magazine*.2
31. Dr. J.F. Hosch in a typescript record prepared by Wallace Wharton of remarks made at a Democratic candidates' forum, March 11, 1938, CHMC, OHS; *Oregon Democrat*, January 6, 1938.
32. Elton Watkins to CHM, January 27 and 28, 1938, CHMC, OHS.
33. Typescript of a memorandum of telephone communication between Wharton and Watkins, January 28, 1938, Martin Papers; Robert E. Bradford to CHM, January 27, 1938, W.W. Sirrine to CHM, January 28, 1938, J.D. Slater to CHM, January 28, 1938, John S. Hodgin to CHM, January 28, 1938; *Salem Capital Journal*, March 1, 1938, CHMC, OHS.
34. Robert E. Burton, *Democrats of Oregon: The Pattern of Minority Politics, 1900–1956* (Eugene: University of Oregon, 1970), 86; Charles Evans to Solon T. White, April 23, 1938, Leo G. Spitzbart to Solon T. White, April 23, 1938, CHMC, OHS.
35. Duane Hennessy, "Labor Big Factor in Martin's Loss," *Oregonian* [date missing, probably late May or early June 1938], CHMC, OHS.
36. Typescript of a speech by Governor Martin at a regional meeting of real estate brokers, Salem, February 18, 1938, CHMC, OHS.
37. Arthur M. Schlesinger Jr., *The Age of Roosevelt: The Politics of Upheaval* (Boston: Houghton Mifflin Company, 1960), 517, 520, 572–95; McKay, 88; Oswald West to James A. Farley, May 10, 1938, CHMC, OHS; Senator Alfred E. Reames to FDR, May 145, 1938, Martin Papers; *Oregonian*, May 15, 1938, 1.
38. Typescript of a memorandum by CHM abstracting a conference between the governor and PWA administrator Harry Hopkins, September 19, 1938, Martin Papers.
39. Ibid.
40. Ibid.
41. *Oregonian*, "Governor Loses in Blazing Defeat," May 22, 1938, 1; McKay, 88; Burton, 87; conference with Harry Hopkins, September 19, 1938, Martin Papers; *Oregonian*, May 22, 1938.
42. Burton, 87.
43. Typescript memorandum prepared, presumably, by Wallace Wharton of a phone call between James A. Farley and CHM, July 15, 1938, Martin Papers.

Chapter Twelve

OLD SOLDIERS NEVER DIE

The head of the present democratic party speaks without authority for the party or its members. His voice is that of a Stalin with a New York accent.
—Charles Henry Martin

How unlovely to grow old at war with the whole world!
—Charles Henry Martin

FOR MARTIN THE BATTLES went on, only the venue changed over time. He established his war-room in downtown Portland at the Hughes Building. From there he directed a withering attack on the National Labor Relations Board, chastised his gubernatorial successor, kept up his obsessive pursuit of Harry Bridges and other radicals, organized a statewide John Nance Garner for president campaign, and grew increasingly disillusioned with FDR. He finally openly attacked the president as a communist and fascist, and counseled anyone who would listen on the inadvisability of U.S. interference in the growing threat posed by Adolph Hitler in Europe.

Still unable to accept any responsibility for the consequences of his actions, the general traced his troubles with working people and unions to the National Labor Relations Act (NLRA), Frances Perkins, and members of the National Labor Relations Board (NLRB), accusing it of conducting "Kangaroo courts." He said he would like to "kick the pants off the National Labor Relations Board," and asserted that the NLRA (the Wagner Act) should be "wiped off the books."

Martin's xenophobic rhetoric escalated when he thought about the NLRB. Aliens or alien sympathizers—John L. Lewis, Harry Bridges, Dave Beck "et al."—were promoting their un-American program "to deprive us of our individual freedom" and had infiltrated the NLRB, Martin charged. In Martin's conspiracy theory, "they have their strangle hold on us through the National Labor Relations Act, an Act put through Congress by them, and members of the Board are their henchmen." Not even his old colleagues in Congress could stop this juggernaut, Martin believed, because "these yellow-bellied politicians go along with them to get the labor vote which their selfish leaders have intimidated and coerced." As a private citizen once again, Martin made it his goal to help bring down the NLRA and destroy what he believed was a Communist-ridden NLRB.[1]

The NLRB enjoyed mixed support during its first two years of existence, but when the Supreme Court upheld its validity in 1937, the NLRB became a powerful agency. During the 1920s, employers had established company unions as a way to blunt the growing threat of independent labor organizations over which they had no control. Employers allowed workers to elect representatives who consulted with management over worker grievances. Employers kept strict control over these unions, rigidly restricting their activities. When workers finally brought grievances against company unions to the NLRB, however, the board moved to outright ban or reorganize the old organizations to provide autonomy for workers. By 1939, the NLRB had banned 340 company unions and reorganized dozens more. The National Association of Manufacturers and the Chamber of Commerce throughout the country vigorously protested the NLRB's power and used its considerable influence in Congress to eventually replace the NLRA with the less stringent Taft-Hartley Act in 1947.

Martin's battles with Secretary Perkins and the NLRB did not go unnoticed by other opponents of New Deal programs. When the invitations to speak against the NLRB began to pour in to his Hughes Building office, Martin eagerly took up the gauntlet. He traveled to Washington, D.C., early in 1939 to testify against the Wagner Act before a Senate committee. Unable to contain himself, the general lashed out against the New Deal and harangued old colleagues on the House side with conspiratorial prophecies.

"I told [Congresswoman] Mary Norton that in my opinion unless the Wagner Act was amended it would go the way of the prohibition law," he wrote to a Portland attorney, "and that the Act would fall into the hands of the gangsters and racketeers. I told her she had better get over some of her New Deal ideas and learn what was going on in the country." But Martin wanted more than to amend the Wagner Act. "I am quite sure that the best thought on the subject would be the repeal of the whole business," he told T. W. Phillips.[2]

At one of Martin's first speeches, the Portland Chamber of Commerce billed the ex-governor's appearance by using the caption, "Shake Hands with Dynamite." Martin evidently liked the explosive metaphor so much that he used it as he traveled around the country. In speeches before the National Association of Manufacturers in Chicago and Miami, the overwhelming popular reception afforded his message by reactionary audiences began to heal his wounded pride.

At a gathering in Chicago, his comrade in arms General Charles Dawes soothed Martin by claiming that in defeat, Martin "was considered a martyr to a worthy cause . . . that . . . [he] was a lucky man in being beaten the way [he] was." Martin warned his audiences against outright repeal of the Wagner Act "because that," he said, "would be a tactical error, because labor, etc., would consider the repeal of the Act as a direct attack on collective bargaining." Abolition of collective bargaining would be out of reach because of its popularity with workers and "even if Congress passed such [an abolition], the President would veto it to enhance his already strong following in the labor unions. . . . When the President signed the Act he said it was a Magna Charta for labor, and I have no doubt he will not antagonize labor now by even approving [any] amendments."

But there is no doubt Martin ardently desired an end to worker's rights. He commended a program proposed by Portlander A.N. Steele to "Repeal . . . the Wagner Act—lock, stock and barrel," to abolish the NLRB, to make "it illegal for an employer to bargain collectively with his employees," and "making strikes, or such collective action, illegal." Martin did not live to see the punitive alterations to the NLRA enacted in the 1947 Taft-Hartley Act by a Republican Congress by then thoroughly alarmed at the strides achieved by labor during World War II nor the increasingly oppressive legislation directed at radicals of every stripe. We can be assured, however, that the general would have congratulated the Republicans and southern Democrats on a job well done.[3]

Though Martin carried on his crusade against the rights of labor, local politics did not escape his omnipresent gaze. Less than a year after breaking ranks with the Oregon Democratic Party to support Republican Charles Sprague for governor, Martin let no opportunity go by to ridicule his liberal Republican successor. "The more I see of the Governor's actions and the more I read of his 'polly-anna' utterances," Martin wrote to Wallace Wharton, his former executive assistant, "the more I am convinced that he is a sanctimonious fraud."

When a group of Martin's admirers presented the state with a bronze plaque commemorating Martin, the general and his dwindling army of followers found Governor Sprague less than considerate. Sprague followed the suggestion of the new capitol architect to hang the plaque in a ground floor hallway. Salem's *Capital Journal* and other newspapers around the state took Sprague to task. "If the basement ever becomes such a gallery and adorned with plaques of famous Oregonians," the *Journal* opined, "the Martin plaque could be transferred there, but at present, with the memory of his services fresh in the public mind, it deserves a better setting." Never mind, Martin wrote to George Putman, editor of the *Capital Journal,* "the Governor . . . [is a] small envious narrow-minded bigot."[4]

When Governor Sprague sat down with Harry Bridges and other labor leaders in 1940 to discuss ways to build trust between labor and management in wartime industries, Martin put Sprague's conciliatory actions down as cynical political expediency. "For some time," Martin wrote, "Sprague has been courting the labor politicians who during my administration brought such disaster on this state. Of course he is out for votes, not the general welfare of the people." In even more blunt terms, Martin ridiculed

> our "War Governor," . . . our . . . rank prohibitionist and . . . Sunday school teacher. . . . [I]n spite of the warnings of my good friends . . . that our Christian idol, . . . the governor . . . had feet of clay, I did not become suspicious until the closing days of the campaign when he came out against the Labor Regulation Bill. Later, when he became Governor and . . . made a trip to Marshfield to meet Bridges, and made a speech extolling the virtues of the C.I.O., sitting on the platform smiling while I was roasted by these "worthies," I was finally firmly convinced that [I] had his character sized up. . . . Who but a cheap demagogue would [do] such a thing as that with a straight face.[5]

Martin provided no less quarter to his old nemesis Walter Pierce. In 1940 when Congressman Pierce voted against a bill demanding Harry Bridges' deportation, Martin chided the former governor. "I think you made a great mistake in your Bridges vote," Martin scolded. "I frankly tell you that people with whom I have talked do not understand why you should have done this." Pierce fired back an immediate response:

> For my part, I can't understand how you and the other friends in the Legion, who have devoted so much of their lives to law and order, could be for the Alien bill. You have given your life to the preservation of law, order, and due processes. . . . The Alien bill was clearly a "bill of attainder," . . . [which] the Constitution strictly forbids. . . . Read it. General Martin, while you and I sat in the same Congress, we never intentionally voted for an unconstitutional bill. You are a good, game old sport, and if you thought you were wrong, you have got the guts to say it. From my point of view, you are wrong.[6]

As his repudiation by the Roosevelt administration festered, Martin became obsessed with the effort to wrest control of the Democratic Party from his local enemies and nationally from Franklin Delano Roosevelt. Not yet six months out of office, Martin turned his sights to that end. When his former House colleague John O'Connor wrote to feel Martin out on the movement by which "sensible" Democrats could recapture the party, the general had already put his own plans into operation. O'Connor warned that "unless the 'sensible' Democrats take hold—and at once—the Republicans will walk in, in 1940." Claiming that a "Third Term" for Roosevelt "is not the greatest menace—although that will be fatal for our Party," O'Connor feared that FDR would tap "one of the radical crowd, now in the saddle" as his successor. "The predominant issue in 1940 will be the 'New Deal,'" O'Connor warned. "That manufactured slogan will be turned against its creators like 'the ill fed, ill clothed and ill housed one-third,'" Roosevelt "tommyrot."

Agreeing with O'Connor "100%," Martin related FDR's perfidious actions in the 1938 Oregon primaries, then announced his own choice as party leader. "I am satisfied from my knowledge of local conditions that if Roosevelt is re-nominated, this State is gone. You can't beat somebody with nobody; so I have come out for [Vice-President John Nance] Garner."[7]

Martin assumed leadership in Oregon of the movement to capture the Democratic nomination for Vice-President Garner. From his office in the Hughes Building, he feverishly organized Democrats across the state throughout the summer of 1939. In September, however, he had to put the brakes on the organization somewhat because Adolph Hitler's invasion of Poland disrupted Martin's plans. "I have been busy in organizing the Garner campaign here in Oregon," Martin wrote to his brother-in-law, "but now with war talk so rampant, we have thought it advisable to go under slow bell for a time." Indeed, though he did not realize it at the time, World War II had begun.[8]

While serving as governor, Martin had praised Hitler and his "brownshirts" for settling communist labor problems in Germany, but Roosevelt was growing increasingly alarmed at the German dictator's actions. During the Depression, as Americans directed their primary focus at economic recovery, they progressively grew more isolationist. Fearing that the United States would be drawn into a European conflict, especially with Italy's aggression against Ethiopia in 1935, Congress passed a Joint Resolution in August of that year known as the Neutrality Act. The measure stipulated that "upon outbreak or during the progress of war between, or among, two or more foreign states, the President shall proclaim such fact, and it shall thereafter be unlawful to export arms, ammunition, or implements of war from any place in the United States . . . to any port of such belligerent states . . . for the use of a belligerent country. . . . The President, by proclamation, shall definitely enumerate the arms, ammunition, or implements of war, the export of which is prohibited by this Act."[9]

The Neutrality Act represented the old trust in a belief that no foreign power could assault the United States because it was protected by two great oceans. At heart, the act proclaimed that the United States had no outside interests worth defending. "I only hope the people in this country who really do not know what a horrible thing war is will not succeed in getting us into it," Martin wrote proclaiming his support for isolationism. "We should stay home and attend to our own business, worship God and build up a good strong National Defense so that none of these outside Devils would dare combat us." Roosevelt, meanwhile, developed a position at polar opposites to General Martin's stance.[10]

Hitler had continued to show his contempt for international treaties and world opinion throughout the mid to late 1930s. He denounced the Treaty of Versailles, marched his troops into the Rhineland in early 1936, tested his military strength in the Spanish Civil War, absorbed Austria in 1938, peacefully invaded Czechoslovakia in March 1939, concluded a non-aggression pact with the Soviet Union in August, and on September 1, 1939, defying ultimatums by Britain and France, invaded Poland.

In his annual message to Congress on January 4, 1939, President Roosevelt had attempted to arouse public opinion to the necessity for preparedness. "All about us rage undeclared wars—military and economic," the president said. "All about us grow more deadly armaments—military and economic. All about us are threats of new aggression—military and economic." FDR called for the United States to arm itself. He requested an increased appropriation for the armed forces and criticized neutrality legislation because the United States would be unable to help Britain and France.[11]

Oregon Senator Rufus Holman cabled Martin on January 12, requesting that the general comment on the president's message and make recommendations. Four days later, Martin assured Holman that the president's recommendations "are sound." "We may have war forced on us again without having allies to protect us until we can get ready," Martin went on. "When the President can recommend $825,000,000 for relief for five months, a little over $500,000,000 is certainly not very much to ensure the protection of the country in these troubled times." In fact, Martin wanted more money spent on preparedness and criticized FDR's priorities. "The trouble is that we are throwing away so much money on 'Alice In Wonderland' stuff that we have not enough left to do the essential things when a grave emergency arises."

As the War Department implemented Roosevelt's directives for preparedness, Martin lauded the progress. Citing his insider access "as a retired officer" to "sources of information . . . more or less secret or confidential,"

Martin told a Veterans of Foreign Wars gathering that mobilization plans met his specifications. The general saw benefits to conscripting and mobilizing young people. Conscription "would provide a splendid training plan for the youths of the country and besides would provide some employment and take the many youths from our streets and public places who have no employment at present." And in the case that the United States did not go to war, the general recommended military training as "valuable in securing employment in civil life."[12]

When Martin called for moving more slowly on the Garner campaign in September, he wanted to test the waters concerning Roosevelt's popularity. He worried that Roosevelt's supporters would press the president for a third term. He ruminated on what he saw as the destruction of the real Democratic Party—the party of Jackson and Douglas, the conservative Democratic Party—complaining bitterly that "there are a lot of wild-eyed new dealers—rubber stamps—who are in favor of anything that is proposed by that crowd now surrounding the President, and who by the way, are not really Democrats." He saw the threats of war redounding to FDR's benefit. "The President is certainly the luckiest man in the world," Martin complained, "just at the time that his ventures were waning, here this war talk comes up to boost him again."[13]

As summer turned to fall, Martin continued his work on Garner's behalf. He waffled now though, not sure if other Democrats would see his actions as public criticism of the president. "Don't get any idea that this is a . . . spite campaign against the President . . . [or] a campaign against the administration or the fine progressive laws which it has placed on the Statute books," he wrote disingenuously to some fellow Democrats. "We are presuming that the President will follow his predecessors in not seeking a third term . . . [and] we Democrats have an obligation to our Party . . . to select a logical successor . . . who can lead us to victory."

When the general castigated the president at a Eugene rally, employing what Mark Hatfield has called Martin's "very earthy language," the business manager at the Eugene Hospital and Clinic, who had previously supported Martin, washed his hands of the general. "Yes it is true," Marvin Warlick wrote, "that many cheered you and had good strong laughs but later some of these same men stated that you had soured and could never expect to get any where with your present attitude. It is easy to criticize and cuss the man who made possible the Willamette Valley Project," Warlick scolded Martin, "but that does not solve our problems. . . . That night you convinced me that you were done for." Martin noted in the letter's margin, "unanswered."[14]

Undaunted, Martin kept up his push for Garner, refining his message for palatability among wavering Democrats by simply standing up for opposition to a Roosevelt third term. By March 1940, his initial optimism that FDR would not run for president again faded considerably. In private he leveled broadsides at FDR. "I am very much discouraged at the outlook," he wrote. "Our people seem to be crazy over Roosevelt. Why, knowing him as I do, is difficult to understand. They simply don't know the man." How dare Roosevelt assume that he knew better than Washington and Jefferson, Martin claimed didactically. "No man is essential in a democracy. Only in dictatorships is that the case. The most sacred tradition in this country is opposition to a third term, the dangers of which were pointed out in the beginning by Washington and Jefferson whose teachings in this respect heretofore have been violated only by Republicans, Grant and Theodore Roosevelt," he claimed. Violating "this sacred tradition" would lead the United States down the road of the banana republics where the only way to get rid of a president "is by assassination or revolution."[15]

Throughout the latter part of 1939 and into the early months of 1940, Martin interspersed his work for Garner with speeches urging that the United States stay out of the war in Europe. Relying on emotions exhibited by his carefully selected audiences, he claimed to "discover no war sentiment here. The general feeling among people here is we must let the Europeans settle their dispute." But Martin did not trust the electorate to identify the problem for themselves; after all, "the average citizen appears to have lost that most important and outstanding virtue of Americanism as we used to understand it, namely, independence of thought and action," so he pointed out the dangers. "There are many conditions in our country which should cause you thought for the future," Martin told one audience.

At home, "the foreign red and the domestic yellow are alike . . . inimical to our free institutions," he said allowing his inveterate racism and xenophobia to creep into the rhetoric. Abroad, "no thoughtful person can escape the conviction that the interests of the United States . . . are terribly involved in the European struggle." Whether the United States sent troops overseas or not, "the basic conditions of our life—economic certainly, and perhaps social and political—are endangered." What to do? "The important task is for us to determine what procedure is best for America and for the western civilization of which we are a part." World War I had proved the fallacy of sending American soldiers to Europe, Martin said assuredly. Should people be surprised? No, because "war is the normal state of man in spite of all the wistful thinking of pacifists," the general asserted. "Our policy," he concluded "should be to prevent these European wars if we can, and otherwise to stand aside while the nations of Europe find their own destiny . . . stand aside if for no other reason than that one strong western nation may be left to preserve the flame of civilization and to lead the way from the chaos that will come to Europe if this war goes on. Somewhere among us that flame must be kept burning."[16]

Eight days later Martin continued his series of "patriotic speeches in the state . . . to arouse the latent patriotism of real Americans and get them to realize how far along the road we have traveled toward collectivism." He claimed public-spirited motives. To the Democratic Women's League he declared that "we are not here . . . to in any manner express any disrespect to President Roosevelt, or to make any attack upon him." But, he said, "there is a difference between the President, a hard working man doing his best, and some of the people who have slipped into subordinate position in Washington." At a convention of bakers held at the Multnomah Hotel, Martin implied that Roosevelt was unaware of the actions of his subordinates. He blasted the "impertinent, petty" Harold Ickes for interfering in the 1938 election and repudiated Secretary of Labor Frances Perkins derisively, "God forbid I should speak with disrespect or slightingly of the lady who, shall we say, is so inept in the Department of Labor of the United States." Without missing a beat, Martin then linked Ickes and Perkins to a group of Communists who had disrupted a White House gathering.

> There isn't a man or woman in the City of Portland, even though they differ honestly on some questions, who would show disrespect to our President. No matter how you disagree with him, you respect the high office he holds and respect the individual who holds that office. Not so a month ago. A month ago the Communists took a little band of misguided young people who went down to Washington, trained and primed to accept the hospitality of our nation, to assemble on the very White House lawn and to insult our President, your President, and mine, our President, in the midst of his speech, with cat calls and jeers. I tell you, as Good Americans, we are not going to have Ickes or anybody like him subject another President to insults by young Communists in this land.[17]

By now, though he refused to say so publicly, Martin had come to the conclusion that FDR constituted a danger to the continued existence of the republic. "I went along with the New Deal at first," an exasperated Martin complained, "but with its objections and leadership development, I am through with it." The general lashed out about his open frustration with his fellow citizens. "How long is it going to take to have the people snap out of the present 'humanitarian bunk'?" FDR "emptied our treasury, loaded our country with a back-breaking debt, but worst of all, has brought a wrong philosophy of life." The country must make a "complete about-face, and go back to the practice of the hardy virtues which [have] made this a great Nation."

Martin moaned that citizens besotted with FDR who were "hell-bent on the President, who they feel will keep us out of war" were suffering from delusion. "As a matter of fact, from my personal acquaintance with him, I know of no one in the country with his temperament who would sooner put us into the war." Martin wanted to mobilize his fellow-minded comrades into "an army of people who practice the hardy virtues, pride, courage, initiative, self-reliance, and hard honest work," to "take control of this country" and to take the nation out of the hands of "the fifth column, with its crowd of whiners, self-pitiers and loafers, enforced by the vicious." General Martin wanted to lead this army and ignite a revival of patriotism that would sweep FDR and his sycophants out of power, but his actions thus far had failed to produce a following. He wanted to lead "right thinking" people in a crusade to save civilization. "I feel the United States is now in the greatest crisis of its history, with its people demoralized through the inroads of the so-called fifth column." When would the public recognize that men like Martin and Charles Lindbergh, whose vision provided "the clarion call," offered true salvation to "patriots" and "the un-thinking masses"?[18]

Charles Lindbergh, promoting isolationism, parlayed his status as an aviation hero into a prominent position with the America First Committee, one of several hundred isolationist groups formed by 1940. Lindbergh early on concluded that the United States, not yet even in the war, could not win it. When encouraging a negotiated peace in Europe with Hitler in 1941, he claimed that if the United States entered the war, "it would mean the end of democracy on this side of the Atlantic." Lindbergh eventually claimed that "the three most important groups which have been pressing this country toward war are the British, the Jewish, and the Roosevelt Administration."

In May 1940, Martin extolled Lindbergh's virtues, expressing the hope that his friend Robert Ruhl of the Medford *Mail Tribune* had "thoroughly reread and digested that wonderful speech of Lindbergh. . . . We must listen to . . . such a man." By August, when General John J. Pershing contradicted Lindbergh in a radio address of his own, Martin turned on the aviation hero. "Timed as it was," he wrote Pershing, "your . . . strong, admirable, radio address . . . was a knock-out blow to Lindbergh. How foolish for a single-tracker like Lindbergh whose reputation is founded solely on one great exploit, to attempt to assume leadership in this great National Crisis! It is beyond comprehension," Martin wrote disingenuously.[19]

When the public did not rally to his banner, Martin, as always, assigned the cause for this failure elsewhere, blaming the other, the foreigner, the dangerous outsider. "I am very much discouraged at the lack of public interest in a patriotic revival here in Portland, . . . especially a revival of love of our country, just as it is, in which all will join, poor and rich," an anguished Martin wrote. "These great masses of unassimilated foreigners in our great cities, all ruled by corrupt rings, whose only thought is of their own selfish interest . . . [are] a danger to our country. These are not the places to look for patriotism. You have to go to the smaller towns and the countryside to find . . . the hardy virtues with an attendant genuine spiritual and moral revival."[20]

During the spring and summer of 1940, FDR maintained a coy silence on a third term. Garner and Postmaster General Farley, whom Ickes and Corcoran forced out of the administration, both openly coveted the nomination but neither managed to gain enough supporters to carry them to the convention. FDR's political managers saw to it that the president's name appeared in numerous state primaries, in all of which Roosevelt won overwhelming victories. Finally, in July, the Democratic convention renominated Roosevelt on the first ballot. Martin must have been particularly galled when FDR dumped Garner from the ticket as the vice presidential candidate, choosing the progressive Henry Wallace in his place. Martin claimed that FDR hoped "to build up . . . strength from 'across the tracks' . . . the same kind of class warfare in this country which ruined LaBelle France." The general had accepted defeat two months prior to the convention. When writing to his brother-in-law he admitted, "our campaign for Garner here in Oregon was ruined by Hitler; not that we ever had any hope of carrying the state, but we could have made a much better showing if this war hysteria had not been present."[21]

The Republicans chose their ticket in Philadelphia prior to the Roosevelt love-fest in Chicago. Wendell Willkie, a former Democrat turned Republican, won the nod over early favorites Thomas E. Dewey, Robert Taft, and Senator Arthur Vandenberg. Willkie picked Martin's Bonneville promotion partner, Oregon's senior senator Charles McNary, as his running mate. The Republican platform denounced the New Deal, promised to amend New Deal reforms, opposed U.S. entry into any foreign war, and demanded a constitutional amendment to limit presidents to a maximum of two terms. By the end of July, Martin made the decision to turn on Roosevelt and support Willkie. He felt his decision showed "courage, independence and patriotism." For the time being, though, he decided to work clandestinely. "I should keep them guessing, with a statement that I am still 'licking my wounds,'" he said of the Oregon Commonwealth Federation, acknowledging its role in his defeat. "Of course, I want to do all I can to help Willkie but I must do it in the most effective manner possible. To come out too soon publicly would cause the Commonwealth Federation and Rooseveltians . . . to switch its fire on me, as an old reactionary sorehead . . . and bolter."[22]

Surreptitiously Martin went to work organizing Democrats for Willkie, once again claiming altruistic motives. "I intend to remain a Democrat," he wrote Robert Ruhl of the Medford *Mail Tribune*, "and work for the cleansing of the Party to the best of my ability." When Republicans pressed him to come out in the open with his support, Martin steadfastly maintained that after consulting with "many of my friends, . . . at present it would be a mistake for me to come out publicly." He claimed countless times, more to assure himself than to assuage the doubts of others, that the "wild-eyed Rooseveltians" would portray him "as a sore-head and a bolter and that my action was dictated by the peevishness of an old man beaten in the recent primary." Nothing he could say of course could mask the truth at the heart of the statement.[23]

After seizing Poland in September 1939, Hitler positioned his forces westward along the Siegfried Line opposite to the French and British allies huddled behind the Maginot Line. In May 1940, the Nazi blitzkrieg swept over Holland, Belgium, and Luxembourg. France surrendered on June 22, 1940. Martin blamed the fall of France on French radicals whom he declared had provided too many "rights" for their people. The French people became demoralized, Martin said, because the French government "advocated all the rights of the people—rights to their jobs, rights to their unemployment insurance, rights to their old age pensions, right of an abundant life—stressed all these things but had nothing to say about their duties and their obligations to their Government or to their Nation." Martin scoffed at notions of class domination in France and the United States. "Then there was the cry that the people were all working for the two hundred families which controlled the wealth of France. You remember," he told a military colleague, "we have only sixty-nine families in this country for which we are working." Martin felt that "to bring out and accentuate this miserable class warfare . . . is so ruinous to the strength of any Nation."[24]

Roosevelt, fully cognizant of the Nazi military threat, realized he must take action to support Britain in her lone stand against the Axis powers. During the late summer of 1940, FDR opened secret negotiations with London for the lease of military bases in British territories in the Western Hemisphere. This "rental" agreement called for the United States to provide fifty overage but fully functional destroyers to help strengthen the British navy. When the two countries consummated the lease arrangement on September 2, 1940, the United States received, in exchange for the fifty destroyers, a ninety-nine year lease for bases in the Bahamas, Jamaica, St. Lucia, Trinidad, Antigua, and British Guiana. The next day FDR justified the arrangement:

> The value to the Western Hemisphere of these outposts of security is beyond calculation. Their need has long been recognized by our country, and especially by those primarily charged with the duty of charting and organizing our own naval and military defense. They are essential to the protection of the Panama Canal. . . . For these reasons I have taken advantage of the present opportunity to acquire them.[25]

While isolationists throughout the country denounced Roosevelt's action as a violation of the Neutrality Act, Martin saw even more sinister motives lurking just under the surface. Congress must not adjourn, Martin warned Oregon Senator Rufus Holman. "We have seen in the past few months actions that parallel the dictatorial actions found abroad, . . . [that] strike a blow at the very heart of our form of government." If Congress adjourned, Martin went on, "having rendered us dangerously close to war . . . [the] radio crooner in the White House" could "create any situation he desired to create." Consumed by his own demons, Martin wanted Roosevelt not in the White House but in the Fairview Home for the mentally deranged in Salem. "It must be borne in mind that any man who has suffered from infantile paralysis and recovered therefrom has brain lesions," Martin babbled to Senator Holman. "Under stress and strain . . . [the lesions] may cause unbalanced actions of the most dangerous character. You can confirm this by consulting with any prominent authority on the mechanics of the brain." In fact, according to Martin, FDR already had exhibited symptoms of his mental instability. "If you will recall the words of his acceptance of the Democratic nomination, you will detect evidence of delusion characteristic of such a mental condition. The doctrine of indispensability is merely one of the forms." There is no record of a reply from Senator Holman.[26]

The general's anger, frustration, and outright hatred and envy of Roosevelt eventually drove him to publicly campaign against FDR. As the 1940 presidential campaign drew to a close, Martin presented a series of speeches ostensibly promoting the thrust of the Willkie campaign—i.e., "No Third Term"—then in its waning days. Willkie declared October 23, 1940, as "National No Third Term Day."

Martin concentrated on Democratic voters. "I am a Democrat, but not a New Dealer," he thundered, confirming Ickes' analysis. "I feel this administration has abandoned the principles of the Democratic Party and has substituted . . . National Socialism sneaking in the back door as in Germany."

Roosevelt was a devil that Democrats should repudiate: "shove the tempter behind us." FDR and those around him had as their purpose a communistic plan to "break our nation up into classes so the group in power can play each class against the other." But "there is no need for such division into classes," the general claimed. "In fact we have grown great as a nation because there have been no class lines." With the will of the people broken, FDR would create "a regimentation of the worst possible type." He would be a Hitler, forcing "a form of National Socialism which is the logical result of the trends developed in our National Government in the past few years." Democrats must forget party divisions, Martin said. "This is not a contest between the Republican and Democratic parties . . . [the] issue is Americanism against demagoguery and destruction . . . [manifested] in the iniquity of the New Deal. We [have] helped to create a monster which must be destroyed before it [turns] on us." After comparing FDR to Hitler and Judas Iscariot, Martin then turned to what he considered the ultimate charge, connecting FDR to the "Red menace." Beware the melodious voice of the "radio crooner," Martin warned, that voice is malevolent, that voice emanates from a "Trojan Horse," that voice soothes to deceive. "His voice," the outraged general brayed, "is that of a Stalin with a New York accent."[27]

On election day, the popularity of Roosevelt and the specter of war led Democrats to remain loyal to the president. Martin felt repudiated once more. For the first time in U.S. history, the voters had decided to give a sitting president a third term. Martin "cast another vote with the Republicans . . . and did what I could to cut . . . [FDR's] majority." Contradicting himself in hindsight, Martin claimed that Willkie never had a chance in Oregon because "Republicans refused to vote for Willkie on account of his having been a Democrat." The general lamented Roosevelt's deviousness: FDR had allowed so many people to claim relief under the New Deal that Willkie never had a chance. "I never had any idea that Willkie could win against 12 million Government checks a month, the city machines, and those living on taxpayers' money."[28]

The tempo of change quickened after Roosevelt's third victory. The United States did indeed enter the war with overwhelming support from the American people and history swept past the anachronistic Martin. The labels that he so dreaded—"reactionary sore-head and bolter"—stuck to him. Beginning the ninth decade of life, his health failing, Martin retired from active pursuits. Louise finally had her husband to herself. Together they tended the garden at their home in Portland's west hills. Other than his family, Martin turned to his cronies at the Arlington Club to succor his reactionary views. During the last two years of his life, he lost even the joys of the club as he lay almost completely bedridden with a lingering fatal illness.

Louise and Charles Martin celebrate the general's 80th birthday with friends at the Arlington Club, 1943. *Oregon Historical Society, 004881*

He maintained a sporadic correspondence with his former assistant, Wallace Wharton, then serving in the office of the chief of Naval Operations in Washington, D.C. Even though bedridden and dying, Martin could not give up the habits of a lifetime. The old hatreds still rankled. Having been defeated by Franklin Roosevelt and unable to strike any effective blows at the president, Martin turned his vitriol on the president's wife, Eleanor.

"Your letters to me have been classic," Wharton wrote. "I have taken the liberty of quoting from them to some of our reliable friends. You express our opinions exactly." Wharton and Martin chortled over Eleanor's "petting the black boys." The South "is greatly disturbed," Wharton reported, "because of the reaction among the niggers." Here at last, Wharton and Martin believed, FDR might yet have his "birds [come] home to roost with a vengeance. . . . Perhaps the Great I Am will pay dearly for Lady Eleanor's jaunts about the country and her inanities." Already several southern states had refused to contribute money to the Democratic National Committee because they disapproved of Mrs. Roosevelt's stirring up of racial trouble, appearing in public with "black bucks." With racial animosity increasing in the South, "the pickling brine gets stronger and more odiferous," Wharton wrote. "It is a sweet smelling kettle of fish."[29]

Martin perhaps breathed easier after Roosevelt died on April 12, 1945. But the relief brought no joy. The general fought on for a while, at war with his own body, but finally met FDR on an equal footing on September 22, 1946. In an obituary, the *Oregonian* rhapsodized on Martin's republican ideals, his battles to see that "neither demagogue nor charlatan ever should rise to control of the nation. . . . What a full life he lived! And how generously he lived it—for this is the measure of fullness . . . constant in purpose, until at length the veil fell over his eyes and he awakened, while his friends said with sorrow, 'The General is dead.'"[30]

Notes

1. *Oregonian*, December 18, 1937; CHM to L.O. Bird, December 29, 1939, CHMC, OHS.
2. CHM to Nicholas Jaureguy, August 3, 1939; CHM to T.W. Phillips Jr., February 18, 1940, CHMC, OHS.
3. Jay W. McCune to CHM, August 28, 1939; CHM to Mrs. Nelson Reed, November 22, 1939; CHM to T.W. Phillips Jr., February 18, 1940; CHM to A.N. Steele, March 11, 1940; A.N. Steele to CHM, March 8, 1940, CHMC, OHS.
4. CHM to Wallace Wharton, October 5, 1939, CHMC, OHS. *Salem Capital Journal*, October 21, 1939; CHM to George Putman, October 17, 1939, CHMC, OHS.
5. CHM to John T. Russell, April 16, 1940; John T. Russell to CHM, April 10, 1940; CHM to L.L. Staley, October 27, 1939; CHM to William G. Hare, April 29, 1942, CHMC, OHS.
6. CHM to Walter M. Pierce, September 12, 1940, CHMC, OHS.
7. John O'Connor to CHM, July 4, 1939; CHM to John O'Connor, July 14, 1939, CHMC, OHS.
8. CHM to L.L. Staley, September 15, 1939, CHMC, OHS.
9. Thomas G. Paterson, ed., *Major Problems in American Foreign Policy, Volume II: Since 1914* (Lexington, Massachusetts: D.C. Heath and Company, 1989), 169–70.
10. CHM to Sam Running, September 29, 1939, CHMC, OHS.
11. Oscar Theodore Barck Jr. and Nelson Manfred Blake, *Since 1900: A History of the United States in Our Times* (New York: Macmillan Publishing Co., Inc., 1974), 420–21.
12. Rufus C. Holman to CHM, January 12, 1939; CHM to Rufus C. Holman, January 16, 1939; CHM to R.H. Ringle, September, 9, 1939, CHMC, OHS.
13. CHM to L.L. Staley, September 15, 1939, CHMC, OHS.
14. CHM to Mrs. Sam Taylor, September 15, 1939; CHM to George Putman, September 13, 1939; Marvin T. Warlick, September 10, 1939; CHM to Miss Nadine Strayer, October 11, 1939; CHM to Mrs. Nelson Reed, November 22, 1939, CHMC, OHS.
15. CHM to L.L. Staley, March 21, 1940, CHMC, OHS.
16. CHM to Rufus Holman, September 30, 1939; Typescript of remarks addressed to a baker's convention at the Multnomah Hotel, Portland, April 9, 1940; Typescript of a speech delivered to the Progressive Business Men's Club, Benson Hotel, Portland, April 4, 1940, CHMC, OHS.
17. CHM to L.L. Staley, May 6, 1940; Baker's convention speech, April 9, 1940, CHMC, OHS.

18. CHM to L.L. Staley, May 6, 1940; CHM to Wallace S. Wharton, May 22, 1940; CHM to L.L. Staley, May 29, 1940; CHM to Robert Ruhl, May 21, 1940, CHMC, OHS.

19. Barck Jr. and Blake, 435–36; CHM to John J. Pershing, August 20, 1940, CHMC, OHS.

20. CHM to J.H. Raley, June 24, 1940; CHM to L.L. Staley, May 29, 1940, CHM to Raley, CHMC, OHS.

21. CHM to Mr. Tugman, July 25, 1940; CHM to L.L. Staley, May 29, 1940, CHMC, OHS.

22. CHM to Mr. Tugman, July 25, 1940; CHM to Dick Tullis, August 14, 1940, CHMC, OHS.

23. CHM to Wallace Wharton, August 30, 1940, CHMC, OHS.

24. CHM to C.A. Robertson, January 16, 1941, CHMC, OHS.

25. FDR to Congress as quoted in Barck Jr. and Blake, 428.

26. CHM to Rufus Holman, September 26, 1940, CHMC, OHS.

27. Allan Valentine to CHM, October 20, 1940; Typescript of speech, October 23, 1940; Typescript of an undated speech, CHMC, OHS.

28. CHM to Richard B. Wigglesworth, December 30, 1940; CHM to L.L. Staley, December 7, 1940, CHMC, OHS.

29. Wallace S. Wharton to CHM, April 9 and June 23, 1943, July 25, 1944, Governor Martin Papers, State of Oregon Archives.

30. Typescript of an obituary prepared by Samuel Holly Martin, undated, CHMC, OHS.

BIBLIOGRAPHY

UNPUBLISHED SOURCES

Archival Collections

Charles Henry Martin Collection, Oregon Historical Society, Portland, Oregon.

Governor Martin Papers, Archives of the State of Oregon, Salem, Oregon.

Grayville Historical Society, Records of White County, Illinois.

Leo Huberman Papers, Special Collections, University of Oregon Library, Eugene, Oregon.

Lawrence T. Harris Collection, Lane County Historical Society, Eugene, Oregon.

National Archives, Records Groups: 94, Box 1097; 165, Records of the War Department General and Special Staffs, War Plans Division, General Correspondence, 1920–42, Box 10, 73; 98, Panama Canal Department, 1915–39, Box 3, 42.

"Red Squad," Archives of the City of Portland, Oregon.

U.S. Army Military History Institute, Archives Branch, Carlisle Barracks, Carlisle, Pennsylvania. Allen J. Greer, to Assistant Commandant, General Staff College, April 13, 1920; Robert C. Humber, "Notes on Employment of Colored Troops," Historical Section, Army War College, 1942; Harry B. Jordan, "Negro Manpower Employment in Combatant Units," December 3, 1924, Prepared for the Army War College; Charles Henry Martin to Colonel H.A. Smith, April 6, 1920, typescript report; U.S. Army War College, "Employment of Negro Man Power in War," November 10, 1925. File 127–25.

Thesis and Dissertations

Feingold, Miriam. "The King-Ramsay-Conner Case: Labor, Radicalism, and the Law in California, 1936–1941." Ph.D. diss., University of Wisconsin-Madison, 1976.

Murrell, Gary. "Murder on the *Point Lobos:* A Parallax Conspiracy." MA thesis, University of Oregon, 1990.

_____. "Perfection of Means, Confusion of Goals: The Military Career of Charles Henry Martin." Ph.D. diss., University of Oregon, 1994.

Published Sources

Books, Pamphlets, and Government Reports

Ambrose, Stephen E. *Duty, Honor, Country: A History of West Point*. Baltimore: The Johns Hopkins Press, 1966.

Army War College, Historical Section. *Order of Battle of the United States Land Forces in the World War American Expeditionary Forces*. Washington D.C.: U.S. Government Printing Office, 1931.

Auerbach, Jerold S. *Labor and Liberty: The La Follette Committee and the New Deal*. Indianapolis and New York: The Bobbs-Merrell Company, Inc., 1966.

Barbeau, Arthur E., and Florette Henri. *The Unknown Soldiers: Black American Troops in World War I*. Philadelphia: Temple University Press, 1974.

Barck, Oscar Theodore, Jr., and Nelson Manfred Blake. *Since 1900: A History of the United States in Our Times*. New York: Macmillan Publishing Co., Inc, 1974.

Beisner, Robert L. *Twelve against Empire: The Anti-Imperialists, 1898–1900*. New York: McGraw-Hill Book Company, 1968.

Bemis, Samuel Flagg. *A Diplomatic History of the United States*. New York: Henry Holt and Company, 1942.

Bone, Arthur H. *Oregon Cattleman/Governor Congressman: Memoirs and Times of Walter M. Pierce*. Portland: Oregon Historical Society, 1981.

Boorstin, Daniel J., ed. *An American Primer*. Chicago: The University of Chicago Press, 1966.

Brandegee, Senator Frank B. *Report of the Committee on Alleged Executions without Trial in France*. Washington, D.C.: U.S. Government Printing Office, 1923.

Brinkley, Alan. *Voices of Protest: Huey Long, Father Coughlin, and the Great Depression*. New York: Vintage Books, 1983.

Brown, Richard C. *The Social Attitudes of American Generals, 1898–1940*. New York: Arno Press, 1979.

Bullard, Robert Lee. *Personalities and Reminiscences of the War*. New York: Doubleday, Page and Company, 1925.

Burton, Robert E. *Democrats of Oregon: The Pattern of Minority Politics, 1900–1956*. Eugene: University of Oregon, 1970.

Coffman, Edward M. *The War to End All Wars*. New York: Oxford University Press, 1968.

Commager, Henry Steele, ed. *Documents of American History*. New York: Merideth Corporation, 1968.

Congressional Record (1890, 1902, 1931–34).

Curti, Merle. *The Roots of American Loyalty*. New York: Antheneum, 1968.

Daggett, A.S. *America in the China Relief Expedition*. Kansas City: Hudson-Kimberly Publishing Company, 1903.

Dalfiume, Richard M. *Desegregation of the U.S. Armed Forces: Fighting on Two Fronts, 1939–1953*. Columbia: University of Missouri Press, 1969.

Dietrich, William. *Northwest Passage: The Great Columbia River*. New York: Simon and Schuster, 1995.

Dodds, Gordon B. *Oregon: A History*. New York: W.W. Norton and Company, 1977.

Dolan, Edward F. *Panama and the United States: Their Canal, Their Stormy Years*. New York: Franklin Watts, 1990.

Dowd, Jerome. *The Negro in American Life*. New York: The Century Co., 1926.

Drinnon, Richard. *Facing West: The Metaphysics of Indian Hating and Empire Building*. New York: Schocken Books, 1990.

Duberman, Martin. *In White America*. New York: Signet Books, 1964.

Duiker, William J. *Cultures in Collision: The Boxer Rebellion*. San Rafael, California: Presidio Press, 1978.

Edson, Christopher H. *The Chinese in Eastern Oregon, 1860–1890*. San Francisco: R and E Research Associates, 1974.

Encyclopedia Britannica. 1960 ed., s.v. "Illinois."

Esherick, Joseph W. *The Origins of the Boxer Uprising*. Berkeley: University of California Press, 1987.

Farnsworth, David N., and James W. McKenney. *U.S.-Panama Relations, 1903–1978: A Study in Linkage Politics*. Boulder: Westview Press, 1983.

Faust, Karl Irving. *Campaigning in the Philippines*. San Francisco: The Hicks-Judd Company Publishers, 1899.

Ferrell, Robert H. *Woodrow Wilson and World War I, 1917–21*. New York: Harper and Row, Publishers, 1985.

Fleming, Peter. *The Siege at Peking*. Oxford: Oxford University Press, 1983.

Foner, Jack D. *Blacks and the Military in American History: A New Perspective*. New York: Praeger Publishers, 1974.

"Fourteenth Biennial Report of the Adjutant General of the State of Oregon to the Governor and Commander-in-Chief for the Years 1913–1914." Twenty-eighth Legislative Assembly, State of Oregon Press, 1915.

Franklin, John Hope. *From Slavery to Freedom: A History of Negro Americans*. New York: Alfred A. Knopf, 1980.

Franklin, John Hope, and Isidore Starr, eds. *The Negro in 20th Century America*. New York: Vintage Books, 1967.

Funigiello, Philip J. *Toward a National Power Policy: The New Deal and the Electric Utility Industry, 1933–1941*. Pittsburgh: University of Pittsburgh Press, 1973.

Ganoe, William Addleman. *The History of the United States Army*. New York: D. Appleton-Century Company, 1942.

Gentry, Curt. *Frame-up*. New York: W.W. Norton and Company, Inc., 1967.

Giles, Lancelot. *The Siege of the Peking Legations: A Diary*. Edited with an introduction by L.R. Merchant Nedlands. Western Australia: University of Western Australia Press, 1970.

Ginger, Ray. *Age of Excess: The United States from 1877–1914*, Second Edition. Prospect Heights, Illinois: Waveland Press, Inc., 1989.

Goldstein, Robert Justin. *Political Repression in Modern America*. Boston: G.K. Hall and Co., 1978.

Goodwyn, Lawrence. *The Populist Moment: A Short History of the Agrarian Revolt in America*. Oxford: Oxford University Press, 1978.

Gould, Lewis L. *The Spanish-American War and President McKinley*. Lawrence: University Press of Kansas, 1982.

Gray, J. Glenn. *The Warriors: Reflections on Men in Battle*. New York: Harcourt, Brace and Company, 1959.

Gunther, Gerald. *Constitutional Law*. Mineola, New York: The Foundation Press, Inc., 1985.

Hamby, Alonzo, ed. *The New Deal: Analysis and Interpretation*. New York: Weybright and Talley, 1969.

Healy, David. *U.S. Expansionism: The Imperialist Urge in the 1890s*. Madison: University of Wisconsin Press, 1970.

History of White County, Illinois. Chicago: Inter-State Publishing Company, 1883.

Hoover, Herbert. *The Memoirs of Herbert Hoover: Years of Adventure, 1874–1920*. New York: The Macmillan Company, 1951.

Huberman, Leo. *Free These Three*. San Francisco: King-Ramsay-Conner Defense Committee, n.d.

Jamison, Stuart. *Labor Unionism in American Agriculture*. Washington, D.C.: U.S. Government Printing Office, 1954.

Jones, Manfred, ed. *American Foreign Relations in the Twentieth Century*. New York: Thomas Y. Crowell Company, 1967.

Just, Ward. *Military Men*. New York: Avon Books, 1970.

Karnow, Stanley. *In Our Image: America's Empire in the Philippines*. New York: Random House, 1989.

Karp, Walter. *The Politics of War: The Story of Two Wars which Altered Forever the Political Life of the American Republic, 1890–1920*. New York: Harper and Row, Publishers, 1979.

Katcher, Leo. *Earl Warren: A Political Biography*. New York: McGraw-Hill Book Company, 1967.

King-Ramsay-Conner Defense Committee. *Not Guilty! The Ship Murder Frame-Up*. San Francisco: King-Ramsay-Conner Defense Committee, n.d.

_____. *Punishment without Crime: An Unfinished Story.* San Francisco: King-Ramsay-Conner Defense Committee, n.d.

_____. *The Ship Murder: The Story of a Frame-up.* San Francisco: King-Ramsay-Conner Defense Committee, n.d.

Kitchel, Denison. *The Truth about the Panama Canal.* New Rochelle: Arlington House-Publishers, 1978.

Kornweibel, Theodore, Jr. *Seeing Red; Federal Campaigns against Black Militancy, 1919–1925.* Bloomington and Indianapolis: Indiana University Press, 1998.

Kovel, Joel. *Red Hunting in the Promised Land: Anticommunism and the Making of America.* New York: Basic Books, 1994.

LaFeber, Walter. *The American Age: U.S. Foreign Policy at Home and Abroad, 1750 to the Present.* New York: W.W. Norton and Company, 1994.

_____. *The New Empire: An Interpretation of American Expansion, 1860–1898.* Ithaca, New York: Cornell University Press, 1963.

_____. *The Panama Canal: The Crisis in Historical Perspective.* New York: Oxford University Press, 1978.

Lanning, Michael Lee. *The African-American Soldier from Crispus Attucks to Colin Powell.* Secaucus, New Jersey: Carol Publishing Group, 1997.

Lee, Ulysses [Office of the Chief of Military History, United States Army]. *The Employment of Negro Troops.* Washington, D.C.: U.S. Government Printing Office, 1966.

Levin, Murray B. *Political Hysteria in America.* New York: Basic Books, Inc., 1971.

Lewis, David Levering. *When Harlem Was in Vogue.* New York: Vintage Books, 1982.

Link, Arthur S. *American Epoch: A History of the United States since the 1890's.* New York: Alfred A. Knopf, 1955.

Lowitt, Richard. *The New Deal and the West.* Norman: University of Oklahoma Press, 1993.

Lynch, George. *The War of the Civilizations: Being the Record of a "Foreign Devil's" Experiences with the Allies in China.* London: Longmans, Green and Co., 1901.

MacColl, E. Kimbark. *The Growth of a City: Power and Politics in Portland, Oregon, 1915 to 1950.* Portland: Georgian Press Company, 1979.

_____. *Merchants, Money, and Power: The Portland Establishment, 1843–1913*. Portland: The Georgian Press, 1988.

_____. *The Shaping of a City: Business and Politics in Portland, Oregon, 1885 to 1915*. Portland: Georgian Press Company, 1979.

Maddux, Percy. *City on the Willamette: The Story of Portland, Oregon*. Portland: Binfords and Mort, 1952.

Mandelbaum, David G. *Soldier Groups and Negro Soldiers*. Berkeley: University of California Press, 1952.

Marable, Manning. *W.E.B. Du Bois: Black Radical Democrat*. Boston: Twayne Publishers, 1986.

Marchant, L.R., ed. *The Siege of the Peking Legations: A Diary, Lancelot Giles*. Nedlands, Western Australia: University of Western Australia Press, 1970.

McAleavy, Henry. *The Modern History of China*. New York: Frederick A. Praeger, Publishers, 1967.

McClellan, Robert. *The Heathen Chinee: A Study of American Attitudes toward China, 1890–1905*. Cincinnati: Ohio State University Press, 1971.

McElvaine, Robert S. *The Great Depression: America, 1929–1941*. New York: Times Books, 1984.

McKay, Floyd K. *An Editor for Oregon: Charles A. Sprague and the Politics of Change*. Corvallis: Oregon State University Press, 1998.

McMurry, Donald L. *Coxey's Army*. Seattle: University of Washington Press, 1968.

Miller, Kelly. *The World War for Human Rights*. New York: A. Jenkins, 1919.

Miller, Merle. *Ike: The Soldier as They Knew Him*. New York: G.P. Putnam's Sons, 1987.

Miller, Stuart Creighton. *Benevolent Assimilation*. New Haven: Yale University Press, 1982.

Morgan, H. Wayne. *America's Road to Empire: The War with Spain and Overseas Expansion*. New York: John Wiley and Sons, Inc., 1965.

Morris, Edmund. *The Rise of Theodore Roosevelt*. New York: Ballantine Books, 1979.

Morris, James M. *America's Armed Forces: A History*. Upper Saddle River, New Jersey: Prentice Hall, 1996.

Moton, Robert Russa. *Finding a Way Out: An Autobiography*. College Park, Maryland: McGrath Publishing Company, 1920.

Mullen, Robert W. *Blacks in America's Wars*. New York: Monad Press, 1973.

Nalty, Bernard C. *Strength for the Fight: A History of Black Americans in the Military*. New York: The Free Press, 1986.

Nash, Gerald D. *The Great Depression and World War II: Organizing America, 1933–1945*. New York: St. Martin's Press, 1979.

Neal, Steve. *McNary of Oregon: A Political Biography*. Portland: Oregon Historical Society Press, 1985.

Nenninger, Timothy K. *The Leavenworth Schools and the Old Army*. Westport, Connecticut: Greenwood Press, 1978.

Neuberger, Richard L. *Our Promised Land*. New York: The Macmillan Company, 1938.

Norwood, Gus. *Columbia River Power for the People: A History of Policies of the Bonneville Power Administration*. Portland: The Bonneville Power Administration, n.d.

Ornstein, Norman, Andrew Kohut, and Larry McCarthy. *The People, the Press and Politics*. Reading, Massachusetts: Addison-Wesley, 1988.

Painter, Nell Irvin. *Standing at Armageddon*. New York: W.W. Norton and Company, Inc., 1987.

Paterson, Thomas G., ed. *Major Problems in American Foreign Policy, Volume II: Since 1914*. Lexington, Massachusetts: D.C. Heath and Company, 1989.

Pearce, Jenny. *Under the Eagle*. Boston: South End Press, 1982.

Phipps, Virginia, et al., eds. *China Journal 1889–1900: An American Missionary Family during the Boxer Rebellion*. New York: Charles Scribner's Sons, 1989.

Plesur, Milton, ed. *Creating an American Empire, 1865–1914*. Buffalo: State University of New York, 1971.

Rauch, Basil. *The History of the New Deal, 1933–1938*. New York: Capricorn Books, 1963.

Richmond, Al. *A Long View from the Left: Memoirs of an American Revolutionary*. Boston: Houghton Mifflin Company, 1973.

Roback, A.A. *A Dictionary of International Slurs*. Cambridge: Sci-Art Publishers, 1944.

Rosenberg, Emily S. *Spreading the American Dream: American Economic and Cultural Expansion, 1890–1945*. New York: Hill and Wang, 1982.

Savage-Landor, A. Henry. *China and the Allies*, 2 Vols. London: William Heinemann, 1901.

Schlesinger, Arthur M., Jr. *The Age of Roosevelt: The Coming of the New Deal*. Cambridge: The Riverside Press, 1958.

_____. *The Age of Roosevelt: The Crisis of the Old Order*. Boston: Houghton Mifflin Company, 1964.

_____. *The Age of Roosevelt: The Politics of Upheaval*. Cambridge: The Riverside Press, 1960.

Schwantes, Carlos A. *Coxey's Army: An American Odyssey*. Moscow: University of Idaho Press, 1994.

_____. *The Pacific Northwest: An Interpretive History*. Lincoln: University of Nebraska Press, 1996.

Scott, Emmett J. *The American Negro in the World War*. Published by the Author, 1919.

Selvin, David F. *Sky Full of Storm*. San Francisco: California Historical Society, 1975.

Sheehan, Neil. *A Bright Shining Lie: John Paul Vann and America in Vietnam*. New York: Random House, 1988.

Sorley, L.S. *History of the Fourteenth United States Infantry: From January, 1890 to December, 1908*. Chicago: L.S. Sorley, 1909.

Stanley, Peter W., ed. *Reappraising an Empire: New Perspectives on Philippine-American History*. Cambridge: Harvard University Press, 1984.

Steel, Ronald. *Pax Americana*. New York: The Viking Press, 1967.

Trask, David F. *The War with Spain in 1898*. New York: Macmillan Publishing Co., Inc., 1981.

Turnbull, George S. *Governors of Oregon*. Portland: Binfords and Mort, Publishers, 1959.

University of Chicago Staff, Social Sciences 1, *The People Shall Judge*, Vol. 2. Chicago: The University of Chicago Press, 1949.

"Unofficial Observer." *The New Dealers*. New York: The Literary Guild, 1934.

Utley, Robert M. *The Indian Frontier of the American West, 1846–1890*. Albuquerque: University of New Mexico Press, 1984.

Vandiver, Frank E. *Black Jack: The Life and Times of John J. Pershing*, Vol. 1. College Station: Texas A&M University Press, 1977.

Walton, George. *The Tarnished Shield: A Report on Today's Army*. New York: Dodd, Mead and Company, 1973.

Weigley, Russell F. *Towards an American Army: Military Thought from Washington to Marshall*. New York: Columbia University Press, 1962.

White, Richard. *The Organic Machine: The Remaking of the Columbia River*. New York: Hill and Wang, 1995.

Williams, William Appleman. *The Tragedy of American Diplomacy*. New York: Dell Publishing Co., Inc., 1962.

Wollner, Craig. *Electrifying Eden: Portland General Electric, 1889–1965*. Portland: Oregon Historical Society Press, 1990.

Wythe, George. *A History of the 90th Division*. N.p.: The 90th Division Association, 1920.

Young, Marilyn Blatt. *The Rhetoric of Empire: American China Policy, 1895–1901*. Cambridge: Harvard University Press, 1968.

Zinn, Howard. *A People's History of the United States*. New York: Harper and Row, 1980.

Periodicals

Brogdon, Frederick W., and Robert D. Ward. "The Revolt against Wilson: Southern Leadership and the Democratic Caucus of 1920." *Alabama Historical Quarterly*, Vol. 38, No. 2 (1978).

Crisis (June, July, and September 1918; March and May 1919).

Du Bois, W.E.B. "The Negro Soldier in Service Abroad during the First World War." *The Journal of Negro Education*, Vol. 12 (1943).

Geary, Thomas J. "The Law and the Chinaman." *California Illustrated*, Vol. 4 (July 1893).

Long, Howard H. "The Negro Soldier in the Army of the United States." *The Journal of Negro Education*, Vol. 12 (1943).

Lowry, H.H. "The Chinese Resentment." *Harpers*, October 1900.

Mercer, D. Tate. "The Panama Canal and Political Partnership." *The Journal of Politics*, Vol. 25 (February 1963).

Ransom, Victoria L. "Officers' Row at Vancouver Barracks." *Clark County History*, Vol. 3 (1962).

Reddick, L.D. "The Negro Policy of the United States Army, 1775–1945." *The Journal of Negro History*, Vol. 35 (January 1949).

[Unsigned]. "The Negro Officer." *National Service with the International Military Digest*, Vol. 5 (March 1919).

Newspapers

Chicago Examiner
Los Angeles Times
Oregon Journal
Portland Oregonian
Salem Capital Journal
Salem Capital Press
Salem Oregon Statesman
Seattle Post-Intelligencer

INDEX